John Sutherland

The
Fields of Dreams

TRAFFORD

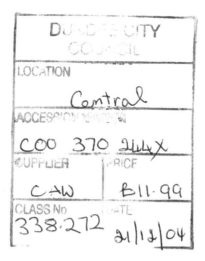
Printed in Victoria, Canada

Note for Librarians: a cataloguing record for this book that includes Dewey Classification and US Library of Congress numbers is available from the National Library of Canada. The complete cataloguing record can be obtained from the National Library's online database at:
www.nlc-bnc.ca/amicus/index-e.html
ISBN 1-4120-2696-2

TRAFFORD

This book was published on-demand in cooperation with Trafford Publishing. On-demand publishing is a unique process and service of making a book available for retail sale to the public taking advantage of on-demand manufacturing and Internet marketing. On-demand publishing includes promotions, retail sales, manufacturing, order fulfilment, accounting and collecting royalties on behalf of the author.

Suite 6E, 2333 Government St., Victoria, B.C. V8T 4P4, CANADA
Phone 250-383-6864   Toll-free 1-888-232-4444 (Canada & US)
Fax 250-383-6804   E-mail sales@trafford.com   Web site www.trafford.com
TRAFFORD PUBLISHING IS A DIVISION OF TRAFFORD HOLDINGS LTD
Trafford Catalogue #04-0524   www.trafford.com/robots/04-0524.html

13   12   11   10   9   8   7   6   5   4   3   2

Acknowledgments

I would like to express my heartfelt thanks and gratitude to Danny Morris of B.P. Dyce, (Aberdeen), who supplied the photographs of the B.P. platforms, also to Scotty Gordon, Jeff Murray, Duncan Blake, Paul Armstrong and George Davidson for some of the others. I would also like to say a special thank you to Steve Mackay, Eddie Slater, Peter Atherton, Les Bell, Maitland Baff, Derek Furlong, Tam Reynolds and David Shearer for their assistance so readily given in the research that went into the preparation of this book. And to my wife Liz for her patience, encouragement and support while writing this Autobiography.

Thanks to everyone who helped with this book.

J. S.

Introduction

Let me tell you something about myself; at the time of writing this I am the wrong side of fifty years of age, born in Greenock in 1953 I left what was fast becoming an employment black spot and moved to the new town of Glenrothes (fife) in search of work in July 1972... After years of menial job changes I wanted to look for something more permanent and Glenrothes seemed to promise that opportunity. Sadly it looked that I had jumped out of the proverbial frying pan into the fire because the jobs I had acquired were mostly general labouring dead end tasks, that led to nowhere, jobs like digging ditches, carrying coal, foundry and factory work and general builder's labourer, don't get me wrong, it wasn't as if I left school with a pocket full of qualifications and deserved something better, but I always thought that there must be something else out there and if there was and I got the chance, I would grab it with both hands.

Then just over seventeen years ago I was given the chance to work in the Oil Industry, It was a job that supposedly earned you good money working two weeks on two off with the prospects of promotion in a relatively short time and earn even more money, that was the carrot that was dangled in front of me and I took it, hook, line and sinker.

Little did I know how much it was going to affect me? Not only in the short term but periodically over the months and years to come... Now! Don't think for a minute that I'm complaining because I'm not. I wasn't press ganged into doing this kind of work, it was my choice, I just felt that life seemed to either run along nice and smooth for some people but mine was a fucking Rollercoaster ride. Full of up's and down's. One of those rides that you pay a couple of quid to get on like the Pepsi Max Ride in Blackpool's Pleasure beach. You know what I mean, you can shout and bawl and scream your fucking head off; but you're on that ride until it stops, with no chance of your money back. That's what my time working offshore has been like. Full of up's and downs. It's great when you're on a high. (Feeling good, not a care in the world sort of feeling.) But when you hit a low, Boy you better try and be ready for it, because when it comes and believe me it will come and without warning too, all you can do is try and hang on in there and wait till the high time comes round again, which it will do. Trust me I know. !

The Men and Women working on one of these steel Monstrosities often well over a hundred miles from the Mainland and only visited periodically by supply boat and helicopter, is a special sort of Individual working towards one goal and that's to return home safely after their two or three week stint offshore. They like me are forgotten soul's for two or three weeks of the month. It's only when were seen back home again that people realize that we have been away. And listen; ask any offshore worker how many times they have heard this. "Is that two weeks already you've been away"? When do you go back? That does your fucking head in. (I know it does mine in). Another thing is. The people asking these questions are the same people that were in the pub the day before I left to go offshore. They are the same people, sitting in the same seats the day I go back into the pub, Talk about Dejavue.(I ask you), It's like entering a fucking time warp, Like I've never been away. The last two weeks didn't exist. I mean let's be honest about this, I've just done two week's Working Offshore, Parted from family and friends so I can earn enough to pay the bill's and have a decent sort of Lifestyle and what do I see.? The same people sitting in the same seats asking silly fucking questions and thinking that I'm the lucky one for having a job. (Having a laugh)? Yeh, I'm pissing myself thinking about it! Don't get me wrong I'm not Tarring everybody with the same brush, (I blame the System) but if your working offshore or worked offshore and your reading this. Then you will know exactly what I'm on about.

Offshore life takes its toll in many different ways it leaves its mark mentally and physically. To leave home every two or three week's (especially if you have a young family) is quite emotional, something you never really come to terms with, Oh I know that once you meet up with the workmates your going offshore with; the banter, the jokes and everyday chit chat takes your mind off home and family matter's, you tend not to show your true feelings, but sitting on the helicopter on your way to the rig your mind starts to wander back to the time you spent at home. Wishing you were going back there instead of going out just starting your two or three week trip.

After all these years I still get a knot in my stomach when I'm going away and I don't suppose I'm alone. What I want to do now is relive some of my experiences and share them with you. Everything you read in my autobiography are actual events that happened on the various rigs that I've worked on. The people named are real, although some names have been changed to protect their Identity.

Some names I would like to give a special mention too, who helped me put this book together are as follows.

My wife Liz, Kids, Michelle, Jason, Nicky and David, My best friend Ian Macleod, My very good friend's and workmates, Jim Pitcairn, Alex (Seldom) Macdonald, Alex (Sooty)Robertson, Jim Fulton, Billy Bell, (R.I.P.) Tam Fitzpatrick, John Conroy, Billy Patrick, Harry Macadam, Tam Adamson, (Station hotel Leslie) Jock Bell, Davie Wright, (Rothes Oak Leslie,) Sandy Herd, Ian (Yano) Bryson, Ian Sturton, Davie Liddell, Eddie Watson, John Leslie, Eddie McKnight (R.I.P.) Eddie Slater, Steve Mackay, Bob Anderson, Scotty Gordon, Les Bell, Sam Graham, Peter Atherton, Maitland Baff, Brian (Ploo) Clark, Gary (Gazza) Johnson, John M Sutherland, Alan Matthew, Jamie Wright, Hamish Muirhead, Blyth (Biffo) Whyte, John (Munster)Munn, Jim Brydon,(R.I.P.) Colin Prentice, Steve Ritchie, Mick Casey, Mick Gower, Brian Cannon, Brian (Robbo) Robinson, Alan (Jenky) Jenkinson, Davy (Chinky) Macdonald, Russell Brennan, Andy Kenyon, Craig (Homer) Davis, Norman Fraser, Fin Paterson, Big John Stubbs, Nat Ritchie, Gordon Findlay, Bobby Booth, Wee Davy Ross, Tony Smart, Keith Robert's, Jim (Smiddy) Smith, Mike Marsen, Brian Gardiner, Duncan Blake, Jeff Freeman, Robbie Anderson, Steve (Sumo) Simmons, Campbell MacAskill, Stuart Campbell, Paul Armstrong, George Davidson, Phil Meach, Paul Richman, Derek Furlong, Val Stephenson, Tam Leahy, Barry (Baz) Raper, Frankie Pearson, John Kyle, Davy Reid, Nigel Evans, Hans Watt, Dougie & Fraser Andrew, and Alan Slessor, The list is endless, If you don't see your name here or somewhere in the book please accept my apologies, If I jotted down every person I worked with or came into contact with in my offshore life this would be a book of names, that's not my intention. I hope as you read on you can relate to at least one if not more of the stories I'm about to unfold. The rigs your about to read about are as follows. The West Intrepid, (Land rig) The Tartan Alpha, The Hutton T.L.P. (Tension Leg Platform), The Forties Echo, The Heather Alpha, The North

West Hutton, The West Omikron, The Stenna Seawell, (Diving Ship) The Bruce, The Harding and finally The Magnus, Each one has a story to be told, it may be funny, it may be sad but whatever. I hope I make it good reading. Just remember its all true.

I have decided to call this book The Fields of Dreams as in the oil fields I've worked in & the dreams I have of one day leaving it all behind as a distant but very fond memory.

John Sutherland

1

The West Intrepid

October 1987 was the turning point in my working life, after years of working in

Dead end jobs I was given the chance to work on the rigs. It came with a phone call from my mate Alex Macdonald who worked on the rigs and was affectionately known out there as (Seldom), the reason being, whenever there was anything to be done work related, Alex was never anywhere to be seen, hence the term (Seldom Seen). Seldom was asked by his boss to supply one more labourer (roustabout as their known in the Oil industry) to make up a crew working on a land rig down South in Lincoln, when he asked me if I wanted a couple of weeks working as a roustabout (as he knew I wasn't working). I told him I didn't know fuck all about shearing sheep, (I'd seen this film on T.V. called Roustabout it was about sheep Shearer's in Australia) no you silly bastard it's a labouring job that will last about two weeks and earn you a thousand quid, are you fucking interested? YEEESSSS was my answer, Ok Then! I will fill you in with the details later on he said and hung up. My head was buzzing; I couldn't get the thought of that thousand quid out of it. I thought I'm never going to be skint again. (Yippee). Do you know that feeling? like when you've picked a couple of winners at the bookies and you start to think heh this is fucking easy, you have a wad of notes in your pocket and your mentally thinking; if I keep this money in that pocket and that money in this pocket it will last forever. (LIKE FUCK IT DOES), before you know it your skint, well that's not happening to me that thousand quid I'm going to earn will be put to good use. Trust Me!

The only thing I had to do now was go see my mate Macleod and ask him to look after the house when I went away as me and my partner Liz had a wee fall out and she went back to Glasgow to stay, then I remembered he would also have to look after the dog, now how the fuck could I forget him (Kaiser), well, what else would you call a German shepherd? He was mental, just fucking mental, he would bite himself and anybody else that was near him just to keep his teeth sharp, but Macleod could handle him. He wont let me down I was positive of that. No fucking way! That dogs bonkers, was all he kept saying, come on I said, its two weeks work and a £1000 to be had, I can't take him with me. Eventually we agreed that he would take him out once in the morning and once at night as long as he had his muzzle on. Fuck knows how the dog was supposed to eat with his muzzle on, but that was Macleod's problem hopefully him and the dog will work it out. I wasn't sure what to do dole wise, as I didn't know when we would be leaving. Should I sign off? Will the job last two weeks? Fuck it I thought, I will sign on this Thursday and if the job lasts two weeks after we get down there and I miss my signing on day in a fortnight, I'll tell them I was away looking for work, which was true! And if it doesn't last two weeks I'll be back home anyway.

Seldom phoned me on Friday morning, it was all set, we travel to Lincoln first thing on Sunday morning catching the early train to arrive in time to start night shift Sunday night. Saturday morning found me pacing up and down waiting for my Giro; I was thinking? If that doesn't come I'm fucked! If it's true what they say that a watched kettle never boils, then a watched for postman never arrives (not at his usual time anyway) but arrive he did! I cashed the Giro bought two electricity power cards paid £5 towards my Gas bill, bought the dog food and dog biscuits, enough for two weeks, (I didn't see any point in me buying messages) then I went home, packed my holdall with what I thought I needed for Lincoln (Seldom said work gear would be supplied) and went to the pub for a celebration drink.

After a couple of train changes Seldom and me arrived in Lincoln about four in the afternoon, we went to the digs Seldom had arranged for us, changed our clothes and headed out to the pub to meet the crew we would be working with, Seldom explained on the train what the wages were and what hours we would be working. It was £5 an hour working twelve hour shifts, plus £25 a day expenses, not bad money considering I was getting just short of £59 a fortnight off the dole. The digs were £7 a night, bed and breakfast, and all I had to buy was food. A quick bit of mental arithmetic got me thinking @ £85 a day over fourteen days that's nearly £1200, lets say a £100 for dig's and another £100 for grub, Yessss, that £1000 is in the bank. We met the drill crew in a pub called (Martha's) in Lincolns city centre, had a couple of pints and at six thirty we headed out in the works van to a place called (Whisby) a few miles from Lincoln, that's where the land rig was working, first impression's as we approached the site were of a huge concentration camp with an eight foot fence all around, right in the middle of a field. Their were huge floodlights everywhere illuminating what looked like a Wee holiday caravan, three big portacabin's, two portaloo's an old railway carriage and a couple of wooden huts all down one side of the fence, in the middle of this camp was a huge steel complex that stretched for over a hundred yards, I couldn't see what was behind the steel complex (but I would find out later). I followed the crew into the railway carriage and stared in disbelief. I thought if (Arthur Neagus) the antiques dealer had seen this carriage he would have come in his pants.(It was ancient)We were supposed to take our breaks in here, wash our work clothes, cook and eat our dinners, generally use this shitehouse when we were on the site.

Let me explain what was in it, a sink with cold and colder running water. some pots, a frying pan, a kettle, some cutlery, a table, two wooden benches, a washing machine and tumble drier to wash and dry our work clothes, about forty small wire mesh cages to keep our food and our personal belongings in, an electric cooker, a small fridge and lot's of hole's in the wooden floor so the rats didn't feel too restricted in their movements, all in all a right little holiday camp. Oh before I forget! Next to the washing machine was a large plain brown cardboard box full of what looked like soap powder, written on the front of the box in felt tip pen in large letter's was F.U.G.G. I found out later on that some wag came up with the idea that while doing the washing, if Daz doesn't dazzle it and Persil doesn't whiten it, then F.U.G.G, it.

The Wee caravan was for the B.P. company man to stay in, as that was the company we were drilling the well for, The three portacabin's were for the Tool pusher, the geologist, the mud man, the drilling engineer, the Cementer, the Mechanic, the Electrician, and a couple of other office staff. The Tool pusher was a guy named Bert Wokke, Ex/mister Holland I was told and I wasn't surprised, you should have seen the build on this guy, (all muscle). He was a fine guy to work for though. His job was to make sure the operation ran smoothly and was in overall charge of the rig crew. The company man from Great Yarmouth, was a right little shite, it didn't take long to suss him out. He strutted about the place glowering at everybody, Seldom warned me on the train going down what he was like, and his job I presumed was to report the progress of the well to his bosses. The rest of the crew were fine! A mechanic named Drew Shaw from (Glasgow), a Sparky, a Driller and three roughnecks all from down South somewhere, and Seldom and me, quite a motley crew I can tell you!

My first nightshift (Sunday) was spent finding out what my job was? Basically I was to make sure their were joints of 5 inch diameter tubes (drill pipe) on this long steel structure they called the Catwalk, once I had put five of these thirty foot pieces of pipe onto the catwalk with the forklift, one of the roughnecks would attach a winch line to one end and pull it up to the rig floor, they joined it to one already up there in the hole and started drilling another 30 feet, they kept repeating this operation till the required depth was reached, sometimes up to 600 feet. When the time came to pull out of the hole for any reason they racked back two of these joints joined together in the derrick (as they called it) calling them doubles. Making a total length of about 60 feet for each double. (All interesting stuff) I thought to myself? But still I hadn't a clue what was going on.

Basically I was there to give a helping hand to whoever needed one, But one job that had to be done regardless of what was going on was to wash and dry the dayshift crews overalls (the dayshift roustabout would do the nightshifts) For me this was a bit of trial and error, how much F.U.G.G. will I use and how many sets of overalls to put in to get them clean, I settled on four pair's at a time with two plastic cups of powder, worked a fucking treat. They came out spotless, a little shorter than when they went in, but spotless nevertheless. Next time I'll cut down a little on the F.U.G.G. everybody wore two sets of overalls as it was so fucking cold down there you needed them on to try and keep warm. It was also while I was doing the washing that I noticed the logo on them, it said Dan Smedvig that's how I found out who I was working for, (Seldom never said.) Piece of piss this, I thought! Imagine paying me £85 a day for this, I was on cloud nine! Whistling away like a fucking canary, a plastic surgeon couldn't take the smile off my face. No. (But very shortly something else will)!

The first night (Sunday) went Ok, but I was starving by the time the shift finished at seven in the morning considering we didn't buy any grub to see us through. Ok. I had a couple of cups of tea, but since I hadn't eaten since Sunday morning I was ready for a cooked breakfast, I was in for a shock. Something the landlady couldn't or wouldn't do was cook; apart from that she didn't get up till nine in the morning lazy bitch. It was a case of help yourself to any cereal you liked as long as it's cornflakes or sugar puffs, So much for bed and help yourself to fucking breakfast. I wasn't too bothered though, I just wanted to get to bed, as I was knackered. In the room was, a portable television, a kettle, three small bowls, with teabags, sugar, and coffee in them, and some of those wee tubs of milk, Three beds, Seldoms, mine, and a roughnecks called (Bob the Dog) I honestly never found out his second name, I always called him bob, One other roughneck called Dave, from (Great Yarmouth) stayed in another room in the digs, The four of us got on fine, the other two (Driller and roughneck) stayed elsewhere, these two kept to themselves, Oh they traveled to and from work with us and got changed into and out of their working clothes in the railway carriage, but they didn't eat with us, or generally mix, they would bring packed lunches and flasks of hot drinks and virtually spent their time on the rig floor.(in the doghouse) I would have thought that's where Bob the Dog would have been but he mixed with us. Only the drill crews traveled to work each day, everyone else stayed on the site obviously for 24 hour cover.

I crawled into bed full of Fucking Sugar puffs and slept like a baby till Seldom woke me at three in the afternoon, we have some shopping to do, he said if we wanted to eat tonight. Now after paying my rail fare, buying my round of drinks, and paying out two nights dig money, (I was running a bit short of cash) the landlady wanted a full weeks money in advance, but after explaining to her my situation, she agreed to wait until I got an advance on my wages, I only had about £15 left, enough to get messages (surely) back home in Glenrothes £15 would buy everything a single man could want. (Enough for a week) but in Lincoln.(OH NO) I'll tell you what I was hoping to get for a £10, In the basket I put two pint s of milk, one loaf of bread, one large tub of margarine, one pound of bacon, two pound of cheese, 3 fray bentos steak and kidney pies. One medium sized jar of coffee, 2 pounds of sugar, and three packets of smash potatoes. Then as she was ringing it up in the till, I noticed I didn't have enough cash, it came to just under £14. I wanted to keep a fiver for emergencies, you know (a couple of pints and some rolling tobacco) if Seldom hadn't been there to help me out I'm sure the woman behind the counter would have taken the steak and kidney pies off me (well done Seldom) fuck you Missus.

Back at work that night (Monday) I explained to the Tool pusher (Bert) what my financial status was, no problem John he said, I go to the bank every second day! Let me know how much advance you want on your wages and I'll have it for you tomorrow. Now I'm thinking fast here! I'm due the landlady £35, I need more messages, and I've still to give Seldom £4 (How about a Hundred Bert?) Would that be Ok, no problem he said see me tomorrow! (Yeeesss). With that sorted, I'm out on the site again looking around to see what the whole complex is made up from. The rig was drilling away and there was three joints of drill pipe on the catwalk, the washing was on universal wash. So I went exploring!

Everything on the site was run by diesel generators, the whole shooting match was fueled by a single 500 gallon diesel tank, which a road tanker refueled every couple of days. This diesel tank was surrounded by sandbags to contain any spillage, about fifty yards away were the generators the diesel tank supplied and this was the warmest place on the whole site. Considering it was near the end of October and its fucking freezing you really didn't want to venture too far away from the generator's, but I couldn't always pick my place of work. Loading up the Catwalk with drill pipe and doing the washing, weren't my only jobs. On the other part of the site was a load of different size tubulars, loads of them, my job was to measure them with the help of a roughneck and write the sizes on them with chalk, that was ok in it's self, but with the site being covered with small sharp hardcore stones that are normally used to build roads, I was finding it quite difficult to stay on my feet. I kept going over on my ankles, and I was wishing now that I had brought my own working boots. These fuckers I had on were the best one's I could find among the ten or twelve pairs lying in the railway carriage, (work gear supplied) I'm sure I heard that somewhere! Now I had worked on the roads before but they always had a big fucking roller flattening the stones as we went along. But not here, these stones were only for cosmetic purposes, once the well was drilled, and all the plant was taken away, the field it was in was put back to its original state, with only a wellhead left as proof of anybody ever being there. That's ok BP are happy, they have the oil. The farmer is happy he's got his money. But what about my fucking ankles? Honest to god they were swollen too twice their normal size. I was in fucking agony, (Everybody but me thought it was funny). Seldom did say, have a word with the driller and he might give you the night off. Well I did! And he didn't his somewhat witty remark about getting a bigger pair of boots fell on my deaf ears. Are you a man or a mouse, he asked? As I limped away to make some toast and cheese! (Fucking Arsehole).

Boy was I glad when that shift was over, when we got back to the digs all I wanted to do was get washed and get to bed. But we stayed up to have a word with the landlady about our breakfast's she agreed we could have a cooked breakfast at 08:30 every morning if we wished, we were happy about that till we saw the breakfast, I remember thinking she should try a hot flame under the frying pan before she took the grub out of it. (Honest to fuck it was revolting) bring back the cereals.

Before going to bed that morning I asked Seldom for a loan of £20 until I got the £100 off Bert that night. I told him I was planning to get up early and go to the chemist's for some tubigrip bandages to help support my ankles and I would meet the three of them in the pub later at five that night, and that's what I did. At work that night (Tuesday) I went to get the money off Bert in his portacabin, and let me tell you it was done out like a miniature house, TV, Video, Sink, Washing Machine, Tumble Drier, Tables Chairs, even two big easy chairs, computer's, phones, cordoned off bedrooms, I bet he even had a shower in there but I can't be certain. This was home from home. I would have moved in with him if he had asked me, but he didn't. I signed for the £100 and thanked him. No problem john he said. If you need more just ask. Well if I could get a £150 just to tide me over the next time your at the bank that would be smashing Bert, I said. See me on Thursday night and I'll have it for you. With that done, I left his cabin full of the joy's of spring until the freezing night air brought me back to reality, after all it was fucking winter. I wasn't needed by the drill floor, so after I put the first wash in the machine I went walkabout. I knew that the machine would take roughly one hour to finish its cycle so I had plenty of time. I wandered to the far end of the site to explore and found loads and loads of pallets of all sorts of different chemicals, these pallets were stacked three and four high next to what looked like to me huge water tanks, open at the top. I later found out they mixed sacks of chemicals into these tanks, and through a series of pipes the fluid chemicals (mud) were pumped into the hole they were drilling. (All good stuff) Just behind these tanks I could see what looked like a large pond partly frozen over, as I got nearer to investigate a voice boomed out (DON'T GO TOO NEAR TO THAT,) well fuck me I nearly shat myself, I didn't expect to see anyone down that end of the site but it was Drew the mechanic he was working on the forklift and had spotted me being a nosey bastard. He explained that what I thought was a pond was actually a man made reservoir a very deep reservoir with sheer sides to it. It supplied the tanks used to mix the mud chemicals. Why the FUCK did nobody tell me about that, if I'd fallen in I would never have gotten out again, The sheer sides would have made sure of that, shouting would have been no good, the noise of the drilling rig would have drowned out my cries for help, I thanked Drew and made a mental note not to go anywhere near that fucking deathtrap again, Back in the railway carriage later on I explained to Seldom about the pond, "Oh you don't want to go near that," he said. Fucking cheers mate,

The eating arrangements were quite simple. As I was the only roustabout it was my job to wash the dishes and try to keep the place clean, Find out what the lads had chosen for their dinner and get it ready for them, It went something like this, usually about 11-15pm I would go and have my meal, I would cook the meal of whoever was next to eat,(we could only eat one at a time depending on what was happening,) I then took over the job that the next man to eat was doing, while eating his meal he in turn cooked the next meal and so on. We only took thirty-five minutes to eat and because there was only four of us (driller and rough-neck staying on the rig floor) it worked no bother, the last man eating about 1-15am Usually it was pie, beans, and Smash, or a fry up, with plenty bread and butter, nothing special. Normally we had plenty of tea and smoke breaks so we restricted our dinner break to roughly half an hour. Sometimes someone would drive into Lincoln for fish or chicken suppers depending on how busy we were. And we would keep them warm in the oven till eating time.

Another shift finished and with money in my pocket I decided to get up early and have a look about Lincoln. I paid Seldom his £24 and the landlady her £35, leaving just over £47 including the change from the chemist shop, the tubigrip was working, my ankles were not Ok but were not as swollen as before, I managed to hobble to the bookies lost £40, bought some more messages then went to the pub to wait for the boys until it was time for work.

By Wednesday night I was getting into the swing of things. Even though I didn't know what was happening on the drill floor, all I knew was they were drilling an Eight and a half inch hole. I thought to myself there's a lot of fucking equipment here just to dig a hole (what do I know). The driller told us on the way to work that night that the company man would be having a fire drill. The Scenario was the diesel tank was on fire and we were to get there as quickly as possible once the driller sounded the fire alarm, this was a horn that would have wakened the dead it was so loud. I suppose it had to be, to be heard above the noise of the rig, anyway on our way to the fire we were each to collect a fire extinguisher from a shed close to the diesel tank. The driller and one roughneck (guess who) were exempt, so that left me, Seldom, Dave, and Bob the Dog to save the day. About half past nine I had just sat down with a cup of coffee forgetting about the drill, when this Fucking siren went off. I hadn't heard it before and even though I knew it was coming I thought world war 111 had broken out, (FUCK ME). It was loud. I started running towards the shed, grabbed the only extinguisher I could find and ran to the diesel tank to find, Seldom, Dave, and Bob the Dog already there with a fire Extinguisher each at their feet, I took my place across from them, we were supposed to form a circle, hearing fuck all due to the noise of this eardrum piercing alarm. They kept shouting and pointing at my feet but I couldn't make out what they were saying, eventually Bert and the Company man appeared and the siren was switched off (thank fuck). All the company man had missing was a fucking Doberman dog because he strutted about looking like a German guard doing his rounds inside a prison camp, (a right little fucking Hitler.) Mustache and all. He looked at each of us in turn and then at the fire extinguishers, when he got to me, he looked down and said what do you expect to do with that? I looked down and noticed it was a red water extinguisher I had picked up, that's what the boys had been trying to tell me. You won't put out a diesel fire with that Sonny, he said, oh I'm not going to use it on the fire; I'm going to wait until the lads have finished with theirs and then cool them down with mine. He just shook his head and fucked off! Bert and the boys seen the funny side of it but he didn't (Fucking Arsehole). If he thought for a

17

moment I was going to be anywhere near 500 gallons of burning diesel with a piddly wee Fire Extinguisher then he was off his Fucking trolley.

The rest of the shift went fine. I attended to what I had to do, but things were happening on the Rig floor and I was getting curious as to what!

It turned out that they were preparing to pull the drill pipe out of the hole, but first they had to prepare some chemicals for mud treatment, I was sent with the Mudman to get the pallets of chemicals we were going to use. It was his job to work out the formula of chemicals used, and it was my job to empty the sacks into the hopper until the right mixture was had. Seldom being the (Derrick man) gave me a hand to empty the sacks (thank fuck) there were loads of them. Seldom's job as derrickman was to ensure the tanks were full of water and liquid mud to send down the hole via the various pipes, also to monitor the whole pumping system. When not doing that he was required to work on the Rig floor usually in the derrick, (which is no place for someone afraid of heights) standing on a wee platform 60 feet in the air without wings or at the very least a can of Red Bull is not my idea of a long lasting career, Ok, he had a safety harness on, but just the same (fuck that) maybe now you'll understand why we always had a drink before work. We were never drunk you understand. Just a wee drop of the amber- nectar to keep out the cold and steady the nerves. After all, this was a dangerous place to be working in, As all drilling sites are.

Mixing the chemicals was a fine enough job, a bit dusty as you can imagine. There was no such thing as a coshh (Control of Substances Hazardous to Health).Assessment sheet, or if there was, nobody told me about it, we did have masks on but they soon got clogged up, so basically we wore nothing. After the sacks were empty we set fire to them, usually the pallets as well, it certainly took the chill off us, if only for a short time. And not a fire extinguisher in sight.

Seldom tried his best to explain the full cycle route the chemical mud took till it ended up back in the tanks, (it went something like this,) The mud in the tank went to two high pressure mud pumps where it was pumped up a metal pipe until it reached the Rig floor, there the metal pipe had a flexible rubber hose attached to it, this in turn through a series of attachments fitted onto the top of the drill pipe and under pressure, the mud was pumped down the drill pipe through the small holes (called jets)in the drill bit on the bottom, whilst the drill pipe was turned at the rotary table on the rig floor creating the drilling action. The cuttings from the drill bit being forced back up to the surface outside the drill pipe, floating in the mud and carried down a metal trough until it reached a series of fine wire mesh screens called (shaker screens) these vibrating shaker screens allowed the mud to fall through into another trough which led back to the tanks, doing a full 360 degree cycle, The cuttings not being able to get through the screens were routed down yet another trough and washed away to the man made reservoir, sinking to the bottom.

There was a lot of activity on the Rigfloor for the rest of the shift, I could see people coming and going, Strangers who I hadn't seen on the Rig floor before, I was wondering what was going on, and I was soon to find out.

Seldom told me in the van on the way to the digs that morning that the well results were not good and that the chemicals we were adding to the mud that night, were to be pumped down the drill pipe so they could pull the drill pipe back to surface without the roughnecks getting covered in mud, he called this (Pumping a slug, that was the term he used.) This mud was heavier than the mud already in the hole. He spoke to me as if I knew what he was talking about and I just sat there nodding in agreement as if I did.

He didn't go into very much detail about what was going to happen, but said we would find out more that night.

At the site that night (Thursday) Bert called us all together and told us we were going to run the 7inch diameter casing in the hole and cement it in. (The well was a Duster). Now even though all this drilling Jargon was new to me, I knew what a duster was, (There was fuck all oil there.) I started thinking! All this time, money, manpower and equipment wasted! We were going to Cement in the well, break down all the doubles in the derrick and put them with the tubulars that were already in racks so they could be bundled up later on, Then start dismantling everything so they could move it all elsewhere. Probably to another drilling site somewhere else. this would probably take us into next week sometime, I don't want to sound selfish here, but I really didn't give a fuck whether their was oil there or not, I was more interested in how much more work we had left before we got paid off and when I heard we would still be here the following week, I felt

19

a little better. The dayshift crew had pumped the slug, pulled the drill pipe out of the hole and racked them back in doubles in the derrick. They were busy getting ready to run the 7 inch casing when we arrived at the site and after our usual pep talk with Bert, we went out to relieve them.

My job tonight was to get the casing joints ready for running in the hole, To get enough on the catwalk to keep the rig floor supplied just like I did with the drill pipe, Only thing was, they were using these up faster than they did with the drill pipe so I had to work it between bundles to put the washing on and go see Bert for my £150 before he turned in for the night The drilling Engineer said that they were going to pick up around twenty of these joints to reach the depth that was required, about 585 feet, So It shouldn't take more than a couple of hours, that suited me fine. On the Rig floor that night were two extra men who arrived that day, I found out that they were called casing hands, their job was to make sure the casing was joined together properly, That was great because it freed up a roughneck who came and let me away from the catwalk for a smoke and a cup of tea, during this break I got the money off Bert who told me his three weeks stint was finished on Saturday, and that a new Toolpusher would take over from then. He also said that since the well was nearly finished, the dayshift crew would also be finishing on Saturday night to either go offshore in the next week or so or else go home until there was somewhere else to send them. We in turn would finish on Saturday morning, have 24 hrs off, then start dayshift on Sunday and assist with dismantling the whole complex.

The rest of the shift was a fucking nightmare. The Rig floor had all the casing it required, the only thing now was to cement it in. That was the Cementers job and I was sent to help him. His name was Sandy..? And he came from Hull. I couldn't understand a fucking word he was saying, I kept asking him to speak slower but it didn't make any difference, He kept rattling on and talking at a hundred miles an hour, I thought this fuckers not coming up for Air, he's going to have a fucking heart attack if he doesn't slow down, his face was so red you could have toasted bread off it, I remember looking at him and thinking. I wouldn't be buying a new fucking suit if I was him. anyway him and me emptied drums of some sort of chemicals into his portable tanks next to his cement unit /silo, Then him running around like a fucking headless chicken checking this and that. And me checking my watch noticing it's been two hours since I last had a cup of coffee. (No roughneck to let me away this time) After some gesticulating gestures from me I was allowed to go for a break while he carried on with the cement job, I was only away about 20 minutes but this gave me the chance to put another washing on and let Seldom know what Bert had told me. I finished off the shift working with this fucking headcase and I was never so glad to see the back of him.

Back in the digs it was Dave and Bob the Dogs turn to have a bath first, we took turns at this as there was no shower in the digs and the water tank only held about 25 gallon of hot water, as you can Imagine we were pretty dirty by the time our shift finished. So we needed a good wash. The first two would use roughly half of the 25 gallon and the next two the rest. As it usually took an hour or two for the water to heat up again we got washed as soon as we got in, the water usually being hot because the immersion heater was on most of the night. After breakfast we usually just went to bed and lay there bullshitting amongst ourselves about life in general or about what happened on the job that night. Dave would sometimes come in and sit for half an hour just to shoot the shit. But this morning was different; we were planning what we were going to do on our 24hrs off tomorrow.

Friday afternoon found me wandering about Lincolns shopping centre, I was looking for a pair of dress trousers and a couple of sweat shirts, the clothes I brought with me were ok, but if we were going out for the night on Saturday as we planned, then I wanted some new gear to wear, I found what I wanted and got back to the digs just as Seldom was getting up, Bob the Dog and Davy were still sleeping so Seldom and me headed out to the pub for a bar lunch. Bob and Davy arrived about half past 3 so we stayed there till it was time to leave for work. We were like four kids the way we were carrying on, laughing like fucking hyenas, everybody in the pub must have thought we were on something, you know, taking drugs or smoking pot, little did they know we were on (a high) because this was our last nightshift and tomorrow night we were going to paint the town red. 24hrs off. (Yes Ya fucking dancer.)

When we got to work that night (Friday) the dayshift crew were waiting in the railway carriage for us, this was unusual because we always changed over on the job, but the reason was the Cement job was complete, And after waiting a few hours for the cement to set, the mud in the hole was displaced to fresh water and pumped back into the man made reservoir, we didn't need it anymore, The drill pipe had been laid down from the rig floor and put back into their racks with the forklift, (boy they had a busy shift)

Bert and the new Toolpusher a guy named (Les Devine) came into the railway carriage to meet us and explain what was happening that night. Seldom and me were to start emptying the tanks back into the reservoir and clean them out ready for dismantling. Then start to dismantle the pipes leading from the tanks, this would take all shift I thought? These pipes called (chicksans) looked to me to stretch for miles, the Driller and the roughnecks were to start dismantling things on the rig floor and below, one of these being the B.O.P. stack. this was a weird looking piece of equipment, but I was told essential for drilling purposes, B.O.P. stood for (Blow- Out- Preventer) it was situated directly below the rig floor, the drill pipe went through the middle of it and if there was any problems while drilling the well, the hydraulic rams set into this stack could be closed automatically stopping any gas or high pressure fluid coming back up the drill pipe, hence the term preventing a blow out. This would only be used as a last resort, another tool they kept on the rig floor was called a (T.I.W.) valve and this tool was the first line of defense. In the event of any indication of problems down the hole this valve would be screwed onto the top of the drill pipe and with the aid of an Allen key turning a device inside this tool it could be opened or closed subsequently stopping anything coming out of the top of the drill pipe and they could monitor the well through various gauges in the doghouse until the pressure was bled off elsewhere.

Seldom and me worked away at our tasks with us both periodically going for breaks giving me a chance to check the washing. Bert told us the Lorries and trailers were booked for Tuesday and Wednesday, The mobile crane was also booked along with the slinging crews for the same two days. It was looking more likely that we would be finished here by Wednesday.

Later that night the Driller came round to ask us what we wanted from the chip shop as Bert was buying us a meal of our choice as a farewell present and that as there was no reason to split the dinner breaks we should all eat together, Bert arrived back from the chippie about 11–30pm and we all settled down to eat. This was the first time the whole crew had sat down to-

gether to eat and to enjoy my meal without looking at my watch
to make sure I didn't take too long, was a treat in itself. We were
all talking about things in general when the washing machine
kicked into spin to finish its cycle. The fucking thing vibrating
so much it was heading for the door, only the flex attached to
the plug on the wall stopped it from succeeding, the strap securing it to the wall was left undone, I only had one more batch of
overalls to do when Bert asked me if I would do a washing for the
Company man as he was also leaving in the morning, he said he
forgot all about it and only remembered when he seen ours playing up, Also as it was getting late he was wanting to get to bed.
Now the reason I disliked this company man so much was, he
would pass you by on the site without as much as a second look,
even though on numerous occasions I shouted hello or nodded
in acknowledgment of him being nearby, so I thought fuck you
mate. (Ignorant bastard) the times he did speak to me whatever
he was saying always ended with ok Sonny, or have you got that
Sonny? Now at 34 years of age I'd been called a lot of things but
Sonny was never one of them. It used to make the hairs on the
back of my neck stand up every time he called me that! But as
Bert was a decent sort I reluctantly agreed and went to the wee
caravan to get the carrier bag Bert said was just inside the door.
Quietly I opened the door, grabbed the bag, checked that there
were clothes in it and headed back to the carriage. When I emptied the bag out I found a pair of jeans, two pairs of socks, two
pair of underpants with skid marks on them, three tee shirts and
a beautiful Shetland sweater all rolled up together, I left them on
top of the machine till the last of the overalls were washed, this
would be in about an hour and I would be back in for coffee by
that time. By the time Seldom and me went again for coffee the
washing machine had finished it's cycle so after taking out the
overalls and putting them into the dryer I put the Company mans
washing in, quickly followed by three cups of F.U.G.G .and set the
machine for a full universal wash, watching the machine going
through it's cycle gave me a perverse sort of pleasure. Although it
was a crying shame to think what was happening to that Shetland
Sweater but I really didn't care, that little fucker treated me and
everybody else like we were something stuck to the bottom of his
shoe Respect is something you earn, not demand and I certainly
didn't have any respect for him.

About five in the morning Seldom and me went for another break and the first thing I noticed was the washing machine was still going, the tumble dryer had stopped and it had been set for one hour, the same time the washing should have taken, but on the dial it said it still had roughly another 15 minutes to go to finish it's cycle, obviously someone had set the machine to do another wash while we were away, (I wondered if they put any F.U.G.G. in as well). When the machine finally stopped it's kangaroo impression, I took the washing out to inspect it, The jeans and socks looked ok, the tee shirts and underpants looked like they might have shrunk a wee bit, But the sweater, that was half the size it was before it went in, a good hour in the tumble dryer should do it no harm. I thought as I put it in, I remember thinking to myself as I put the bag of washing quietly back into the Company man's caravan. (You won't be wearing that sweater again Sonny). The curtains of his caravan were still drawn when we drove off the site that morning ready to start our 24 hrs off.

The four of us had decided that we would get bathed as usual, have breakfast then get to bed until three in the afternoon, get up, do our ablutions, get dressed, then out for four. The pubs didn't open till 5o'clock so we could have a look about for an hour, maybe have a meal to soak up the drink we intended to have.

At the digs it was Seldom's and my turn to bathe first, so we tossed a coin to see who would go first between us, I won, so I stripped down to my boxers, grabbed a towel and headed for the bathroom, when I got there the door was locked and I could hear voices, the noise of me trying the door handle prompted a voice(I recognized as the landladies) to shout, I'll be out in a minute, then I heard the splash of water (you know) the sound of someone getting out of the bath. I went back to the room and Seldom said, fuck me that was quick, then seeing I was still dry he asked what was up, I told him the landlady was in the bath. You're Fucking joking? He said! No, and that's not all, her fucking husbands in there with her, Bob said I hope they haven't used all the hot water, I bet they fucking have Seldom said, and he was right, when I got back to the bathroom it was empty, and so was the hot water tank, (well empty of hot water anyway) The bath water was still running down the plughole and my first instinct was to put the plug back into the hole and at least save some hot water, but then I thought maybe those two were shagging in there,(well what would you think) so I just let the water run away, I tried the hot water tap again and the water was only luke warm, so back in the room with Dave being there this time, we decided to have breakfast first, hopefully by then the water would be warm enough for at least two of us to get washed and the other two could get washed when they got up. Dirty bastards was all Bob the Dog kept saying, that's our fucking hot water they used. Dirty fucking Bastards. At breakfast it took us all our time not to mention what happened when the landlady served us, she muttered on about how she and her husband were going to Grimsby for the day, to visit their son, that's why they were up early! We told her we were finished working nightshift and would start dayshift tomorrow (Sunday) I was hoping she wouldn't ask for the dig money until I had asked Les Devine for another advance on my wages, I only had about £85 left and was needing that for the weekend, I wasn't due her anything until tomorrow, the start of a new week, but thankfully she didn't ask.

Washed/shaved and dressed for the kill, the four of us walked into the City centre certainly smelling, if not looking, like four poofs, I don't know where Dave got his bottle of Aftershave, I'd never heard of it before, (or again for that matter) but as the rest of us didn't have any, we were happy to try some of his (Big mistake) I could still smell it days later. When the pub doors opened at 5 o'clock we were the first ones in, we decided to pace ourselves so we would last till at least closing time, so for the first couple of hours we stayed on pints of beer, at 7 o'clock there was only about 8 people in the place so we decided to move elsewhere, after all, there was plenty of pubs to choose from.

A couple of pubs and some pints later, we settled in one which, although it didn't have live music was busy enough. A juke box in the corner was playing away merrily and that's what we were getting, quite merry. Dave at the bar ordering the drinks, got talking to two women who were seated there, two (VERY BIG) women, I thought to myself what the fucks he up too when I saw him chatting these two up, I watched him pick up the tray of drinks and head in our direction followed by this pair, Look lads! He said. I've managed to persuade these two ladies to join us, I sat looking at these two and thought, I don't believe he had much persuading to do, The last time these two were taken out, they were holding onto their parents hands. I don't want to sound cruel, because it turned out they were sisters and a very good laugh, they didn't care about what people said or thought, their philosophy was, As they didn't have any control over peoples opinions of them, it was water off a ducks back, they said they had under active thyroids and glandular trouble.yeh I thought, you've both got glands that are greedy bastards.(Lincolns own Fran and fucking Anna) Dave and Bob seemed quite smitten with the both of them, so when Seldom disappeared for a while, I went to phone Macleod just to see how he was coping with (Kaiser) he was ranting and raving something about taking him to the vet just as the pips went, I was trying to tell him I had no more change left, when the phone went dead, ah well I thought, (everything seems ok there). I just got back to the table when Seldom arrived back, when I asked where he'd been, he said he went to buy a bottle of aftershave and asked the girls if they would like to smell it?, yes said one of them,! Then he took the top off the bottle and held it under her nose, well fuck me did she not start laughing, (I mean hysterical laughter.) she was laughing that much she fell off the fucking seat, it was so funny watching her, everybody else nearby was laughing, but I couldn't for the life of me figure out what the fuck she was laughing at, I had a quick look to see if my zip was undone, but it wasn't that, then I looked at the bottle Seldom had bought, after shave my arse. It was a bottle of Amyl nitrate (gold rush) this stuff is supposed to lower your inhibitions, if you have any that is, it's supposed to be a sexual stimulant, well it certainly stimulated her, she didn't stop laughing for about five minutes that was to be our party piece for the next couple of nights. We always had a bottle of rush with us wherever we went. I don't know why, it never done us any good! Not with getting off with women anyway. Waste of fucking money!

I don't remember how we got home, I don't even remember leaving the pub, but when I woke the next morning I was fucking dying, it took a couple of minutes to focus on the room, I couldn't believe what I was looking at, the TV was lying upside down on the floor, surrounded by teabags, coffee and sugar, all the bowls were empty, there was a couple of dark patches on the carpet and I dreaded to think what they were, maybe we spilt something, I didn't remember, Seldom was lying on the edge of the bed, I remember thinking what the fucks he lying like that for, then I saw the wet patch on the other side, I thought Oh no, this is a fucking nightmare, it took a couple shakes before Seldom woke up, his first words were, you dirty bastard, you pissed my bed last night, I denied it, but he said I got up during the night stood by his bed

26

and started pissing on him, I didn't remember, so maybe I did, but its certainly not something I've done in the past, Bob the dog wasn't in his bed and neither were the covers, he was lying on the floor still fully clothed and covered in sick, Christ what a mess, as much as we tried, we couldn't waken him, all he kept mumbling was (fuck off) so we left him sleeping, we tried to tidy the place up a bit before we went and got Dave and headed for work, We didn't do much that day, we were in no fit state, I don't think Les was too impressed but he didn't say too much. (If he did I don't remember) we also had to tell him Bob the Dog was ill in bed, By the time we finished that night we were feeling a bit better, we had decided we would have a quiet night tonight, get back to the digs have a wash then head down to Martha's for a couple of pints, back at the digs we were climbing the stairs me in front of Seldom and Dave when I stopped dead, standing at the top of the stairs with her arms folded and her face looking like she'd been eating a lemon was the landlady. (Yooouuu) she said pointing at Seldom, I asked you when you first came here if you suffered from incontinence and you said no, I would have put a rubber sheet on the bed if I'd known. At that I burst out laughing. Oh you think its fucking funny she said?, the way she said that nearly made me lose control of my bodily functions, I slipped past her and entered the room, the first thing I saw was Seldoms mattress folded in half, lying on the floor next to an electric fire presumably to dry it out, she was ranting on and on about how she kept a spotlessly clean house, I couldn't help looking at the cobwebs hanging from the ceiling as she said that, Seldom was trying his best to pacify her but she wasn't having any, she wanted £70 to replace the mattress, £70 are you fucking daft woman? Seldom said, you haven't heard the last of this she said as she left the room, your not getting £70 off me, you could buy a whole new fucking bed for that, Seldom shouted after her, his face looked like thunder, what the fuck are you laughing at he said, looking at me, this is all your fault, wait a wee minute I said, I'm not so sure it was me that pissed the bed, aye it was you alright, he said, on that note we got washed and changed and headed out to the pub, on the way we were discussing what the landlady had said and thought ourselves lucky she didn't throw us out, she's still not getting fucking £70 off me, Seldom kept on saying. We were only in the pub 10 minutes when the barmaid shouted Seldom to the phone, when he came back he didn't look a happy chappie, it

27

was Les Devine, the landlady somehow got the site number and complained about what had happened, Les said to get it sorted or we could find ourselves out of a job if B.P. got to hear about it, that was that then, we would have to pay her the £70 or find ourselves out of a job, I told Seldom I would give him half, I should fucking think so, he said. It was only when we got back to the digs we realized that Bob the Dog was missing, all his clothes and personal gear were gone, we thought he was out when we first got back, not noticing everything was gone, I liked Bob he was a good laugh. I fondly remember him whenever I ask someone to recite (Roberts retriever ran away) without using the rrrrsss, (Bob the dog fucked off)! It would be a few years later before I met the Dog again and get his explanation of why he fucked off.

At work next day (Monday) Les asked if we sorted out the landlady thing, to which we said yes, well we will tonight. I asked him for £150 advance and got it off him at dinner time, that whole day was spent dismantling everything in sight, we would be out of here by Wednesday for definite, back at the digs I gave Seldom £35 and he gave the landlady £91 for the mattress and three days dig money, I gave her £21 and told her we would be leaving on Wednesday.

That night we decided to try a different boozer, we got a couple of bottles of rush out of the sex shop just in case we found some unsuspecting women to try it out on, In the pub we were in full flight, laughing, and joking, just generally making fools of ourselves, and having a wee sniff of rush now and again, Seldom succeeding in getting some women to sniff, what he called his Aftershave, Oh it was working alright, after they sniffed it they would laugh so much they dropped their handbags, they dropped their drinks, they also dropped their inhibitions, the only thing they didn't drop were their fucking knickers. the barman watching us closely would only serve us half pints of (Scrumpy) cider, (this was potent stuff) to see how we handled it, we were the centre of attraction, but we attracted the attention of some of the local lads, tasty looking fuckers they were too, they didn't like the idea of us working down there and wanted to know why local labour wasn't employed. Now this was turning nasty, until Dave stepped in and offered to employ them for a couple of shifts, this seemed to pacify them, the arrangements were for them to be at a certain pickup point at 6-30am the next morning, they seemed quite happy about this and when Dave told them they would earn

£60 a shift, they were acting like long lost pals, when we were on our own again, I asked Dave what the fuck he thought he was doing, don't worry about it, was all he said, Next morning we were standing waiting for the van, it was fucking freezing, it must have been minus 2 degrees, when it finally arrived 15 minutes late, the driller said he had a problem starting it, the windows were still frosted over even though the heater was full on, driving to work we passed the place Dave told the lads in the pub to be at and standing there were two of them, Dave rolled down the window gave a shout, then stuck two fingers up at them, you should have seen their faces, they started running after the van fucking and blinding, promising vengeance, I had visions of them turning up at the site, but that didn't happen. I made a mental note not to go anywhere near that pub again!

That morning the Lorries and mobile crane arrived along with the slinging crew and we spent the day loading them up, the site was half empty by the end of shift, tomorrow would definitely be our last day.

That night we ventured into Collingham for a drink, in the Kings Head pub the first thing we noticed sitting mounted behind the gantry was an 6-1/2 inch diamond drill bit, how it ended up here and how much the landlord paid for it is anyone's guess, but according to Seldom it was worth a few grand, As Smedvig were not the only drilling company working in the area, Kentings were also down there, so somebody somewhere knows something. Talking with the barman he told us that some drilling crews stayed there from time to time, so maybe that was payment for their digs, if it was then they must have stayed there a fucking long,long time.

Wednesday seen the majority of the equipment off the site, the only things that were left was, one of the potacabins and the railway carriage, presumably to be lifted later. The man made reservoir would be drained and filled in and the fence surrounding the site would be taken down by the contractor who erected it, the mobile rig itself, was on its way to Great Yarmouth for storage. So by 4'o/clock we were finished. In his portacabin Les explained that the balance of my wages would be sent to my home address in the next day or two. Les expressed the hope of meeting us again somewhere else in the not too distant future, also that he would be putting in a report about the good job we did, to head office, (I hope he doesn't mention the mattress). So that was that then, we got dropped of at the digs, collected our belongings and headed to (Martha's) to say cheerio to everyone, In there we were drinking half pints of scrumpy with vodka coke chasers, So you can Imagine what sort of state we were in by the time we got to the railway station, I remember pushing Seldom up and down the platform on one of those two wheeled luggage trolleys until a guard told us off, Dave was still swaying on the platform as Seldom and me boarded the first of the two trains we needed to get home, Dave waiting on a connection going south, he was heading back to Great Yarmouth, I don't know why he didn't travel with the rig? I don't remember much about the journey home, I do remember waking up with Seldom kicking me, I was lying in the walkway using my holdall as a pillow, Seldom was shouting, hurry up this is our stop,(or words to that effect). When we got off the train I noticed we were in Inverkeithing (Fife) what the fuck are we doing here? I asked him, the next stops Dundee he said, I looked at my watch it was after midnight, the pubs were shut and it will have to be a taxi home, he said. So half an hour later and a fare of £8 between us, the taxi driver, who I named as (Dick Turpin) the robbing bastard, dropped us off at the Glenwood shopping centre close by to where we both lived. After arranging to meet at the pub later that morning we split up, Seldom going one way me another. Now after being away for a while be it on holiday, away working, or just visiting family or friends, there's no better feeling than the feeling you get when your back home, that's how I was feeling walking up my path. I can't describe it; it's just a good feeling. But that feeling was to change very shortly, The first thing to hit me when I opened the door, was the smell of Dog shit, the second thing was the Dog, he shot by me like a thing demented, stopping on the grass to hunch his back with his tail in the air, the poor thing only had diarrhea didn't he. He looked so pathetic the way he was whimpering and looking at me as if I could do something about his problem. I couldn't get angry with him if I wanted to; I went to him and started to clap him, rubbing his ears the way he liked and telling him re-assuringly it was ok. When I got into the house it wasn't too bad, there was shite on the carpet just inside the door, at least it wasn't up and down the stairs like I first Imagined, an hour later the mess was cleaned up and the house smelling of disinfectant. I kept my eye on him the rest of the night, In fact I kept two fucking eyes on him, but he was fine, I put it down to excitement, you know how dogs have that sort of built in sixth sense, well he must have known I was coming home, and just got a wee bit too excited.

That morning I went to sign on, answered the usual questions, you know. Have you done any work in the last two weeks? To which I was going to tell them, I was up half the night cleaning Dog shite off the carpet, but as they have no sense of humour in these places I didn't. I went down to take Macleod out for a drink just too say thanks for looking after Kaiser and him and me met seldom in the pub, Seldom told me to expect a phone call from, (Louis Laing) Oh aye,! I said, is she still going out with Superman,

It turned out that that was his bosses' name and that I could be offered a job offshore possibly in the next week or so, I could hardly contain myself, I was grinning like a fucking Cheshire cat, I phoned Liz in Glasgow to tell her the good news and she said she would come back only if I promised to behave myself. To which I agreed.

Saturday morning found me waiting for the postman, the two letters I was waiting on arrived. One with an Aberdeen postmark on it, this was the first one I opened and my heart sank when I saw what was in it. A cheque for £344-70p. It was broken down like this, Days worked 11@£60 =£660 +11days expenses @£25 =£275. As I didn't hand in my P45 they charged me emergency Tax, the expenses were tax free, so by the time they deducted the advances of £400 and tax and fucking national Insurance I was left with nearly £345. I could hardly breathe, I was starting to hyperventilate, All I could think about was where's my fucking £1000 I had a lump in my throat the size of an Ostrich egg I couldn't swallow, It took a while to sink in where it all went too, but that didn't make it any easier to take in. the other letter was my Giro and I had calmed down a bit by the time I went to cash it, I was on my best behaviour by the time I got Liz off the Glasgow bus later that afternoon.

It was later the following week when the phone call came from Louis Laing the (Smedvig Rig Manager) and he asked me if I would go offshore with Seldom to the Tartan Alpha. on the 24,th (you can guess what my answer was) I was over the moon, I phoned Seldom to tell him but he already knew, I had enough time to organize things like signing off the dole and sending my p45 to Smedvigs office in Aberdeen, then the days dragged by until finally it arrived, I'm going offshore.

2

The Tartan Alpha

On our way to the rig on Tuesday November 24, I had everything in my bag that Seldom said I needed, you know things like towels, soap, toilet rolls and a change of clothes in case we got ashore for the weekend. All the things a new start in the Oil Industry would need. I felt a right cunt at the check/in at Bristow's Helicopter Base in Aberdeen, when the security guy started taking everything out so everybody in the queue could see, first time offshore mate he asked? I only nodded, trying to hide my embarrassment. Still I bet that wasn't the first time he saw anything like that. And it probably wouldn't be the last. After I got over my initial embarrassment I saw the funny side of it, (cheers Seldom I should have known better) On the chopper I was as excited as a kid on Xmas morning, full of expectations, but not knowing what to expect, All I knew was, Liz was back, I had a new job, Yep things were looking up. Things were taking a turn for the better. I had heard you earned good money working offshore, with two weeks off to spend it, what could be better than that.I silently vowed to myself that I would work out there for a couple of years, save some money, buy my house, maybe buy a wee business, generally stick in and work towards those goals, Yep no doubt about it, I was on a high.

Looking around I noticed that some of the lads on the chopper were sleeping, others were reading, and some like me, were just looking at nothing in particular. I started to wonder if it was like me, their first time going offshore.

The journey to the rig took less than an hour, but it seemed longer, The noise of the rotor blades prevented us from having a conversation other than shouting at each other, so we just settled down, until we reached the rig, That in itself was an eye opener for me, although I didn't know what to expect, I had visions of something completely different. After checking in at the heli/ admin, and having a quick meeting with the Offshore Installation

Manager, (O.I.M). who took great trouble in letting us know that we were all one big happy family out there, I followed the rest of the crew to our cabins, (not in the main accommodation) we headed back up to the helideck to a place they called the annex, (I called it a fucking container) because that's basically all it was, next to it was another container they called the gym. That was for working out in if you had any energy left after your shift, (I can tell you now I was never in it.) The annex was used only for the drill crews, (Derrick man, Roughnecks, and Roustabouts) the Driller and assistant driller stayed in the main accommodation. That was my first taste of the type of segregation that I was told was rife in the North Sea by the Operators and the Contractors.

The Oil company we were drilling for was Texaco, and it soon became apparent that we and the other contractors on board were second class citizens.we were only there for as long as the drilling program lasted, depending on what was happening, this could be anything from 30 days to 1 year or longer.Back in the annex I found we were sharing four to a room, two on shift two off shift, adjoining the room was a toilet, shower, and a sink.We would be starting work at midnight that night, working a week of nights then the last week on days, I wasn't too bothered and also too excited to sleep so Seldom took me to see the storeman who rigged me out with overalls, boots, hardhat, and gloves. His name was Malky Mackay known as the (Welt) for reasons known to anybody who saw him naked in the shower, Malky explained to me that I was going Roughnecking as their were enough Roustys on the crew and I would be working on the rig floor, even after explaining I knew fuckall about Roughnecking he said I would soon pick it up. Talk about being thrown in at the deep end. It's a myth that just because your six feet tall you will make a good Roughneck. But I will give it my best shot. Malky took me to meet the dayshift Toolpusher, a big bearded Dutchman called (Hans van dyke) after one or two questions about what experience I had Roughnecking, (I told him about the land rig) he said I would do fine, and hoped I settled in ok.

On the rig floor that night I met the driller. a right unhappy chappie called Dennis, his assistant, (Stevie Roberts) who by the way was never allowed on the controls or the brake in the doghouse, for some reason known only to the driller, Stevie from Plymouth was such a quiet unassuming guy well liked by everyone, then there was Alan Sher from Glasgow (Big Jake) as he like to be called, he was a mountain of a man, well over six and a half feet tall, but a big gentle giant, then came Seldom and me, one of the Roustys a guy called Jimmy English spent most of his time on the rig floor although he wasn't classed as a Roughneck, (he was what was known as relief rousty)

Anybody reading this, who has worked offshore in the drilling game, especially in the late eighties will know what I mean when I say it was hard going for a novice like myself working on the rig floor, I was willing enough to work hard but just couldn't co/ordinate. I kept thinking I'm going to get seriously Injured here, What with the drill pipe being sent down the hole at a fair rate of fucking knots, me wondering if the driller was paying attention to what was happening, instead of fucking shouting Slips, Spinners, and make those fucking tongs bite.(I thought this fuckers nuts.)

On one side of the rig floor was a huge drum of steel cable, called the (Draworks) this cable was somehow reeved through sheaves on top of what I was told were the blocks, this was a huge heavy looking piece of machinery hanging from this cable, attached to the blocks were two steel arms (bales) about twenty feet in length and attached to these were the elevators which closed around near the top of the drill pipe allowing it to be picked up and lowered into the hole, (The top 12 inches of the drill pipe (tool joint) was thicker than the rest of It, so it didn't slip through the elevators) I was demented, down on the land rig we used doubles of drill pipe, here they were trebles, about ninety feet in length, the derrick looked twice as high and there was fucking hundreds of these pipes (Stands) they called them. The slips they used in the rotary table to secure the drill string while we joined another one onto it, weighed a fucking ton, it had three handles on them for easier lifting, but it felt like I was lifting them on my own. The spinners were used to spin the stand into the one already in the rotary table, making the threads meet, but even these had a fucking mind of their own. Once you released them from the strap holding them tied to the wind wall, they took off in any direction but the one you wanted, and once you finally got them onto the pipe and spun it in, it was a struggle to get them secured back to the wall, they were supposed to be on a counter weight for easy handling, but I had to wrestle these fuckers back, my arms were hanging off and we were only two hours into the shift. The tongs we were using were a fucking nightmare too, these were used to tighten up the joints once the spinners had spun them in as far

34

as possible, these too were supposed to be on counter weights for easy handling, all I can say is, it was anything but fucking easy, Seldom was up the derrick, about 80 feet in the air, it was his job as derrick man to grab hold of the elevators and latch them onto the next stand of drill pipe to go in the hole, just like he did on the land rig, only thing was, on the land rig their was only about twenty odd stands, here there was fucking hundreds, he wasn't going anywhere for a while, In fact, whenever were tripping in or out the hole Seldom spent nearly the whole shift up there, only getting down when someone went up to relieve him, and that wasn't very often. Tea breaks seemed to be few and far between, any time I asked the driller if I could go for a cup of tea or a smoke he would shout, Ten minutes, hurry up. Now the smoking shack was on the skid deck below the drilling package, and it took you two fucking minutes just to get there running down the stairs and four to get back, (I know, I timed myself) so much for taking your time to do things, and walk, don't run at anytime! Whoever brought these rules in never worked in drilling. I used to light two fags and smoke them alternately so I didn't burn my fucking lips! This would have been a good opportunity to give up smoking, if I wanted too, dinner breaks were a fucking joke as well, by the time you left the drilling package, made your way to the Main Accommodation, took your work gear off, in the dirty locker room, washed your hands, went to the galley, ate your meal, went back to the locker room got dressed, had two fags it was time to head back to the rig floor, twenty five minutes is not enough time to enjoy your meal,(it is if you're a fucking seagull) but I'm not.

I crawled into bed after my shower when the shift finished, every fucking bone in my body was aching, Big Jake who was sharing the room with me, lay on the opposite bunk trying to tell me it would be easier that night, as we would be drilling again, he said the dayshift crew would finish running the rest of the stands into the hole and that they would be drilling by the time we went out, he explained the reason they had pulled out the hole was to make a drill bit change, also change part of the B.H.A.(bottom hole assembly) this he said was a configuration of different shapes and sizes of steel assembly's attached to the bottom of the drill pipe and on the bottom of this was the drill bit itself, Big Jake was right, for the next week or so we were drilling away, giving me enough time to take in my surroundings while holding a scrubbing brush, and with a bucket of rig wash at my feet, scrubbing anything that didn't move, only stopping periodically to connect a joint of drill pipe to the ones in the hole, on the rig floor there was a hole in the deck called the (Mouse hole), in this hole they kept the next single joint of drill pipe to be picked up by the elevators ready for drilling, I hadn't noticed It before as It was covered by a steel plate when not in use.

The driller, an unhappy looking Chappie as I've already said, would hold (blow-out drills) these were to keep us on our toes so to speak. Unknown to me the Oil field we were drilling in, was rife with gas, and high pressure problems down the hole were common, so when the driller sounded the alarm with a horn in the doghouse we were to stop whatever we were doing rush and put our gas masks on, and operate the air winch which always had the T.I.W.valve attached to it, lift it onto the drill pipe, screw it in using the handle on top shaped like a ships steering wheel for faster turning, then tighten it up using the rig tongs, and then close the valve with the Allen key. It was always left in the open position, and the Allen key was always kept on the window ledge below the doghouse window. This would stop any fluid or gas coming out the top of the drill pipe. We never knew if it was a drill or the real thing, so as soon as we heard the alarm we went into action, We all had our own personal gas masks, this was called an (ELSA) escape life saving apparatus, we normally kept these somewhere at the back of the doghouse, each in a different place, so we would know exactly where our own one was at any time. When the alarm was sounded we would run and put these on, the small bottle of oxygen when fully charged gave you ten minutes to secure the rig floor and seek safety, and it was our job to make sure they were full. As I said we never knew when the alarm went off if it was the real thing or not, we would wait for directions from the driller. One time the alarm went off and with the driller shouting Blow-out we all ran and put our masks on, after donning mine I found I couldn't turn the valve to get air, it was too tight, I looked at Seldom and saw him laughing inside his mask, the bastard only tightened my valve didn't he. But its amazing the strength you get when you start panicking, And I managed to turn it on. Seldom did it for a joke, later on he said he knew it would only be a drill that's why he done it. Well I didn't know when the next drill was going to be or if it was going to be a drill for that matter, but when I found where he stashed his apparatus I tightened his valve with a stilson, at the next drill you should have seen his face when he couldn't turn the valve on, it was all red and purple, his cheeks were blowing up like a fucking puffer fish, I couldn't stop laughing, all I can say was I'm glad it was only a drill, Seldom was calling me all the stupid bastards under the sun, when he finally got a breath, obviously he had a wee memory lapse, the good thing that came out of it all was he never fucked with my (Elsa) again. When I thought about it later it was a daft thing to do, but you never think about that at the time do you? We managed to get the T.I.W. valve on and secured in good time, but the driller still wasn't happy, (too fucking long)! Was all he would say?

Heading to the canteen (galley) at dinner time, I wondered what would be on the menu, T, bone steaks or fresh salmon, maybe lobster, all the things I had heard you had a choice of eating while offshore, but I was brought back to reality by the chef when he informed me, (Yes mate of course you have a choice, you can take it or fucking leave it) I remember getting up early one night, feeling peckish I put my boots and hard hat on(these had to be worn when outside the accommodation and we were outside in the annex) and carrying my trainers I headed to the galley for something to eat, in the galley I settled down with a plate of mince and tatties, when I heard one of the catering staff tell the chef that I was nightshift, they were making such a big fucking deal about this, that I picked up my plate and headed to the counter, hey mate, I said to the chef, what's the problem. No problem he said, I know I'm nightshift, I'm also hungry, but if this is somebody's dinner I'll certainly give it back. With that, I emptied the plate into the slop bucket, feeling disgusted with that sort of attitude I went to the laundry to get my washing. We could only put our work clothes, not our overalls, into the laundry; these had to be washed in the drilling shack on the skid deck, below the drilling package. The dayshift and nightshift roustys washed these, this was yet again the sort of segregation that drilling people had to put up with, the reason our overalls could not be washed in the same machines as the rest of the platforms were they were too dirty. So drilling had their own washing machine and tumble dryer, (One big happy family).

Lifeboat drill was usually held on a Sunday morning, but it was common practice to muster at the boats two or three times a week, it could be at any time of the day or night depending on when the alarm went off, Now drilling worked from 12am to

37

12pm and vice versa depending on shift rota, the rest of the platform worked from 7am to 7 pm on the same rotation, only thing
was, when the boat drills were held on a Sunday it was usually at
7am, when half the drill crew were sleeping, it was ok if you were
on nightshift which you normally were the first week, but the
dayshift crew had to get up, and muster at the lifeboats, wearing
their lifejackets, this could take up to half an hour standing down
there fucking freezing, until someone, usually the (O.I.M.) decided that everything was ok, and you were allowed to stand down,
the 7 to 7 workers would either go to work or go to bed. But the
dayshift drill crew, what about them? They still had 5 hours before they started shift, and their all wide awake by now, just one
more example of ah well its only drilling, When you muster at the
lifeboat there was a large board on the wall with plastic cards in
slots, on these cards were the names of everybody who was allocated too that certain lifeboat, once you got there it was your
job to take out the card with your name on it and turn it round,
when all the cards were turned the lifeboat musterer then knew
that everybody was accounted for, I remember one time we were
wakened at 4am while working dayshift and headed down to the
boats, its was lashing rain, howling wind, and fucking freezing,
we were all huddled together trying to keep warm when I heard
a voice shouting SUTHERLAND SUTHERLAAAND I shouted,
here mate, I'm Sutherland, your not here he said, oh I'm fucking
here alright!, your not here, you haven't turned your card. Please
believe me when I tell you I wanted to throw this fucking arsehole
over the side. Ok, I forgot to turn my card, but the way he was
carrying on was fucking ridiculous, only in the offshore industry
would you get away with that attitude, if that had happened on
the beach I would have knocked the bastard out, but if I had hit
him that would have been the end of my offshore career, with
Texaco anyway, so I went and turned the card and said to him,
I'm here now.

N.R.B. (not required back.) Was a term used a lot offshore, it
was used for things like, your face not fitting, your attitude, or
even talking back, maybe refusing to do something you thought
was dangerous. that kind of thing, your name would be entered
into the invisible black book that the oil companies denied ex-
isted but everybody knew did, even though nobody saw it, it was
a form of blacklist, if you were ever N.R.B.'d from a particular
rig then you could near enough guarantee you would not be em-

ployed by the same oil operator on a different one, that's what would have happened to me if I had hit that musterer, and he knew it. Even though he was in the wrong, he was employed by the oil operator, I was just a contractor. (Cannon fodder)

Big Malky went home and another store man nicknamed "Hen Broon" came on, he was a tall lanky lad hence the nickname, he was a genuinely funny guy, and very easy to get on with, I always remember anytime I went to the store looking for something, Hen always said, I haven't got what your looking for mate, but it's on the next boat, I'm certain that's the first thing trainee store men are taught to say, " its on the next boat mate" I was in the cinema one night with Hen and a few others we were watching the film psycho and when it came to that bit in the film where Norman Bates sets about Janet Leigh in the shower Hen was getting a wee bit carried away, he was shouting, GO ON GIVE IT TO THE BITCH, FUCKING GIVE IT TO HER, I turned to him and said, steady on mate its only a fucking film, Later on while telling Seldom about Hen's antics he explained that some years ago Hen and his partner had a wee disagreement with her ending up with quite a few puncture holes about her person, Hen lost his liberty for a while over this. So there you are you just never know who you're sitting next to at the pictures.

We changed onto dayshift on Tuesday doing a crazy change over, we started at 8pm Monday night worked till 4am Tuesday, when that were dayshift came out and worked till 12am and then we came out to relieve them, they going home when the chopper arrived with the other crew, usually about 4pm. I was getting into the swing of things now, the spinners were getting that wee bit easier to handle, so were the tongs, but the driller, he was hard work, any time one of us went for a break we would bring him back a cup of coffee, by the end of shift their would be about six or seven cups of cold coffee sitting on the doghouse window he never drank one of them, but we still kept bringing them just too piss him off, the only time he left the doghouse was when the Toolpusher came up to relieve him for dinner or a smoke break, and when he did go for a smoke he never mixed with us he used the pushers office which was at the end of the catwalk so he could look out the window and keep his eye on us. we pulled out the hole a couple of times during the following week (round tripping) they called it, that's pulling everything out the hole making whatever changes that were needed, be it changing the drill bit or part

39

of the B.H.A.then running the whole lot back in again. I don't know if I told you or not but another name for the drill pipe is (string).as in drill string.

They were still drilling away when we boarded the chopper bound for Aberdeen, in my bag I had 5 cartons of fags, Seldom told me that's what we were allowed, obviously nobody told the customs guy, because when I didn't have enough money to pay for them, he took 4 cartons off me, outside waiting for us was a wee guy called John Smith, he was the Dan Smedvig courier, john had with him a list of names and when he called mine out, I went and got £50 in cash and a cheque for nearly £800 off him, now this was the life I thought, £850 for two weeks work, you canny beat that. I'll never spend all that in two weeks, or so I thought, I couldn't wait to get home to show Liz what I earned, but first stop was the boozer that was the start of the slippery slope, but I didn't know it yet.

When I finally staggered home all I had left was the cheque. The £50 in cash was gone, A couple of quid in silver was all I had left in my pocket, I suppose I was acting the big oilman home from the rigs, throwing his money around like there was no tomorrow, buying drinks for people that I wouldn't normally give the time of day too, but I didn't care their was still £800 left remember,

Liz didn't say too much as usual, when I sobered up next morning I noticed in the mail a letter from Dan Smedvig it was my joining Instructions for the Robert Gordon's Institute of Technology (R.G.I.T.) in King Street, Aberdeen. I was to attend on Monday 14th December at 8-30 am for a 5 day survival training course, it was outlined what the contents of the course would be on a daily basis finishing at 4-30 pm on the Friday.

I travelled to Aberdeen on the Sunday night, Dan Smedvig had booked me into a boarding house on Bon Accord street, 10 minutes walking distance from King Street, already in the digs was a rig bag with boots, coveralls, hard hat, and a couple of pairs of gloves. that I was required to take with me to the course, On my arrival I filled in the registration form giving my personal details, their must have been over 50 people all attending the same course as me but later we were split into three groups, my group were going fire fighting for our first day.

On arrival at the fire station two Instructors spent most of the morning showing us videos of fires and explaining the ingredients needed for a fire to exist, after lunch we were shown the different types of fire extinguishers "I recognized the water one" also the different types of hoses and connections, the firemen lit a couple of different types of fires and we got a chance to put them out using the Extinguishers. They showed us how to use the oxygen mask and how to check the cylinder was full, then they kitted us out in groups of four with oilskin trousers, firemens jackets and hats, fully equipped with the oxygen masks we were to enter this darkened building and using the technique they showed us, were to find our way out again. That was easier said than done, we were all holding onto each others jackets doing the fucking conga dance inside this smoke filled building, unknown to us one fireman was already in there watching our every move, one part of the building was blocked off so we had to crawl through what I can only describe as a wire cage, finally we emerged outside again, feeling somewhat claustrophobic the first thing I did was light a cigarette, I was needing the nicotine, once all the groups were finished that exercise we were to enter another building this time without wearing breathing apparatus. The only snag was, this building had a fire burning in it, I was in the first group led by a fireman who told us to take off any jewellery we were wearing as it got very hot in there, he wasn't fucking kidding, I was feeling quite ill with the heat by the time we got out of there, I noticed a guy in the next lot to go in was wearing an earring, aye I mean a big fucking earring, but when I said to him he'd be better taking It off, he just gave me a stare that said mind your own fucking business, I thought ok pal, then when I saw him ten minutes later he was wishing he had listened to me, his fucking ear was all swollen and angry red looking, Do you know that feeling you get when your proved to be right? Well I had that feeling when I saw him. "Told ya"

Back in the classroom later on, we each filled in a questionnaire about the day's events, what we learned, if anything, and what we thought about the contents and the course Instructors. I must admit It gave me a good idea of how to approach a fire, how to test a door for heat, how to search for an opening in a smoke filled room, all these things were new to me and hopefully would give me an idea of what to do in the event of me ever coming across a real fire.

The next two days were to be spent finding out all about the lifeboats, Tuesday in the classroom learning the theory about compass bearings, the survival kits, water, food rations, that sort of thing, even though I was paying attention I didn't really take much of it in, all the talk of steering west by north west, and east by nor,nor east simply went over the top of my head, All I was thinking about was having a curer after the night before, there wasn't much to do in the digs at night except look at the four walls, there was no television in the room and as the landlord didn't supply an evening meal, It was down to the chip shop after the course then off to the pub, I had stayed a wee bit longer than I had intended so I was feeling just a little bit fragile in the morning, Anyway at dinnertime, although they supplied a meal at the course myself and three other lads headed to the pub, the Instructor didn't have a problem with this, as long as we weren't late back, or under the Influence so much that it showed. We didn't let him down; we were back in plenty of time after having two or three pints each. The afternoon was similar to the morning session and I was feeling better after the beers, even so I still couldn't grasp the compass bearing theories,

Wednesday morning first thing, we were split into groups of six and taken to our allocated lifeboat, there we were kitted out with our life jackets and shown the inside of the boat, how to start and stop it, how the release mechanism that was holding it in the air at the pier worked, (davits) they called them. Once everyone was familiar with this, the boat was lowered into the water and we were off, everyone was given a shot at steering the boat, Steering the compass heading the Instructor gave us, It was getting a wee bit choppy and the wind was picking up a bit so the Instructor kept us inside the breakwater, he told us that maybe in the afternoon, if the wind dropped a bit, we would head out into open water, I wasn't looking forward to that,! I'm a landluvver at heart, the sea hold no pleasures for me, only fears. At dinnertime only four of us out of the same boat headed to the pub, we all had the bar lunch of the day plus a few pints, but still got back in plenty of time for the afternoon session, The Instructor Informed us that as the wind had dropped sufficiently we would be heading out into open water, Now the wind might have dropped a bit but it was still quite choppy, a bit too fucking choppy for my liking, but he new best so off we went.

I didn't know If I suffered from seasickness or not, I'd never been on a boat before, so when the Instructor asked everyone if they did? I shook my head like everyone else, All I can say is, it was getting a bit uncomfortable out there, I looked about the boat and noticed that one guy was looking quite grey, he told the Instructor how he felt, The Instructor Informed him of the chain reaction that would occur, if he was sick inside the boat, and asked him to stick his head out overboard if he felt sickness coming on, everything seemed to settle down for a while, then it was someone else's turn to steer the boat, the guy who was next was an ex/fisherman with a big bushy beard, he was like the rest of us, going through his R.G.I.T. so he could work Offshore, he wasn't long at the wheel when the Instructor gave him a new heading to steer, in correcting the course the boat gave a violent surge and started to dip and rise, this was enough for the guy who was feeling queasy, he made a bolt for the open hatch and started throwing up, this made the rest of us, who were sitting on the benches either side of the boat start to boak, then when the guy who was steering the boat ducked his head back inside to tell us he liked nothing better, than to feel the sea spray on his face, that was enough for us we all dived for the hatches and started throwing up. Stuck to the guys beard were bits of fish, chips, and mushy peas, what he thought was sea spray was actually the spewings from the guy with his head out the hatch, seeing it stuck to this guys beard set off the chain reaction the Instructor warned us about. I can tell you now, returning to the pier later that afternoon; we were a sorry fucking sight. The rest of the day was spent looking at flares, how they worked, and how to set them off, The ones I was Interested in were the hand held ones, ones that stayed lit even under water, these, I was told, took the oxygen out of the water, and I got to thinking about a couple of fish pools not far from where I stayed, a couple of these would come in handy. They didn't work exactly as I thought they would, but I will explain about that later! Wednesday night was spent the same as the last two. Chippie, pub, bed, in that order.

Thursday was a day in the classroom learning all about the basics of first aid. How to put the patient in the recovery position, apply tourniquets and bandages, resuscitation, how to feel for the pulse or heartbeat. How to co-ordinate between applying pressure to the sternum then give mouth to mouth, giving (C.P.R.) Cardio Pulmonary Resuscitation, they called it, all good stuff I thought? One or two lads on the course looked like they had previous experience when it came to playing with the blown up dolls, but that was their business, who am I to cast dispersions on their private life.

That was the longest day of the of the course, and after filling in the usual what did learn and what did you think of the course questions, we were out of there, one more day and I was going home.

Friday morning was spent at the poolside learning all about the life raft, all the safety equipment that was attached to it, how to erect the roof canopy of it, to keep out the elements, why the need to throw out the sea anchor, all the things you would need to know about if you ever found yourself adrift in one of these, after every one was conversant with the workings of the raft it was then thrown into the pool and everyone took a turn of turning it over, I didn't see the point of this because it was the same upside down as it was upright, but that's what the Instructors wanted so who were we to argue, once everyone had a go at turning it over, which by the way was no easy feat, we then all got into the water and had to climb into it, being helped in by the person already in it,

The second half of the morning was spent doing exercises in the pool climbing up ropes, simulating being lifting out of the water by helicopter, all this while wearing one of the biggest bulkiest life jackets I've ever seen, I was knackered by the time we went for dinner, I was still on a liquid diet so some of us headed for the bay view bar just across from the course,

The afternoon found us back in the pool, this time we were taught how to escape from a ditched helicopter, (H.U.E.T.) helicopter underwater escape training. I didn't like this one bit, and I wasn't the only one,but we were told if we didn't complete this exercise, we would be given a restricted certificate stating the person didn't complete the whole exercise, I supposed that meant you couldn't travel in a helicopter, and if that was the case you wouldn't be going offshore, so what was the fucking point of spending all week training to go offshore then at the last hurdle you don't finish the course, It didn't make sense to me, especially if you were paying for the course yourself, so as much as I didn't like it I was determined to last the distance, we were again split into groups of four this time, if you were a non-swimmer you put on a red hat, blue if you could swim, in the water were two divers, to help if you got into difficulties, they tried to keep only one non-swimmer in a group(guess who?) your right. Even if I could have swum like Johnny fucking weizsmuller, I was getting a red hat on my knapper. In the huet we were to settle into our seats while the Instructor went through what was going to happen, first we would be lowered into the water until only our heads were sticking out of it, then we undone our safety and swam to the poolside, (I floated) then the next lot did the same until everyone had done this part of the exercise, the next bit was in two parts, once we were seated again in the huet, we were to be lowered again like the first time, until only our heads remained out of the water, then we would be raised out again, but this time we would be lowered back down again pretty quickly, right under the water, the huet was then turned 180 degrees still under the water, we were supposed to wait until it settled then count to 7 then release our seatbelts and swim to the surface, All I can say is I'm fucking glad I was in the first group to go, If I had to stand and watch what was going to happen, I'm not so sure I would have went through with it, It was terrifying to watch, I was visibly shaking, I tried to laugh it off by saying to the others it was cold eh?, but I was silently shitting myself, to think you had to do this every three years was frightening, but I had done it, I was quite pleased with myself, especially when one guy couldn't bring himself to do it, there was also a young girl who refused as well, I don't know if they ever did do it, the last I seen of them was being led away by one of the Instructors.

The last part of the exercise involved everybody jumping off the high tower in pairs, into the water, which by now was very rough due to the wind machine they used to simulate bad weather being switched on, make our way to the life rafts, climb in, help everybody else in, put up the canopy, throw out the sea anchor, simulate cutting the securing ropes, then once everyone was safely accounted for we started looking out our safety equipment, I enjoyed this part of the exercise, there was little chance of drowning due to the size of the life jacket I had on, the only danger was of breaking your neck when you hit the water, but I landed safely enough. The exercise over we all got changed and met back in the classroom to receive our certificates from the Instructor, fill in yet another questionnaire, then we all headed off in different directions, On the train home I silently pondered over the weeks events, and some of the characters I had met, not knowing then, that I would meet some of them in the years to come and we would reminisce the stories of our very first attempt at survival training.

Arriving home that night, Liz met me in the pub with the news that my passport had arrived while I was away, It was only a year passport, Seldom told me I would need one for Identification purposes, I knew from experience that Seldom was a wind up merchant but even I knew he wasn't kidding, It also came in handy because with the mail was a letter from Dan Smedvig (recruitment) informing me to report on Tuesday 22 December at 12o'clock for a medical in Aberdeen at Aberdeen industrial doctors. And to bring some sort if I, D, with me, I thought that's the day I go offshore? I haven't had much time at home, So much for 2weeks on 2 weeks off, but I wasn't too bothered, I did what needed to be done to secure at least the survival certificate, even if the job with Smedvig didn't come to much, I was warned not to expect to much, as work in the drilling Industry was either a feast or a famine, so I prepared myself to take each trip offshore as the last,

Tuesday came and I boarded the train without Seldom, he would get a later train and I would meet him at the check/in, if he had travelled with me it would have meant him hanging about Aberdeen for a few hours more than needed, this time would be better spent with his family, I hadn't been for an offshore medical before, so later when it became clear to me that I'd spent more time answering questions about my parents illness's, whether they had problems with their hearts, headaches, backaches, blood pressure, angina, vagina, thrombosis, tuberculosis, hypnosis, whether they smoked, coughed, took a drink, had all their own hair and teeth, or any of the other 30 ailments in the list, I was pretty pissed off, because the next page asked me If I also had any of these ailments, from the time I was seen by the doctor, where I was measured, weighed, whispered too, (as a deafness test) found out I was colour blind, had my blood pressure tested, piss tested, had my bobby felt, and finally had a finger stuck up my bum, I was back on the street in twenty minutes flat, It took twenty minutes to fill the fucking form in, how the fuck was I to know if my parents had any of these ailments I could hardly pronounce most of them, all I knew was they were alive and kicking, what more does a son need to know than that? Apart from that they didn't even ask me for Identification, I could have been anyone.

Back on the rig again, we were greeted with loads of Xmas decorations hanging from the roofs and walls of the accommodation, a Xmas tree was standing in one corner all lit up with fairy lights, this was the last thing I or any of the crew wanted to see, It was bad enough being out there at that time of year without being reminded of It, I don't mean to sound like scrooge, bah humbug and all that, but I was quietly pleased when I found they didn't decorate the annex where we were living. We found out they were drilling the six and a quarter inch section of the hole that should be finished in a day or two. So things should be fairly routine for a while, As we didn't start work till midnight we were all to attend an Hydrogen Sulphide (h2s) course, this would take approximately two hours, what it involved was giving us an indication of what this type of gas was capable of, and what affect it had on people who came into contact with it, basically at up to 5 ppm (parts per million) you were reasonably safe, but from 10 ppm onward you were in danger of losing your sense of smell, followed by unconsciousness, then death . not a gas to fuck around with, I can tell you, this gas was heavier than air so it floated downwards, I often used to wonder when the alarms went off, if it was a gas alarm as was the norm, then if they knew that h2s was possibly the cause for the alarm going off, then why the fuck were we going to the lifeboats, where eventually this gas would float down to where we were waiting? The rule of thumb was, if you could smell rotten eggs you were ok, so get out fast, once you stopped smelling them, you were finished, say goodbye, end of the road, life expectancy nil, so you never had anybody taking egg rolls or egg pieces to the rig floor, even if you were fucking lucky enough to get them, "just in case". I wondered why they didn't give us this course last trip.

The whole platform was manned by one of five categories, Production, Drilling, Construction, Services, and Catering, the latter four were all contractors working for their specific companies, contracted out to do work for the operator, that being (Texaco) the Production workers were usually employed by the Operator Or whoever's platform or rig it was, i/e B.P. Shell, Conoco, etc,etc and the majority of these people had a certain air of esteem about them. It was plain to a blind man that if you didn't have the same type of logo on your overalls on as they did, then you were not one of the big happy family that the O.I.M. who took the time and trouble to tell everyone that came onboard were. We were treated as Incomers, as If we didn't belong there. But the stupid thing about was, If drilling didn't drill the wells, there would be no need for the production workers. And if there was no

Production workers there would be any need for drilling, so we actually needed each other. But somewhere along the way, they seemed to have forgotten this, I don't know if it was the fact that we were contractors, that we were treated this way, all I can say is, it wasn't a nice atmosphere to work in. It was usually the ones who were employed as contractors before being taken on by the operator who were the worst offenders.

This certain breed of the workforce tarred all of their colleagues with the same brush that they themselves were tarred with, and it was a shame because most of the workforce were there to do a job and get home to their families, just like everyone else, How the wearing of a different pair of overalls could change a working mans attitude to another working man was beyond belief, but I was to witness this obscene act of snobbery being carried out on other Installations by the workforce of other Operators.

On my second nightshift (wed) I hurt myself when, while making up a joint of pipe in the hole, the tongs slipped jarring my shoulder, I carried on until the end of shift, then went to see the medic, after some questions about what happened, and who I worked for, it became very apparent to me when he found out I was working for drilling, that he wasn't Interested, try some deep heat rub on It, he said, giving me a tube, you will be alright in a day or two, well it wasn't alright that night, I could hardly lift my arm, all the driller kept mumbling was fucking pussy, So much for his man management skills,(wanker) Anyway I carried on until the end of shift, thank fuck we weren't pulling out the hole, I would never have been able to do It.

Xmas eve (Thursday) and we were messing about behind the doghouse cleaning and scrubbing, my shoulder still hurt a bit, but at least I could move it, we were wishing each other a Merry Xmas just after we came on shift. We were still drilling away, but we only had another 6 joints, about 180 feet to drill, till we reached total depth (TD). And when that happened we would circulate the mud down the hole for a while, then we would pull out, I was dreading pulling out the hole, there must have been over a hundred stands of pipe down there, I expressed my concerns to Jake and Stevie who both said just take your time, we probably wont pull out on our shift, But Santa Clause dressed as a driller had other ideas, he was horsing on as usual giving the odd bellow from the doghouse window when a connection was required.. 5am and the breakfasts had started, the crew going off in pairs for their fry up, trying to time it between connections. When it was my turn to eat, I noticed outside the galley, on the wall was a sheet of paper with eating times for Xmas dinner, Managers, Office staff and Production, 11.45am till 12.30pm. Drilling and Services 1.00pm till 1.30 pm. I made a promise to myself that I wouldn't be having Xmas dinner at that time 1.00pm. I would be in my scratcher sleeping, when I got back on the rig floor we discussed it among ourselves we couldn't make up our minds whether to go or not, bit eventually we all agreed they could ram it, I didn't fancy hanging around for an hour just to have Xmas dinner and neither did the rest of the crew, but fate was to take a hand in this decision.

At about 9.30am Xmas morning we were getting ready to make another connection when the driller shouted twice, BLOWOUT. BLOWOUT, here we go again I thought, as I ran to get my mask. Xmas morning and this bastards got us doing a drill, a few seconds later we were picking up the T.I.W. when clear liquid started to come out the top of the drill pipe, this liquid was getting darker and higher by the second, by the time we had the T.I.W. valve on this stuff was spewing 60 feet in the air, and all other directions, we were turning this valve as fast as we could till we could get the rig tongs on to tighten it up, once this was done, the driller was screaming at us to close the valve, but we couldn't find the Allen key, this water, oil, and mud, was shooting out the top of the drill pipe like mount Vesuvius, it was like a fucking volcano, and it was covering everything,us included, I couldn't see a fucking thing, I was down on my hands and knees feeling blind for the Allen key when the driller found it and closed the valve, the fluid immediately stopped coming out of the drill pipe, the driller ran back into the doghouse to do what I don't know? But we just stood there looking at each other, the silence was actually deafening, if you know what I mean! Once the adrenalin had stopped pumping in our bodies, we retreated to the back of the doghouse to take in exactly what had happened, the whole rig floor was covered in this fluid, it was dripping everywhere, we were soaking wet, right through to the skin, from start to finish the whole thing was over in about 3 minutes, but you should have seen the mess! The driller gave us the all clear to take our masks off, then we really seen the state of the place, it was going to take more than one bucket of rig wash to clean this up. Soon everybody and his dog were on the rig floor, Inspecting the mess and seeing what was happening in the doghouse, we were standing in the background shivering in our wet clothes, even our welling boots were soaking inside, we were told to wait for Instructions from the driller. After about half an hour when It looked like nobody was bothering about us, we took turns to go in pairs and get dry overalls, these were ok but our working clothes underneath were still wet, and we finished the shift like that. So much for the fucking drill I thought to myself! At 11.45am when the other crew came out, they already knew what had happened, there wasn't much to tell them, except wish them a merry Xmas, so it was a quick handover, down in the smoking shack we were going over the events that had happened, each of us wondering where the T.I.W. Allen key, had got to, I mean it was always sitting on the doghouse window ledge,! It never moved from there, even after a drill it was always put back in the same place, the only thing we could think of was the driller had it, then intending on having a drill, he we would make us look right cunts when it came to closing the valve and we couldn't find the key. That was our theory anyway, whether it was right or not we'll never know. After getting out of our coveralls and with our work clothes still wet, we decided to pay a visit to the galley, on opening the door, we were stopped by one of the stewards who informed us we couldn't come in as our meal wasn't until 1.00pm we could see everybody sitting with their Xmas hats on, laughing, and joking, generally enjoying themselves, and their meal. Some looked up and seen us standing at the door and what a sight we must have looked covered in dirty brown slime, with our clothes sticking to our bodies, Oh said Jake we don't want to come in, were only here to tell the camp boss to ram his Xmas dinner up his fucking arse, after wishing the steward a merry Xmas we left and headed back to the annex for a shower, Jake went in first, and he was only in there a couple of minutes when I noticed water coming from under the bathroom door and running into the room, the fucking drains had backed up, Jake oblivious to this, until I told him, it took us over twenty minutes each to get showered, what with waiting for the water to drain away before it entered the room again. Jake took the dirty washing to the laundry to find there was no laundry being done on Xmas day, Ho.Ho.Ho. How does that saying go? It never rains but it pours.

On shift that night the driller gave us all a dressing down for what he called a fucking fiasco that morning, I couldn't look at him without thinking, you bastard, you had that Allen key all the time, and now you are blaming us for not finding it. He gave us all a big lecture about how important it was for things to be kept in their proper place before handing us each, an Allen key. I said merry Xmas when he gave me mine, and the look I got off him would have made milk turn sour.

For the next couple of days they pumped kill fluid down the well in an attempt to halt the pressure build up. This would have been a couple of easy days for us if the place hadn't been in the state it was in, it took us this time to clean up, I mean two crews cleaning for 48 hrs and it still looked like shit, that's how bad it was!

After the well was stable, it took about 18 hrs to pull slowly out of the hole, lay down the B.H.A. and rig up to run the 4-1/2 inch casing, running the casing was going to take another 12hrs or so, and once this was run they were going to cement it in, and rig down, this was the last well in the drilling program, and they were going to (cold stack) the rig because drilling weren't expected to be back onboard for at least 9 months maybe longer only the maintenance crew would remain onboard.

Our crew were involved in both operations of pulling the second half of the drill pipe out the hole; we had laid down about half of the B.H.A. when the other crew came on shift... That night we came out to finish off running in the 4-1/2 inch casing. Running the casing was quite straight forward, there was two casing hands on board so we got regular tea breaks, the crane landed a bundle of 7 joints on the catwalk and one of the roustys latched one of them at a time to the pick/up elevators, all we had to do then was pull it up to the rig floor and the casing hands connected it to the others in the hole. (Piece of piss). Big Jake told me the other crew had been asked to stay on for an extra two days to help break down the drill pipe, and the drill collars racked in the derrick. But first we would have to lay down the riser sections and the mouse hole and skid the rig to skid to an empty slot to do that, the pusher didn't think it was worthwhile bringing out their relief's, as there wasn't enough work after the pipe and collars were laid down to keep two crews busy. The other crew agreed to stay on, with the promise of them getting off on new years eve, and we stayed on nights until the early hours of Thursday morning, then changed onto days, they had us doing another daft change over, we started shift on Wednesday night at 8 00pm until 4 00 am on Thursday morning then started again at 12 00 midday and worked till 10 00pm, the rest of the platform had most of Xmas day and new years day off, but drilling carried on as normal, It was just another day as far as they were concerned. HAPPY NEW YEAR.

As there was only our crew onboard the powers that be, decided that we could work 7am till 7pm for some reason, they thought we would get more work done on this shift, the tool pushers went off leaving the driller in charge. and for the next 5 days we dismantled everything in sight, every thing that could move was moved, Seldom was busy in the pump room, pumping what fluids were left back to the supply boat, then cleaning his tanks and dismantling and greasing the pumps and parts, The roustys were busy back loading the tubular, chemical containers, tool baskets, etc, while we were busy dismantling the B.O.P. rams, tongs, spinners, elevators, slips, etc, etc, all greased up ready for storage in the sackstore, our final shift and a half was spent spraying a protective plastic coating on every thing that was left, the driller gave us a talk on how to use the spray guns that came with the drums of fluid plastic, the Idea was that once you had the air gun set too spray and the fluid was coming out of it, you were to make slow sweeping motions over the area you wanted to cover, and once it was covered the fluid hardened into a plastic covering, therefore sealing the equipment from the elements, this was called cold stacking, when the rig was ready to operate again the plastic was easily removed and below was equipment free from rust and ready for use. We were also told how much this stuff cost, over $500 a barrel, (as if we were giving a fuck). We were told to use it sparingly. On our last shift Seldom appeared on the rig floor and wanted a shot of a gun. Jake said he could have his and he would go for a smoke, no sooner had Jake left, when Seldom started playing silly buggers with the gun, he was messing about with the nozzle so the fine spray was now just a jet of fluid, he was holding the gun at his waist like a fucking gun slingers, and like the cowboy quick draw McGraw he would point it at the area he was covering and squeeze the trigger, then long jets of this stuff would start running in big dollops down the pipe work, I was laughing like fuck, until I saw the company man coming onto the rig floor, it was too late to warn Seldom by this time, so I carried on with what I was doing, fine spraying the air winch on other side of the rig floor. Seldom didn't see the company man watching his animated antics of shooting every gunslinger on the rig floor, until it was too late, the look on his face when he did, was priceless, this guns fucked, he shouted to the company man! Aye and so are you, the company man said back, clean it off and do it again, and stop fucking about, I couldn't stop laughing, and I laughed all the harder when he asked me to give him a hand.

We finished at 2.00 pm that day (Tuesday), the chopper was due in at 4.30pm so after we got showered and changed, and packed our bags, we headed off to watch a film in the cinema, we had all seen the film that was on before, so Jake and I went to see the radio operator to see if he would change it, his answer was, there's other people in their cabins watching the film that was on, so the answer was no, or words to that effect, Jake let him know in no uncertain terms what he could do with his film, I butted in to try and defuse what was going to become a major argument, look mate I said, you have three video recorders there, surely their not all watching three different movies,? It was beginning to annoy me thinking that the other people he was talking about were lying in their bunks watching fucking movies, while in the annex we were lucky to have running water, I was fed up being treated like shite! Surely you can turn one off and put a film we've not seen before on for us? I don't think I like your attitude, this tosser said, you drilling people are all the same, You think you can get what you want all the time, well I'm telling you no, that done it for me. before he could say anymore I tried to grab hold of him, but Jake caught hold of my arm, holding me back, saying this fucking wankers not worth getting the sack for, I knew he was right, so I told the bastard exactly what I thought of him, and what he could do with his videos. Then Jake and I stormed off.

On the chopper going home, with no paper to read, and too excited to sleep, I tried to see how many seagulls I could count before it got too dark to see, I can't remember how many I counted, but I did start to think that maybe I didn't do myself any favours in arguing with that radio operator, I kept thinking If he reports me for swearing at him, that might not go down too well with my employers, I tried to put it out of my head, telling myself, fuck him, he was in the wrong! But then again he worked for the operator. I was just a contractor.

John Smith again met us off the chopper, and gave out the pay cheques and 50 quid in cash to each of us, he didn't have any answers to the questions the crew were asking him, all he said was the office would be in contact with everyone, informing them if or when they would be going offshore again, I suppose I was a bit paranoid about what happened on the rig because I could swear he was looking at me when he said the word, If.

On the train going home we were partying, after all this was the new year, Liz picked Seldom and me up at Kirkcaldy train station and we headed home, stopping off at the boozer on the way, we led the high life for over a week, Buying the things we couldn't afford too for a long time, all the time waiting and hoping for a phone call or letter from Dan Smedvig with the news of whether I was going away again or not. Liz and me decided that as things were looking up and we were getting along better, it might be a good Idea to set the date for getting married, we had spoken about it before but something always came up to put us off. Liz and I had both been married before and were wary of going through the hassle of it all again. Liz like myself had two kids, (Nicky and David) by her ex/ husband Sam, they stayed with him and his new partner. My two (Michelle and Jason) were looked after by my ex/wife Barbara, so as we were on our own it seemed that getting married was the right thing to do, who knows it maybe settle us down.? Then Liz phoned me at the pub one day to tell me that Louis Laing had phoned, and would I call him back? I was a bit apprehensive when I did phone and the few short minutes it took for the receptionist to get him felt like forever, when I did manage to speak to him I started to fear the worst, he asked me how things went on the Tartan, and if I had any problems, when I said no. I was waiting for him to mention the radio operator! But when he asked if I was available to go offshore the following week, I was over the moon. I was to check/in at Bristows Helicopters on Thursday 21st Jan at 7.ooam and go out to the Hutton T.L.P. more details would be sent in the post later, I phoned Liz and told her the news, then I phoned Seldom, he told me he was going to a different rig from me, and that was the last time that Seldom and me would work on the same rig together, I was on my own now. Two days later the letter arrived from Dan Smedvig. Hutton T.L.P. here I come. At home Liz said she would arrange for the banns to be posted while I was away. And try to arrange the wedding for Saturday the 16th of April.

Tartan Alpha

3

HUTTON T.L.P.

Thursday 21st Jan I was sitting in Bristow's waiting to check in for the Hutton Tension Leg Platform (T.L.P.) looking around to see If I could recognize anybody, when Big Jake appeared, he was going out with me, he Introduced me to another couple of guys that I would be working with, Steve Mackay, (roughneck) Bill Clarke, (rousty pusher) known as (Bradford Bill) John Stubbs, Con Masterson, (crane operator) and some other lads in the crew. Altogether there were 13 of us on the chopper who worked for Dan Smedvig. This time it took over two hours to get to the rig, stopping off after an hours flying, in the Shetland islands (Sumburgh) for fuel, on arrival at the rig we were waiting to check/in at heli/admin when I started to sway a little, I remember saying to myself for fuck sake stand still or someone will notice you, I had a few pints the night before but not enough that I wasn't steady on my feet. A quick look around told me I wasn't the only one swaying, then I thought this fucking thing is moving, Bill the pusher who was standing behind me said the rig moved constantly in a figure 8, it was more prominent in bad weather, the reason it moved like this was it was held in position by 4 long steel tubes connected from the platform to a mooring template on the sea bed held under tension to stop the platform rising and falling with the waves, instead of the legs sitting on the sea bed, the rig actually floated above it, held in place by these tubes, a great feat of engineering and the first of its kind to be used anywhere in the world.

When I eventually found the room I was staying in I was very Impressed, It had 2 bunks, adjoining shower and toilet, and a portable television, now this was more like It, a room to myself, the place was spotless, even the outside decks were spotless, all the walkways, stairways, skid deck and pipe deck, everywhere I looked was pristine clean, It was going to be a treat working here I thought to myself. Once we were settled in we were to go and meet the tool pusher, another Dutchman called Rinus Marrs, he informed me he had a full crew of roughnecks, so I would be working as a roustabout, he called Bill Clarke on the P.A. system and Bill came and took me round to show me around the place. Where to muster, when the alarm went off, the quickest way to the lifeboats, the locker room, the galley, and the tea shack on the pipe deck called the (Blue lagoon) I think the only reason they called It this is because it was painted blue, the good thing about it was you could smoke in there, that way you didn't have to go into the main accommodation unless you wanted too. The first week out there we worked nightshift, then the last week on days, we did one of those stupid fucking short changes our first day on, we started at 12pm worked till 8pm, off till 4 am then worked till midday. We were doing more fucking hours than the local spar shop

Bill was a funny cunt, he was an ex/wrestler and was a practicing masseur, anybody on the rig who had aches and pains would call on Bill to give them a massage, payment was usually half a carton of fags, or a full carton depending on the session he gave you. There was hardly a shift went by without Bill being called away to use his expertise on someone, I will get back to Bill later.

There were 6 roustabouts on each crew plus the rousty pusher I couldn't believe it. There was even a dedicated clean up crew working for a company called Lassalle, who were high pressure cleaning all the time, no wonder the place was spotless. One of the roustys worked as firewatcher for the welder, normally for 6 hours of the shift. The rest were kept busy around different parts of the rig. I/e pipe deck, sackstore or wherever needed. 2 roustys I remember well are Big John Stubbs, from Sunderland who remains a life long friend and Billy Campbell, from Dundee; I believe Billy is now a crane operator with Maersk. (Hello boys)

Con Masterson an Irishman from Enniskillen Co Fermanagh was the crane operator working with us for the first week, Con and I became very good friends and our working relationship could not have been bettered, a classic example was. Con would not be rushed into doing anything. So when Bill sent me to get him out of the blue lagoon, Con said, sit down Johnny and have a cup of tea, It was only about half past 12am we were only on shift about 40 minutes. Then the night Tool pusher another Dutchman called Hans Van Berg came into the tea shack and said to

Con and I, evening gentlemen it's a bit early for a tea break, it's a lovely night out there, Con's reply was. I couldn't tell you, I've not been out yet; the pusher turned and walked out the door again saying. I hope it stays nice for youse when you do decide to go out,

Con gave me my first taste of crane operating; he showed me all around the crane explaining the levers, the radius system, and the workings of the (mipeg) safety system. Generally how the crane operated. I was more than Impressed; this is the job for me I thought? I was glad they had their full crew of roughnecks, I wasn't to bothered one way or the other where I worked, But if I had a choice I would have picked working the deck, There was so much more freedom on the deck and I was to learn so much more about the workings of the rig, the different tools, the different tubulars, all manner of things I would never have learned in the confined space of the rig floor,All we did up there was either join them together or dismantle them. Ignorant of the fact of what they were, or what they did. But the Icing on the cake was there was nobody screaming and shouting all the time, like on the Tartan.

I was really enjoying working on the T.L.P. as it was commonly known, the comradeship and banter among the various contractors was second to none, but alas the production workers employed by the operator (Conoco) were aloof to the other workers on the rig. Once again I witnessed first hand the second class citizen saga, noticeably in the seating arrangements in the galley and the cinema, A classic example of Ignorance was witnessed one day in the galley, one of the stewards had moved the tray that the soup spoons were kept in, to a different place, this Conoco worker who was looking for them, kicked up such a fuss that everybody in the galley was watching him, the steward told him where the spoons were but he wasn't having it, the spoons have always been kept here, they shouldn't be moved from here! With that somebody shouted, for fuck sake somebody go and get that cunt a spoon before he takes a heart attack, you should have seen the look on this guys face as he made his way to where the spoons were now kept. I would never have believed that anyone could carry on like that, if I hadn't witnessed it for myself, the next day outside and inside the galley some of the rig crew had put up posters, with a drawing of a spoon and an arrow pointing to where they were, with the caption of, LOOK SPOONS.

One day after shift Big Mackay, Jake, Bill, some others and myself were sitting in the cinema watching a film, when some of the production workers came in demanding we rewind the film as it wasn't supposed to start till 1.00pm. They were promptly told to fuck off, they didn't like this, so one of them went to get his supervisor and complain. and by the time he got back the film had been stopped, rewound, and started again, It used to piss me off, as these people were supposed to be working until 7 00pm I wondered how long do they get for their dinner? Anyway Big MacKay started farting I mean letting off rippers. Jake soon followed suit, then me, followed by Bill, before long it was starting to smell like an African village, every now and again someone would let one go, we could hear the production guys voicing their disgust, but when Mackay let this fucking ripper go, I rifted, a right belly burp. Straight after him, then in a loud voice I said, I should never have had that fifth pie, well you should have heard them then, that greedy bastard had five pies, one of them said, I know, I heard him, said another. We were in stitches, I couldn't stop laughing, even when these punters kept on shushing us and telling us to keep the noise down, that made us laugh all the louder, eventually they got up and left, With Big Mackay shouting after them, for fuck sake lads give the film a chance, it's only just started. That set us all off again; I went to bed that day with a sore stomach from laughing so hard.

The rig had three cranes on it, one on the west side, one on the east, and one in the center, the center crane was the one we normally worked with, but if it was bad weather and with the rig moving constantly in a figure 8, it was quite dodgy doing lifts, you really had to have your wits about you on the deck. To compensate for this they had a mechanical contraption called a (Hustler) on the pipe deck, this was used to carry Tubulars to the rig floor in the bucket attachment the hustler had fitted to it, to try and explain the workings of this is not easy. but if you can Imagine the rig floor being 160 feet from the deck with a steel ramp at a 60 degree angle leading up to it, it should give you an Idea of its workings, attached to the rig floor leading down to the pipe deck is what is known as the vee door, this is a steel ramp with sides on it, this is attached to the catwalk section at the bottom, and down the middle of the vee door and catwalk runs a gear chain, the bucket attachment hooks into the gear chain allowing the bucket to travel along the catwalk and up to the rig floor and back again, in bad weather we would roll whatever tubulars we needed onto the catwalk, and with the help of hydraulic rams we could juggle the tubulars onto the bucket and send them to the rig floor. Only certain personnel were trained to use the hustler, and by the end of my first trip I was one of them. At start of shift if Bill was going to be busy doing his masseur thing as he normally was, he would give me a list of things to do, or jobs that needed done, If their were any crane lifts to do he would give me the radio to bank the crane, I was becoming Bills right hand man, the other guys on the crew weren't too bothered about this, as most of them didn't want the responsibility, but this was right up my street, I always saw myself as a leader of men, and here was my chance.

I slotted in quite well on the T.L.P. everybody, apart from the production guys were more than helpful, and we all worked together as a team. I had been told that we could be there for possibly a year or more, that sounded good to me, and when I phoned Liz at home to tell her about the possible security for a year, she said that's good because we get married when you get home. She had it arranged for my second weekend at home, and would explain the details when I got there.

That first two weeks on the rig flew in, and we were at the heliport meeting the, ever faithful John Smith before we knew it, this time though I was just under a £100 less in my wages because I was roustabouting not roughnecking. But I thought you can keep the £100 it's not worth the hassle, If that's the difference in pay for all the shite you have to put up with on the rig floor, I'm surprised they have any roughnecks at all. But I suppose it all depends on who your driller is.

Back home again and Liz and me were making arrangements for the wedding, we arranged for a minister from the village of Leslie just outside Glenrothes to marry us in the house. This was arranged for 2.00pm on Saturday the 16th April. I had already arranged for Macleod to be best man so everything was set, apart from the wedding cake and the reception, Liz was going to arrange all this, my first week was spent on the drink, this was becoming the norm. Liz didn't take a lot of drink when we first met, but now she was drinking on a regular basis, she wasn't drinking as much as me, but I think she felt that If I was doing it then she should join in, the gambling was beginning to get out of order as well, but as Liz was looking after the purse strings then I wasn't worried. She would buy the drink for us both and pay for my bets and I was still getting pocket money from the wages to spend on whatever I wanted, Liz never complained about being short of money so I thought everything was ok.

Saturday morning of the big day arrived, at 11.00am I was going out with the boys, with orders to be backed home at 2.00pm. don't be late were Liz's last words, ok I shouted back, then I headed to the pub with the gang, Macleod, Jim Pitcairn, Alex Robertson, and Tam Fitzpatrick, we didn't bother with a stag night or hen night, every night in the pub could be mistaken for both, But today I was determined to be on my best behavior. The reception was to be held in the lounge of our local (The Rothes Arms Hotel) and we all had a quick look in to see the set up. The wedding cake was sitting majestically on a table and there were tables and chairs all set out for our guests, I was very impressed by what the manager had done for us. The food was still under wraps for later.

At 1 45pm we all left the pub to walk home it would only take us 5 minutes to get there, on arrival we were ushered into the living room to wait for the minister, Liz was in the kitchen, Its bad luck to see the bride before the wedding, her bridesmaid said shutting us in, the minister duly arrived and when Liz appeared she looked a million dollars. The ceremony took place and everything was going well until it came to exchanging rings, My fucking fingers had swollen up and I couldn't get it on, Macleod went and got a bar of soap, and after some anxious moments I got the ring on, everything went well after that, there was no more hiccups until we arrived at the reception. All our guests had already congregated there to congratulate us and after this was done and the toasts were over, some of the lads and me disappeared into the bar to watch the horse racing, this didn't go down to well with Liz and she let me know in no uncertain terms that she wasn't happy. I tried to laugh it off, but if she wasn't happy about me fucking off to watch the racing. She was fucking livid when the stripper arrived, Macleod only went and hired a strippogram didn't he, all fucking hell broke loose, Liz trying to strangle Macleod for trying to ruin her big day, all the women taking her side and giving hell to their men who thought it was funny. People were falling over tables and chairs; there were sandwiches, chicken bits, volavongs and drink laying everywhere. I finally got Liz home and tried to calm her down, some guests came with us and we started drinking in the house, one thing led to another until Liz and me ended up arguing about a cassette tape playing in the recorder, it ended up with Liz throwing the cassette at me hitting me just above the eye, cutting it, when that started to bleed she noticed what she'd done and calmed down. Some start to wedded bliss, fuck knows what the people in the pub were thinking, but next morning I went to pick up the wedding cake and was told by the manager, your wife's barred, I knew him quite well so when I explained what happened with the stripper he reluctantly agreed that as there were mitigating circumstances she was allowed back in, on the condition she apologized to everyone, so there we were in the pub on the Sunday afternoon me with a black eye, Liz looking very sheepish and Macleod keeping out of her way incase he got a right-hook, all in all a very memorable weekend.

I returned to the rig still sporting this black eye, telling anyone that asked that I'd had a wee accident at home; some were wondering if it showed up in the wedding photos, thankfully these were taken beforehand

On the rig we had some funny characters, just like most rigs offshore had. You needed guys like these, if only to take your mind off more serious matters and give some light relief to your routine tasks, Bradford Bill was one of these characters, we were preparing to skid the rig this day (moving from one slot to another) and Bill as usual was busy doing his masseuse bit in the accommodation, he gave me a list of jobs for the lads on deck to do and once these were done, I was to phone him and let him know, one of the jobs to be done was for the bottom three steps on the east and west side of the rig stairwell leading up to the BOP deck to be removed, so they didn't snag up on anything when the rig was moving. I gave this job to a lad who was even greener to offshore life than me, but the job Itself was simple, all he had to do was take out four bolts on each set of steps and remove them, they were light enough for one man to lift on his own so he didn't need any help, once he had removed the stairs, he was to put barrier tape, at the top and bottom of the stairwell, to stop anybody from trying to go up or down the stairs, or at the very least make people aware of work going on in that area, once he had done this, he was to tell me, so I could mark It off my job list, I gave the other lads the rest of Bills job list, and went to do one of my own, Later in the tea shack the lads were reporting that their assignments were done, and I was marking them off one by one, they were all finished apart from one, The stairs. I went round to see how the lad was getting on, but he was nowhere to be seen, one side of the stairs were off and barriered off, but not the other side, I spoke to Big Mackay who told me he had seen him hobbling towards the accommodation, I went looking for him and found him sitting down, rubbing his knee, he looked in pain, so I phoned Bill to let him know what was happening, I asked the lad what happened,? And he said he tripped and landed on his knee, when Bill arrived, I went out and finished taking off the stairs

When we were ready to skid, everybody available was posted 360 degrees around the rig, each with a radio to contact the mechanic if he saw anything that would hamper the skidding operation, the skidding operation in Itself was something to see, to watch hundreds of tons of steel slowly moving across the deck, pushed and pulled by 4 big 5000 psi hydraulic rams was something else, once the rig was in its new position everything was assembled again, and the rig could start its operation.

Next morning I heard that the lad who hurt his knee was given light duties, he was sweeping out the storeroom when I seen him, when I asked him how he was doing he said he was in fucking agony, looking at him I wasn't surprised, he looked gray, later on I found out what had happened to him, after he took the bottom set of stairs off, he put barrier tape across the handrails, then did the same at the top. Then as he made his way to the other side via the BOP deck, he noticed that the refuse bin was needing emptied, so picking it up he ducked under the barrier at the top, made his way down the steps, ducked under the barrier tape at the bottom, forgetting the steps were missing and fell 4 feet to the deck injuring his knee. Everybody thought that the swelling in his knee would subside, in a couple of days, so Bill took it upon himself to look after him, when I asked him two days later, how the lad was doing,? He said that he was on the mend. That night after shift I went to the guy's room, to check on him, as soon as I opened the door after knocking I was greeted by a shout of FUCK OFF YA BASTARD. Then noticing it was me he said oh its you Johnnie, I thought it was that cunt Bradford Bill, then he told me the story of how Bill was going into his room and after putting hot towels on his knee, he would massage his knee for about ten minutes, telling him not to be a big baby when he complained of the pain he was in, It turned out that the poor cunt only had a cracked knee cap, no wonder he was complaining of the pain, but in Bills defence he was only trying his best.

One time when I got on the rig, the boxer Richard Dunn was there, not as a celebrity, he was working as a scaffolder, I couldn't believe it, the man who fought Mohammed Ali alias (Cassius Clay), The great white hope of great Britain, now erecting scaffolding offshore, Richard was a giant of a man towering over everybody on the rig, I used to go to the gym to watch him work out and very Impressive it was too, he would show video tapes of some of his fights charging £1 which went to charity, I sat through several of them as he talked us through them, the one I went to see more than five times was his fight with Muhammad Ali in the late seventies, Richard held the British and Commonwealth heavyweight crowns in 1975, he challenged Ali in 1976 for the world title and in Munich on the 24th of May they fought, he would talk us through each round, and when it came to the fifth round he stopped the tape to tell us that this is when he thought he had the beatings of Ali, then in a clinch Ali said to him, start counting Richard your going down, and sure enough down he went, not to get up again, he told us that in the dressing room later when he spoke to Ali, all he could ask was, where the fuck did you get that punch from, he said Ali just laughed. Richard was a good ambassador for the sport, he was also very easy to speak too, none of the look at me I'm a celebrity shite you get from some people, Richard Injured his ankle some months later and that was the last I saw of him, I did hear he was spending his time at a youth center somewhere down south.

The trips were going in fast and furious now and we were always kept busy on the deck, there was always something to do, I didn't care, it got the time in and the 2 weeks seemed to go faster. (But not as fast as the 2 weeks on the beach).

One day Bill and I had an awkward lift to do with the drilling crane, the lift weighed about 9 tons, but we had to find its centre of gravity first. The thing we were lifting was called the Diverter Running Tool, it was large and round at one end and at the other end was a 10 foot joint of drill pipe, called a pup joint, but it was awkward to lift until we could find its centre of gravity, Bill and me had this tool slung up ready to test its balance, we had everybody off the deck, we had barriered off the area we were working in so everything was set, there was plenty of room for us to get out of the way once the tension on the slings had been taken up by the crane, Bill radioed Con to lift the load just off the deck, so we could see how it looked, as Con started to lift it, it looked as if we had got it right first time, then one of the slings slipped and the pup joint end came down heavily on the steel beams it had been resting on, not only that, it sliced straight through a thin electric cable that none of us had seen, we repositioned the slings and successfully moved the running tool to where we wanted it, that done, Bill went to report the damaged cable and believe me when I tell you the hullabaloo that went on over this was unreal, you would have thought we had killed someone, We had to make sketches of what we were doing, write out a report detailing what happened, they wanted to know things like the sea state, the wind direction, the wind speed, who was Involved, was the area cordoned off, were P.A. announcements put out before the lift was done, we were at it for hours, The end result was Bill was demoted to roustabout and I was given a written warning, what for I don't know, it was only an electric cable for fuck sake, but that's how the system worked out there, you really had to have your arse covered all the time, I would do so in future, that was one lesson I learnt, Bill finished his trip as pusher but I could sense there was no way he would come back next trip as roustabout and I was right,

Bill said he would give me a lift home when we got back on the beach, and we both traveled down the road together, on arrival in Glenrothes I took him home to meet Liz and the three of us headed off to the pub, as the night wore on, the usual antics started in the pub, darts, dominoes, playing cards, then as the drink started flowing the usual crowd started arm wrestling, now as I've already said Bill was an ex/wrestler, built like the proverbial brick shithouse, and my money was on him. My big mate Jim Pitcairn,(who worked offshore on the Fulmar) and myself were rubbing our hands, we thought that once the money started to change hands at the arm wrestling we would play our ace in the hole (Bill), but it didn't work out that way, Bill was beaten in his first of three heats, and Jim and me lost a £10 each, the second heat started with me telling Bill to stop fucking about and break the other guys arm, Its all right lad Bill said, its in the bag, but he was beaten again, another £20 down. waiting on the third heat to start we sat with Bill asking him what the fuck he was playing at, don't worry boys, he said, I'm saving myself for the last heat, get your money on, Jimmy and me put £40 each on him this time, only to see him get beat yet again, I couldn't believe it, how this powerful looking cunt could get beat by the skinny bastard he was arm wrestling, beggared belief, but beaten he was, and Jimmy and me were down £60 each, Liz wasn't to happy about it, I think she wanted a shot to try and get our money back, but that wasn't to happen, still the night ended in good humor with us sitting up till the early hours drinking and talking, Bill left the next morning promising to phone us when he arrived home, when he did phone that night he said he was going to concentrate on working at home building up his own clinic in Bradford, and that he had been thinking about it for a while, I think with what happened with the escapade offshore, that was just the push he needed, he said he wouldn't miss the offshore life, not for a second, but I thought the offshore Industry has just lost one of Its characters! Liz and I visited Bill and his family in Bradford some months later, and he was doing very well then, and to this day, he's still doing very well. (Good luck Bill)

Sitting on the chopper on the way back to the rig, your mind starts to wander, and you wish you were going the opposite way, with the noise in the chopper being too loud to hold a conversation, you settle yourself down for the journey, that's when I got to thinking, that the drink and gambling, were taking over my life, Liz never complained about how much money I was going through, but I had a good Idea I was spending as much as I earned, I made a promise to myself that next time home would be different.

Back on the rig again, I was called to the tool pushers office, here we go again I thought, more fucking paperwork, but no, the pusher told me that as Bill didn't turn up for his check/in and as they had heard no word from him, I was to stand in as rousty pusher, not bad I thought, I'm an Arsehole one trip and a hero the next. I didn't let on what I knew about Bill not coming back, that was up to him to tell them, The pusher said I was to stand in until they got an experienced guy out to take charge, the boys on deck were quite happy about my promotion, they knew me well enough by now to know the job wouldn't go to my head, and that I'd behave just as normal.

Being rousty pusher was a piece of piss, I would go to the toolpushers office 7am or 7pm depending on which shift I was working, there I would find out what was planned for the deck, or the rig floor, or whether there was a supply boat due, and I would organize my shift to suit, at these meetings was an agency sub-sea engineer who was standing in for the regular guy (Rocky) who was off sick, now this guy was blatantly trying to stitch up Rocky, he didn't have a good word to say about him or his work, he constantly complained that this was wrong, or that wasn't right, or coming out with verbal shite like, I would have done it this way or that way, or I don't know why he did it that way, when this ways easier, this guy was a complete wanker, hoping to get a permanent slot in place of Rocky. Every day he would sit waiting his turn to speak, with a Vicks nasal spray stuck up his nose, moving it from one nostril to the other, it used to really piss me off, watching and listening to this guy, then one morning as the meeting finished I stayed back to speak to the pusher, that's when I noticed the drawer this guy kept his nasal spray in, later that day some Tabasco sauce accidentally on purpose found its way into his nasal spray, at the next morning meeting at 7am we were all in the office except this guy, about 5 minutes later he appeared, apologizing to the pusher for being late, saying he felt he had a cold coming on, he sat down in his usual seat and started rummaging in the drawer for his spray, I couldn't look at him when he took the top off it and jammed it up his nose, giving it a squirt, 3 seconds flat and he was coughing and sneezing like fuck, It took me all my time not to laugh, but my sides were sore holding it back, I couldn't get out of there quick enough, that was the only morning that I never heard him slag someone off, maybe it was because he couldn't fucking speak?

I was rousty pusher for 2 trips until they sent out a guy called Jimmy Stewart to take charge, Jimmy came from Dundee and him and me had a good working relationship, Jimmy was as easy going as myself and Bill for that matter, the jobs got done without all the shouting and bawling that I was used to on the rig floor, so It made it bearable to go to work knowing there would be none of that, periodically I would go up to rig floor to relieve the roughnecks for dinner, but barring that I stayed well away, I was quite happy working the deck.

One day Jimmy asked me to go down to the well bay (that's where the oil and gas well heads were) and monitor the gauges of a certain well head, I was to write down the pressure reading of three gauges, top hole pressure gauge, annulus pressure gauge and down hole pressure gauge every 15 minutes. It was a boring job but someone had to do it, there was always plenty of papers down there to read so I wasn't too fussed, Every now and again I would get a phone call from the wire line supervisor asking me to either open or close the annulus valve, attached to this valve was a big fuck off wheel that had to be turned 30 odd times one way to open the valve, and 30 odd times the other way to close it, nothing hard about that I thought as I sat down to read the paper, out the corner of my eye I saw this guy watching me, I didn't know who he was as I hadn't seen him before, the next thing he's standing next to me and in a real southern hospitality American accent asked, what yah all doin boyyy,? I said, I'm reading the paper! What yah all supposed to be doin boyyy? he asked again, I told him what I was doing and away he went, I wondered who he was, he was wearing a pair of Conoco overalls but there was no name on his hat or none that I could see anyway, About half an hour later this guys back again, only he's about 30 feet from where I'm sitting and he's shouting, BOYYYY, BOYYYY, I'm thinking what the fuck does this cunt want?, I know It's me he's shouting on and I'm trying to ignore him, but he's getting closer all the time, sounding like foghorn fucking leghorn, with BOYYY, BOYYY, ringing in my ears, he gets up to me and tells me to get the green sample bottle sitting on a bench across from where I was working and take it to the chemist lab for analysis, I told him I couldn't leave here until I'm relieved, he said phone your supervisor and tell him the company man wants you to run an errand, so that's who he was, the new Company man! Eh! anyway I phoned Jimmy and told him what was happening, he said he would be down himself in 5 minutes, I told the company man that someone was on his way, and I headed to get the sample bottle, when I got to the bench there was 6 sample bottles there, all looking the same colour to me, I shouted to the company man, what colour did you want? The green one boyyy, he shouted back, I picked up a bottle, held it up, and said this one? NO boyyy, the fucking green one, I tried again with another bottle, asking him if it was this one? Goddamm BOYYY are you fucking colour blind. Yes I said! Well he didn't know where to look, he just lifted a bottle and fucked off, Jimmy and I had a good laugh when he showed up, and I told him what had happened.

Things were always happening on the rig floor and that impacted on what we were doing on the deck, if they were drilling we were busy sorting out tubulars, ready for the next stage of the operation, if they were running casing we were busy on the deck supplying the rig floor with the aid of the hustler, whatever was happening we were always busy doing something.

One Saturday morning when I was dayshift, I was wakened up at 8 am in the morning and asked if I would escort an injured person back to the beach, this roughneck was cleaning out a mud drip tray, below the BOP's and while crawling on his knees he knelt on a steel spiral nail which entered his leg at the soft fleshy part just below the knee joint, there was only about 4 inches of this nail protruding from his leg and as these nails were about 8 inches in length, that meant that about 4 inches of the nail was embedded in his knee, it looked fucking sore, the guy was doped up with pain killers and a chopper was on it's way to take him off the rig and get him to hospital, It didn't take me long to get ready, and it took even less time to get the camp boss to open the bond and stock up with fags, I had found out that the chopper was flying into UNST airport in the Shetland Islands, from there we would travel on the fixed wing down to Aberdeen where an ambulance would be waiting for us, I got to thinking, surely if customs were at unst they surely wouldn't stop and search an injured party or his escort, once I got the fags, I phoned Liz to let her know I was getting 2 nights in Aberdeen, (no chopper flights on Sunday) she said she would come up and meet me at the airport, I was right about customs, we were rushed from the chopper straight onto the plane, which had some seats removed to give the injured guy more leg room, once we landed in Aberdeen we were met by John Smith, but no ambulance, we had to wait about 20 minutes for it to come, by that time I found out I was spending the next 2 nights in the Skein Dhu hotel at Dyce Aberdeen, John also gave me £40 expenses money, non returnable he said. When the ambulance did turn up John said there was no need for me to travel to the hospital, and they left without me, I was standing at the bar in the airport when Liz appeared. And we had a few drinks before we checked into the hotel. The weekend off the rig fairly broke up the trip, Liz and I went to the hospital on Saturday and Sunday nights to see how the guy was doing, his wife thanked us for our concern, and we left them alone, I never met the guy again, but I believe he made a full recovery. During the day Liz and me spent the time seeing the sites in Aberdeen, the weekend was over before I knew it, and I left Liz in bed on Monday morning when I went to check/ in at 7am for the flight back out to the rig with only a week left to do. She would take the 5 cartons of fag's home with her. Well done the customs guys.

The next week was dragging a bit but someone on the rig was going to make sure that it was going to be anything but boring, The guy I'm talking about was the spitting image of Terry Hall's Puppet, remember the ventriloquist who had Lenny the lion puppet on his knee, he had his own show on TV for a while, well this guy also called Lenny was the puppet's double, but I'm not going to call him Lenny the Lion, I'll call him Lenny The Lying Bastard, I'm not saying everything he said was lies, but lets just say half of what he said was untrue, and the other half was made up, Lenny took great pains to let anyone who would listen, know, that he fought in Aden in the early sixties, serving with the Argyll and Sutherland Highlanders, under the command of colonel Mitchell, Mad Mitch as he was later known, Lenny would recite stories of his combat days, mentioning units he served in, squads he fought with, how many guerrillas he killed and maimed, and various other escapades of great daring, the only thing was, every time Lenny told these stories, they sounded nothing like the first time he told it, Lenny liked nothing better than to hold court in the tea shack, and talk us through his escapades, talking of the medals he won, and the commendations he received, yes no doubt about it, Lenny was a hero, and he wanted everyone to know that If it wasn't for the likes of him, then the world would be over run by Guerrillas and Terrorists, and mad Political Extremists, we had a lot to thank him for, and according to Lenny we take things far too much for granted, Then something happened that had the whole crew buzzing, one of the roughnecks had to go home on compassionate leave, and an agency roughneck came out to take his place, Now rigs are small places, just like villages, and with the drill crew being a close knit community it didn't take long before this new guy got to hear about Lenny's war stories, funny that he said, because I was in Aden, fighting with the Argyll's, un-der Mad Mitch, and he didn't remember Lenny, Lenny was not to be perturbed, oh aye, Lenny kept on, I was there alright, fighting right alongside you, Lenny wouldn't let it go, I suppose this guy could have shot Lenny down in flames with just a few simple questions, but all he said was, in my cabin I've a photograph of everybody that was in the unit, I will bring it to the galley after shift, that was enough for me and the rest of the guys, Lenny you lying cunt, we've caught you out at last! We couldn't wait till finishing time, the hours dragged by, then at last, there we were, all sitting around the table with this guy's photo of the whole unit in front of us, we were all looking trying to pick out Lenny, we could pick out the roughnecks face, but couldn't pick out Lenny's, finally Lenny arrived, he slowly got his meal at the counter and made his way to the table, everybody at the table moved their chairs round a bit to give him room to sit, Jake, Big Mackay, and me were standing behind him looking over his shoulder at the photo, and then at him, trying to see any resemblance, come on then Lenny, Big Mackay said, where are you in the photograph, Lenny stopped eating for a moment, looked at the photograph and said, I remember taking that photo, I was speechless, I was looking at Mackay, he was looking at me, everybody was looking at each other, all fucking speechless, then everybody burst out laughing, what could we say? We all knew Lenny was a Walter Mitty, but his explanation for not being in the photo was priceless, Lenny you lying fucker. I take my hat off to you. And give you ten out of ten for effort.

Sitting in the boozer, my first week-end home, my mate Paul asked me if I wanted to go fishing, we hadn't done that for a while, so we arranged to leave very early in the morning, so as not to be caught by the bailiff, we were going to the fishing pools he knew about, a couple of miles drive, outside the village of Leslie, we would drive to within a ¼ mile of the place, park up and walk the rest, at four in the morning it was pitch black as we made our way to the pool, It lay in between the hills so we wouldn't be easily spotted, when we got there Paul was setting up his rod, and I fetched from the boot of his car my large holdall, where's your rod Paul asked,? Don't worry about any rod, I said, all we need is right here, showing him my fishing net and the 2 flares that I got at the survival training, what the fuck have you got there, he asked,? holding out his hand as I passed him one of the flares, he taking it and looking it over, right I said, all we do is, strike the flares, throw them in the water, wait till the oxygen in the water is used up, then the fish will float to the top, I will scoop them up with the net, fill the bags and then were off, Ok he said, lets strike them together and throw them both in, that way the oxygen will be used up quicker, Ok I said lets do it, we both fired up these flares together, and fuck me, the whole place lit up like a belisha beacon, we could have been spotted from the satellite Soyuz 2, I half expected a fucking Nimrod to fly over us to see if we were in distress, we both threw the flares into the pool, grabbed our gear and ran like fuck, we were running and laughing like a pair of school kids playing truant, I could feel my bladder about to burst I was laughing that hard, we must have fallen about three times, but we were going that fast, we just rolled head over heels and kept running. I don't know to this day, if the flares did take the oxygen out of the pool, all I know is we had the oxygen taking out of us, we didn't get our breaths back for about 20 minutes by the time we got back to the car.

Liz and I went to Blackpool for a belated honeymoon, staying in a rented flat for 5 days, we saw all the sights, Pleasure beach, Golden Mile, that sort of thing, just to get away from the usual routine at home, But mostly so we could talk about us, most of my leave was being spent in the pub and the bookies, and as much as I would promise myself on the rig, that things would change the next time home, they never did, Oh I would stay in for a couple of days on my 2 weeks off, but that was only because I was fucking suffering from the drink, and couldn't get out of bed. At the pub I was drinking 2 double vodkas and tonic, at a time, with a beer chaser as well, Liz used to line up my vodkas on the table like wee soldiers, and I would knock them down one after the other, I would go into the pub with the Intention of having a couple of pints, but once I had a vodka, I wouldn't leave until I was drunk, Liz and I agreed this would have to stop, we were beginning to argue quite frequently now and we were only married 4 months. Liz said there was no point talking to me, when I was on the drink, as I didn't take anything in, and all the promises I made when I phoned home from offshore came to nothing when I got back on the beach again, something had to be done, we had to compromise somewhere along the way, and we agreed that, I would have a day out, day in, system, and cut down on the drink on my day out, It sounded ok to me, but how long will It last,?

On the chopper on the way back to the rig, I started thinking about what we agreed on and I was determined to do my bit, I started thinking about the time on New Years Day in 1986 when all Liz and me had was a half bottle of vodka, 2 cans of beer, 3pound of potatoes a steak pie and 2 selection boxes, we were making rollups out of the ashtray that's how bad off we were, but we were happy, and it was up to me to make sure we were happy again. It's amazing what goes through your head sitting on that helicopter.

Rinus Marrs (Toolpusher) and John Norris (Company man for Conoco) were both supposed to be on a diet when we got on the rig, each determined to lose some weight before the end of the trip, It was funny as fuck watching these two try to out do each other, Rinus was standing in front of John in the galley queue one day looking at the trays of food, when Rinus holding his plate in one hand scooped 2 pieces of fish onto it saying, the fish looks nice John, Norris just grunted and said, the fucking steak looks better, as he grabbed 2 bits and surrounded them with chips, you should have seen the look on Rinus's face it was a fucking picture, another time they had finished their meal and both of them walked out of the galley together, only for John to come back/in 2minutes later and sat down to eat a pudding, then who put his head round the door to catch him, Rinus it took a few days before Rinus caught on to what Norris was up too, and when he did that was the end of the diet.

Things were pretty slow on the rig and everyone was cleaning up their respective areas, mine was the pipe deck, and armed with the pressure wash/down gun, I was busy blasting the dirt of the steel beams dividing the bays, I stopped every now and then for tea, as nobody was being pressured to get the jobs done, not by Jimmy Stewart anyway, just before breakfast, I noticed my right foot was wet, I took off my Wellington boot and found a crack in the sole which was letting in water, I went inside to get changed, took my sock off, put it in the tumble dryer in the laundry, and went for breakfast, when I came out again the sock was dry but the boot was still wet, in the toilets next to the laundry there was one of those electric hot air hand dryers, attached to the wall, Ideal for drying the inside of my wellie I thought, so there I was holding the wellie over the air nozzle with one hand, while hitting the start button with the other, this dryer only stayed on for about 30 seconds then it switched itself off, so I had to keep hitting the button to keep it going, things were going nicely, the wellie filling up with hot air would soon dry out, then I saw Rinus's reflection in the wall mirror, he came in to use the toilet and when he'd finished he turned to wash his hands, that's when he spotted what I was doing, morning Johnny he said, Wellingtons cold. There was no answer to that, he actually thought I was heating them up before I put them on, this was a man who took great pride in telling us, that the first wage he earned as a roustabout was what he used as a benchmark to live on, now this man was in his late 50's when I met him, and he was a rig superintendent, if he was living on a roustabouts wage, all I can say is, he must have had some bank balance,

Last shift again and everybody was hyper as usual, I can honestly say there is no better feeling than the one you get, when you know your going home, every one is on a high, and that's when the tom foolery starts, on the rig were fire monitors, placed strategically around the platform, unmanned but ready for action, all you had to do was open a valve, and the monitor would be charged up with a continuous flow of water, a long bar acted as the on, off, valve switch, kick this bar down and a jet of water would shoot out anything from 60 to 90 feet, lift it up again and the water would stop, if you quickly opened then shut the valve, you got a ball of water shooting the same distance, you could regulate the end nozzle to give a water jet, a spray, or a ball, when we were fucking about, it was always on the ball position, there was balls off water flying through the air right left and center, if you were hit by one of these you were soaked, not wet, I mean fucking drowned, our favorite time was at the production teams shift change, they had to go through these air lock doors to get into their place of work, the idea of these doors was, close one, then open the other, well, the outside door was slow closing, something to do with the configuration of the hinges, it wasn't as if they needed oiled or anything like that, it was the way they were designed, they were just slow to close, and that was right up our street, by maneuvering one of the fire monitors, we got it pointing straight at these doors, and from where we were, we could not be seen, at 6 30pm when these guys came out we were ready waiting for them, our luck was right in this night, normally there would be 2 of them, maximum 3, but this night there was 5 of the cunts, Big Mackay and me could hardly contain ourselves, Ya fucking beauty I said, just like rats in a trap, Big Mackay was holding the monitor, and I had my boot on the bar ready to kick it down as soon as I got the word, steady, steady, Big Mackay was saying, he was sounding like a fucking bombardier on an aeroplane,, Steady, then he shouted NOW, fuck me my foot slipped and I ended up on my arse, I scrambled back up kicked the bar down and this fucking torrent of water went straight into the first airlock door, two guys in there were trying to pull the door shut, the others stupidly trying to open the other one, but the end result was they all got soaked, right at the start of shift, poor bastards, predictably they went and grassed drilling off, and we were all summoned to the office and warned that it was a disciplinary offence if we were caught tampering with safety equipment, we knew that anyway, but it was worth getting a lecture, just to see the look on their faces, apart from that we didn't give a fuck about them. These were the same guys that demanded you give up your seat in the cinema, if they couldn't find an empty one, oh yes, you might find that hard to believe, but it still goes on today, on some rigs out there, that's the segregation bit coming in to effect, the second class citizenship, rearing its ugly head once again, the production team against the contractors, well in that last contest it was contractors 1, production wallahs 0, Game Fucking On.

The next morning the crew were still on a high after lasts nights events, and also because we were going home. We were supposed to check/in at heli/admin at 9.30 am. usually about ½ an hour after the production guys checked in, they crew changed on the first chopper, we were on the second, but when we arrived carrying our bags, there was an eerie silence about the place, usually it was bustling with activity, with people laughing and joking, others telling each other what they had planned to do for the next two weeks, that sort of thing, but something was different today, we could sense something was wrong, there was a lot of speculation, that maybe one of the choppers had broken down, and that there was going to be a delay, then over the Intercom the O.I.M. said he wanted to address everyone on the rig, and we were all to make our way to the cinema, the place was packed, people were standing, others sitting on the floor when he came in, and he broke the news to us about the tragedy that befell the Piper Alpha. Seemingly there had been a fire and explosion on the rig, and that there was a considerable loss of life, that was all he could tell us at the moment. Everybody was stunned, you could have heard a pin drop in that cinema, then people started to drift out, once the initial shock of what we had just been told had sunk in, I started asking questions to no one in particular, just the group I was standing with, what did he mean a fire and explosion? How much damage was done? When he said considerable loss of life, how many was he talking about, everyone asked the same questions that I was asking, but there was nobody there to give us answers, we couldn't get into the television lounge to watch the news, it was packed out, so they linked it up to the cinema and we watched it in there, that's when it really hit home to us, what had happened, watching newsreels of the rescue boats, and the rescue helicopters, made me feel quite helpless, it really made me aware of the potential danger I was in just being here, I really didn't give much thought to it until that day. I felt quite foolish thinking about the night before, how we laughed and joked when we soaked those production guys, and called them for everything when they grassed us up, all I can say is, its wrong, when it takes something like this to happen before everybody comes together and acts like a workforce should, disasters like this one doesn't differentiate between the logo on your overalls, it affects everyone. As long as I live, I will never forget Wednesday 6th July 1988 when 167 oil workers lost their lives, and what was going through my head on Thursday morning waiting to go home, it was a miracle that anybody survived that fateful night but 62 did. Only to relive that night over and over again, (there but for the grace of god)

The lord Cullen report that was published much later, promised safety was paramount for the working people of the rigs, and although I witnessed some changes in the coming years, I personally believe to this day, that the cheapest commodity out there is the workforce.

I did 2 more trips on the T.L.P. after the disaster, but it was a changed place to me, I began looking at things differently, I kept asking myself, do I want to work in this industry? Should I try for a job onshore? I was all mixed up, I really didn't know what I wanted to do, when I was home I was drinking just as much, despite the fact that I promised Liz and myself that I would cut down, drinking was my way of forgetting, it took my mind off other things going on in my head, I hated it, when it was time to go offshore again, that's when the butterflies started in my stomach, and each and every time I get ready to leave for the rigs those butterflies start again, At first I really enjoyed working on the T.L.P. Then I came to loathe the place, so I was happy in a way when the drilling contract changed hands, Dan Smedvig, were being replaced by, Noble Drilling, the crews were to be dispatched to other rigs, and I was going to the Forties Field after my 2 weeks off.

Richard Dunn promotional poster

In the Tea Shack

Piper Alpha Memorial

4

FORTIES ECHO

Saturday 24th September at 12 noon, that was when I was to check/in for the Forties Echo, now I ask you? What sort of check/in is that, If you stay on that rota you'll only be home for one full week/end, Anyway, I was in Aberdeen in plenty of time, actually I was in the Criterion bar just across the road from the railway station at 10am, I was needing a curer from the night before, I was supposed to report to BP in Wellheads road for my check/in, and I was there at 11.45, once I had checked/in and seen the pre-flight video, we were taken by mini-bus round to Bristow's for the helicopter flight, there was only 7 of us on the chopper, and the flight took less than an hour, I thought I was going straight to the rig, but they flew us to an accommodation barge called the Iolair, this was where we would be staying when not on the rig itself, then I was told we were to be taken by shuttle helicopter, at the start and end of shift, to the Echo weather permitting, the barge itself was massive, accommodating up to a couple of hundred personnel at any one time, my room was fine, clean and tidy and obviously as it had 2 bunk-beds I was sharing with someone already on shift, I was told that I would be working nightshift, so I had a couple of hours to kill until the 6 pm flight, wandering about the Iolair was like a maize, just rows and rows of corridors, I got lost a few times, and if the truth be known, I wanted to go home. I felt that sixth sense telling me, I don't like it here. I found the cinema, the TV lounge, and the galley where I had my evening meal, then I got fags out the bond, before going to check/in at 5.45pm for that nights flight.

Travelling to the Echo itself was something else, the pilots were straight out of a Vietnam War film, one pilot took great pleasure in turning round in his seat, wearing a baseball cap turned back to front, sporting dark glasses and asking everybody, are you buckled up? Ok then, lets fly, then the chopper would lift, hover for a few seconds, then dive straight for the sea, only to level off before it hit the water, I thought this guy's fucking nuts, he shouldn't be flying choppers, he should be in a nut house licking the walls, instead of giving us flight suits they should have given us nappies, I was fucking shitting myself. I soon found out this was not to be an isolated case this happened on a regular basis, when I think back they gave us an extra £25 a day shuttle money, they should have called it danger money, the chopper did 2 runs to the Echo as there was only 6 at a time in the chopper, The Echo wasn't a very big place and there was not many accommodation rooms to be had, that's why the drill crew travelled to the Iolair every day. As there was only a certain amount of personnel allowed on board at any one time, if there was a need to send over service hands then 1 or 2 of the roustys would get the shift off, I met Les Devine out there, he remembered me from down in Lincoln, he was the day tool pusher,

They were doing a work/over on the rig when I arrived, this consisted of pulling the old completion string out of the hole, and running in a new one, how this was going to last 2 weeks had the beatings of me,, the crew consisted of a rousty pusher and three roustys me included, then there was the Driller, his assistant,(AD) the derrick man, and 2 roughnecks, on the rig itself was the OIM, the Company man, the medic, a couple of mechanics and electricians, some production guys and a couple of catering crew.

The guys I was working with had been in the forties field for a while, and were quite clannish, what I mean by that is they didn't talk to you or act like any of the crews I worked with before. A classic example was if they were busy on the floor and we were quiet on the deck, the crew I was supposed to be working with would fuck off somewhere and hide, I thought this was a game, they went and hid, and I was supposed to find them, I knew they wouldn't be in the smoke shack as none of them smoked, apart from that the smoke shack was inside the accommodation block facing the O.I.M.'s the company mans, and the tool pushers offices, anytime you went for a smoke, one of them would appear, have a quick look at his watch then disappear again, if that didn't give you a hint that your being timed, one of them would come back again and stare at you, I went looking for them one day and found 2 of them sitting in the mechanic's workshop with their feet up reading papers, when they spotted me, one of them said, we better not all get caught in here, Listen you pair of cunts, I said to them, you might think I came down with the last fall of rain, but I've got both your measures, and I'll be watching you's. they must have went and grassed me off to the rousty pusher, because he tannoyed me and asked me to clean up the sack/store, that would keep me out of the road for a while, I was getting a bit pissed off with their attitude, and it wasn't long before it all came to a head

I was relieving on the rig floor, for dinners one day, the job in its own was easy enough, they were using 3/1/2 inch drill pipe to go fishing for the rest of the completion string, they already pulled over half of it, now they were going in for the rest, it didn't bother me going rough necking again it got me away from the deck for a while, what did bother me was when I came down from the rig floor the rousty pusher wanted me to clean up the sack store again. Now I knew for a fact that one of the roustys had done practically fuck all, since we came over here, apart from that, he had 2 days off, to make room for a service hand, this rousty had a bad habit of pulling out his knife and sharpening it, any time the rousty pusher gave out jobs, and this guy would get easy street, now I don't know if this guy had threatened the pusher or not, but the pusher was wary of him that's for sure. Anyway I told the pusher in no uncertain terms, the he was taking the piss out of me, and that he could go and get himself a plate of backbone out of the galley, then go and tell Jim fucking Bowie that he is to clean up the sack/store, because, I'm fucking not, I spent the rest of the trip sort of isolated, oh we all worked away together, but there was no crack, no banter, when we got back to the Iolair at night there was more crack with guys I didn't know, than there was with the guys I was working with, I don't know if they had a pow wow between themselves, but I wasn't giving a fuck, I wasn't taking any of their shite and they knew it.

Everything on the Echo was so disorganised, you would stop half way through one job and start another, then another, some of the jobs would be left half done, boats would appear out of no-where, you would be busy doing something, when a boat would turn up without any notice, how anybody kept track of what was happening had the beatings of me, after shift we would get to ride the mare of steel, back to the Iolair, where although I couldn't find fault with the food or my room, somebody put me next to the anchor chains, which would bang against the barge in an monotonous clanging motion, if it was supposed to send you to sleep, then I'm sorry, but it had the opposite effect, I hardly slept a fucking wink.

The job didn't last 2 weeks, within 10 days the work/over was finished and so was I, I wasn't sorry to leave the forties, but I would have liked to work in the main field either on the Alpha, Bravo, Charlie, or even the Delta, guys that I've spoken to over the years have spoken highly, not of the rigs themselves, but the camaraderie of the workforce itself, in the immortal words of the Operators, there's no job so important that time cant be taken, to have a bit of crack.

Back at Bristows taking off my flight suit, I could see customs were there, 2 guys and 1 woman, I knew I was over the odds with 4 cartons of fags and 5 packets of tobacco so when it was my turn to go through the woman asked me if I had anything to declare, I don't know why I said what I did, but I said, yes, you're the ugliest woman I've seen in 10 days, well you should have seen her face, she went through my bag with a fine tooth comb, emptying everything out, fags, tobacco the lot, then one of the customs guys gave me a frisk down, whispering in my ear, that was a silly thing to say, even if it is true, I swear I spotted a wry smile on his face, she confiscated everything, even the fags I was allowed to bring off, oh well me and my big mouth, in all honesty she wasn't that bad looking, outside John Smith was waiting with my £50 cash and the balance in cheque, I asked him if he knew where I was going next, but he said Louis would give me a call, I was looking to see if any of the crew had held back, but they were gone, I never met any of them again after that, and I don't suppose they remember me, but if the punk rocker Johnnie Rotten, ever sang the song, made famous by Frank Ifield, it would go like this,(I'll remember you, ya bastards)

Iolair

Forties Echo
New platform with accomodation barge alongside

5

The Heather Alpha

After checking in at 12am at Bond helicopters in Dyce Aberdeen, I was soon on my way in a Dauphin helicopter with 9 other guys, it was Tuesday October 18th, and freezing cold, we doglegged the journey through Sumburgh airport to pick up fuel, and altogether it took us just over 2 hours to arrive at the Heather platform. First impressions of the rig were deceiving, but the crew I would be working with were a friendly bunch, when Mike Beale the rig manager phoned me with the details the previous week, he said that I was going out as rousty pusher, and on arrival at the heli/ port I was to make myself known to the driller Colin Freeman. Colin a big Englishman introduced me to the rest of the crew, Davie (Chinky) Macdonald from Glasgow was the assistant driller, Brian (Robbo) Robinson from Sunderland was derrickman, but he was going out to join the other crew, Graham (Rotary- Dog) Dunnaway, from Montrose and 2 lads from Skye, Willie and Rab McDonald, (no relation) made up the roughnecks, on the deck was Phil Robertson, from Aberdeen, Terry Machlin from down south somewhere, and a guy called Rab, from Buckie who made it plain to me, that the office staff were a bunch of wankers for sending out some cunt from another rig as rousty pusher, when he was doing a great job of standing in himself, I let him rattle on for a bit, then I told him that I was the cunt. Oh don't get me wrong, it's not your fault, he said; I will help you all I can! And he did.

I was given the usual tour of the rig for new guys, by one of the safety reps; I was shown where to muster, and where my lifeboat was, and the quickest way to get there. This is the galley, this is the smoking teashack, this is the non smoking teashack, this is the television room, this is where you do your own washing, this is your room, that was the extent of the induction, when I got back upstairs with this guy, I was completely out of breath, I was asked to fill in a questionnaire to explain that I knew the layout of the platform, Lets be honest about this I've just arrived on this platform, and for 15 minutes I've been following this guy around, he's been walking in front of me, talking about this, and that, pointing this way, and that way, all I've been doing is making sure I didn't lose sight of him, because if I do, I'm lost. Everybody say's sure, I've got all that, but in all honesty they haven't a fucking clue. The only way you will find your way around, is to spend time searching out locations yourself, going from A to B and back again, a 15 minute Induction, following somebody who's probably missing their tea break, is not the way forward.

I was told we were doing the first week on nights, so we had a few hours before starting shift, I went down to my room to change and found somebody sleeping in there, I quietly got changed, then headed out to the recreation room to meet the guys before shift, The day Tool Pusher was Hans Van Dyke from the Tartan, he welcomed me and explained that the rig was drilling the 10 and ¾ inch section of the well, and in a couple of days we would be running the 9 and 5/8's casing, In the teashack at 6 30 pm we were working the more civilized shifts of 7 till 7. I met my relief, his name was Dougie (The Blade) Steele, Dougie was from Dundee and he had been on the Heather for more than a year, Dougie explained that everything was ready on the pipedeck for the casing job, and that until they were ready on the rig floor for casing, there was fuck all happening, I thought that's great, it would give me time to find my bearings, so after a quick fag and cup of coffee Phil showed me round the place, where all the tools were stored, where the sackstore was, where the cement, & barite, tanks were, he showed me the laydown areas for the containers, baskets, and half-heights that came off the supply boats with equipment in them, where the bulk hoses were and which was which, I had a feeling that I was going to enjoy working here, Later we went to see the storeman for some gloves, when who was sitting there but Big Malky (The Welt) Mackay, he said he came here right after the Tartan, we bullshitted for a while, then he asked if everything was ready for the boat, boat what fucking boat I asked? There's a boat due in at 9 30 tonight, he said, did dougie not tell you? No, Dougie didn't fucking tell me, is their much on it, I asked? Not for us Malky said, but I don't know about the rest of the platform! Seemingly the normal routine was for the platform deck crew to work the boat on dayshift, but when they finished at 7pm, the rig crew took over, that was all very well if the boats came in during the day, but as I was told they had a real bad habit of coming in at night, when I saw our backload and offload sheets there was about 30 lifts altogether for drilling, but this rig was a fucking nightmare as far as manifests were concerned, only one came off the boat for offloading purposes, but each department on the rig had their own, altogether there was four different backload lists, Production, Construction, Services, and Drilling, when the boat did arrive, I didn't have a fucking clue where any, apart from drillings backload were, I was trying to juggle with four sheets of paper on a clip board, with the rain pissing down smudging the ink, the crane operator was getting on my tits asking silly fucking questions like where do you want this, or that, in the end I called a halt to everything, everybody into the teashack I said, until I can make some sense out of all this nonsense, eventually we got organized and everything fell into place, the shift went quickly enough and I was fucking knackered by the end of it, the cargo was all finished but the boat was still sitting there pumping mud when the Blade appeared at 6 30 am, sorry about that mate, I forgot all about the boat coming, said the bold Dougie, through that experience, I never believed the Blade again, when he said, there's fuck all happening,

I went into the smoking shack on the pipedeck as I knocked off for only my 5th fag of the night before heading for the accommodation block, and who was sitting there smoking a fag? Dennis, the Driller off the Tartan, I couldn't believe it when he greeted me like a long lost pal, it's good to see you Johnny, he said, I heard you were coming as rousty pusher! I thought, this guy's changed? Maybe I've summed him up all wrong? Then he said I hope you're going to keep these bastards on their toes, they've had it too easy for too long. DOn't you worry Dennis, I'll keep an eye on them! I said as I left. I bumped into the blade outside and asked him what Dennis was doing here, Oh him, he's the nightshift Tool Pusher, fuck me, I thought, where was he during the night, Probably in somebody's nightmare, Oh and by the way, the Blade shouted after me,! He's sharing a cabin with you,

The operator we were drilling for was Unical, formerly known as, Union Oil, the rig used to have a double derrick but was reduced to just one, it was well bye it's sell bye date by the looks of things, everything was either falling apart or had fallen apart, outside on the pipedeck there were places you couldn't go in hours of darkness it was out of bounds, you wouldn't want to go to these places in daylight never mind darkness, inside the accommodation quarters it was clean enough but badly needing at least a coat of paint, the rooms held 4 bunk beds, adjoining shower and the biggest fucking toilet pan this side of America, it was like a bidet, with a spring loaded toilet seat, if you weren't careful it would have your dangly bits off, no question, you had to pull the seat down, then sit on it, remembering to hold onto it when you stood up again. Truly a medieval form of castration. The Blade was right, Dennis was in the bottom left bunk, I was in the top right, but there was none of that night, night, sleep tight, shite, or anything like that when we turned in, it was lights out and sleep. Don't get me wrong Dennis didn't dislike me, he disliked everybody, that was his way, and nothing you did or said was going to change that, he was there to do a job and being nice to people was not in his pact with the devil, his attitude didn't bother me though, as far as I was concerned, as long as my work was done, he stayed off my case, and that's the way I liked it.

After shift you had to do your own personal washing, the catering crew changed the beds, hovered the rooms, and made sure you had clean towels everyday, but as for doing the laundry that was your job, outside the television room were three washing machines, and two working tumble dryers, the only thing was if you left your washing in the machine unattended, you would come back and find it lying in a soggy heap in the corner, that's why someone always stood guard over the machines when the washing was on, the skirmishes I saw out there, when some poor bastard came back to find his washing dumped in a corner, was not real. The roustys washed and dried the coveralls for the crews in a washing machine and tumble dryer inside a place called the annex, (I'll come back to this place later)

Sunday morning was the usual time for the weekly boat drill, this in itself was quite painless, we would all muster for the lifeboat we were in, in the recreation room at 7 am fully fitted out in our life/ jackets, this suited both crews as we were either just starting or finishing the shift, none of the carry on of getting out of bed like you had when we were working 12 to 12, the drills lasted maximum 20 minutes, we also had the option of going to bible class at 9am if you were remotely interested, I don't remember anybody from drilling going to one of these sessions, all I know is if there was a swear box in the vicinity it would have been overflowing, the drill crews would have made sure of that, I remember sitting in the tv lounge one Sunday morning with the crew, watching a very entertaining adult movie, when the door opened and a guy shouted, does anybody want to come to the bible class, all I can say is, if this guy had never heard bad language before, he heard it that day. Lots of it, I bet the shouts of shut that fucking door ya idiot, was still ringing in his ears, by the end of bible class that day.

I only got Dennis for 1 week out the 2, (thank fuck,) his back to back was a guy called Russell, a tall happy go lucky sort of chap, Russell had had a bad injury losing half his foot in an accident on a rig, this earned him the nickname from the crews of 18 inches, because he only had a foot and a half, one day a new roustabout (Terry Machlin) asked me who he was, and I told him that's Russell, the night pusher, 18 inches to his friends, now Russell walked with a distinct limp obvious for anyone to see, but this rousty obviously picked me up wrong in my description of Russell, because sitting in the galley having a cigarette one night after my meal,(you were allowed to smoke in there) this rousty turned to Russell and said, I bet you do alright with the women, eh,? I beg your pardon, Russell asked? He said again, you'll do alright with the women if you've got 18 inches, honest to fuck I didn't know where to look, Russell's face went bright red, the rousty looking at me wondering what he said wrong, me looking everywhere else but at Russell, I thought I was going to bust a gut trying not to laugh, Russell stormed off in the huff, the rousty asking me, what's wrong with him? Until I told him! I think once Russell calmed down a bit, he saw the funny side of it, well, he didn't make an issue of it anyway.

At home on leave after my first trip I was sent on a 2 day slinging and banking course, I thought it a bit strange that I had been doing the job for that long on other rigs, then all of a sudden I was needing training, but Unical insisted that all the deck crews had a certificate of competence, I was sent to Sparrows training centre at Tyrebagger hill just outside of Aberdeen, and for the next 2 days we went round this place slinging up everything and anything we could see, it was a good laugh and the Instructors made the course quite enjoyable, there was 8 of us on the course, but I was the only one staying in the Dee Motel, the others on the course who were working for different contractors stayed elsewhere,, anyone who has stayed at the Dee before they knocked it down to build Boots the Chemist will possibly relate to the place.

In the bar on the Tuesday night before the course I was given a luke warm pint of beer, when I complained to the barmaid she said that it had been like that all day, the coolers weren't working. I said she should put a towel over the handle or at least let the punters know that the beer was warm. That fell on deaf ears, I decided to get a pint of cider, at least that was cool, then when I heard a guy ordering a pint of beer. I told him, the beers warm mate, when he complained, he got the same answer as me, I kid you not, this woman kept pulling pint after pint of warm beer for the next hour or so telling anyone who complained that the coolers weren't working. Ordering my evening meal was a fucking joke, when the waitress came to take my order, I told her I wanted soup, a well done steak with onion rings, and french fries, no gravy, no peas or tomatoes, and no sweet, cheese/ biscuits or coffee. Now 20 minutes later she appeared with the soup, 10 minutes after that she brought a basket of bread rolls, I'd eaten the fucking soup by this time. All the time I'm looking out the windows watching the people on the artificial ski slope going up and down, finally she arrived back at the table to would you believe it,? Ask me, how I would like my steak. By this time I had lost the plot. I'd like it fucking now, I said. She scurried away, and I felt a bit of a cunt for snapping at her, maybe she's new and just finding her way, I thought? But when she arrived back with steak, onion rings, peas, tomatoes, gravy all over it, and potatoes as a side dish, I just looked at her,

I tried to eat the steak, but a fucking alligator couldn't have chewed that, in the end I got up and walked out to complain at the reception desk, but after standing for 5 minutes with nobody turning up, I went to my room in the huff, the rooms were outside in blocks of what looked like flats, it took a few minutes to find where I was staying, and when I did find it, the smell of dampness when I opened the door was breathtaking, the room itself was clean enough, although everything was old looking, in the bathroom was a what seemed like a 10 watt bulb, you could hardly see unless the hall light was on, but the icing on the cake was when I pulled the cord for the light above the mirror, it wasn't working, the bulb was done, I could see by the dark bits at both ends that it was done, it was one of those long slim bulbs that you slide in at one end and it snaps into place at the other, there was no use trying to have a shave in there, not without a bulb anyway. So away I went, bulb in hand, to the reception desk on arrival a woman I took to be the receptionist was sitting behind the desk, good evening sir, she said, can I help you,? Yes I said, can you give me a replacement bulb for this one, I'm sorry sir, that's the handy mans job, ok then, I said, can you get the handy man to change it? Sorry sir, he's off duty at the moment, and wont be back on again until tomorrow, if you give me your room number, and leave the bulb in the sink I will get him to change it, when he's back on duty, now I'm looking for Jeremy fucking Beadle at this point, surely someone's going to jump out and point to a camera saying, Ha,Ha you've been framed, but when that didn't happen I said to her, look, why don't you give me a new bulb, I will give you the old one and I will fit it myself, and we can pretend I was never here, sorry sir, it's Motel policy that the handy man does all the repairs, and he's not here at the moment, I felt like fucking screaming, I was only wasting my time talking to this woman, so back I went to the room, believe me when I tell you it's not easy shaving in near dark by feel alone,, when I left the Motel on Thursday morning for the last day of the course, that fucking light bulb was still lying in the sink handyman my arse,, two things must have happened, either she forgot to tell him, or they ran out of bulbs. No wonder they knocked the fucking place down.

The last day of the course went well and at the end of it I was given a certificate of rigging and slinging competency that meant that now if I fucked up at least I was competent at it, there wasn't much time of my leave left so I enjoyed it as only I knew how.

The crews seemed to change a lot on this rig for reasons that were numerous, one of

those being the liquid mud flow line system, this line was part of the cycle where the mud left the tanks, went down the hole brought back up the drilling cuttings to go over the shakers before ending back in the tanks again, this system worked well on all the other rigs I was on, but the flow line on this rig ran in an incline, therefore 1 roughneck and 1 rousty was always working at the flow line when we were drilling, they were using shovels to keep the cuttings moving, this was a cunt of a job, it was bad enough shovelling these cuttings all day, but with the heat off the liquid mud, it made it intolerable at times, there was no respite from this job, if the cuttings were allowed to build up it was a fucking nightmare to clear. In the end they decided to get an engineer out to look at the job, and sort the incline out, it should have been a downhill gradient, not up. The day this guy arrived on the chopper was one the rig crew had long been waiting for, the guy himself was away doing his rig induction, when the Helicopter Landing Officer (H.L.O.) informed me that the guys equipment was on the heli/deck waiting to be uplifted, I sent one of the roustys to bring his gear down to the pipe deck, informing him that he was to be careful with it, as some of it was fragile, I shouldn't have said fuckall because the next thing I knew was he was sliding 1 of the 2 cases marked with stickers saying FRAGILE on them, down the stairs leading from the heli/deck. he was carrying the guys tripod over his shoulder while bumping the other case down the stairs still holding the handle, I shouted to him to stop, but it was too late, by this time both cases lay at the bottom of the stairs, all scraped and scored. With the Fragile stickers hanging off them when I got to him and asked him what the fuck he was playing at? He said the cases were too heavy to lift, and he thought the easiest way to get them down without hurting himself, was to slide them down the stairs, I couldn't believe it, I was still shaking my head when the engineer turned up, having finished his induction, one look at the cases said it all. Then he looked at me, and it took me all my time not to laugh, not at the state of the cases but at him, he was the spitting image of the silent movie star Ben Turpin, he had one eye looking east the other looking west. I thought we've got a Marty Feldman look alike here, He opened one case and everything looked fine, but the theodolite in the other one had a broken lens, oh well then, he said! that's that job fucked until I get another theodolite out, ok mate, I said, sorry about that, but these things happen, that's when the rousty said, can you not just eye it in mate, that did it for me, I couldn't hold it in any longer, I just burst out laughing, the more I looked at this engineer, the louder I laughed, the more I thought about this guy eyeing the flow line up, had me in hysterics, I had to walk away, I was ready for wetting myself, 2 days later the chopper brought out another case with a replacement theodolite in it, and the guy set about his task, he was on the rig for 4 days measuring up, taking all sorts of readings, I was on the rig for another 2 or 3 trips after that, and the flow line was still the fucking same, I bet its still the same to this day.

At the check/in going out to the rig again for xmas, the rig manager Mike Beale met us at the heliport, he introduced to me a new roustabout who was joining our crew, this lad had never been offshore before and the rig manager told me to look after him, I expressed my concerns about the amount of turnover on the crew and that sending out guys as green as the grass was not a good idea, especially at the drilling stage we were at on the rig, we were going to be really busy and what we really needed were experienced men, the Heather was not a suitable training ground to send anybody, but that fell on deaf ears as usual, as long as the rig was fully manned it didn't matter how much experience they had, it was bodies that counted. the guys name was Mark Riggall from Sunderland, Mark was a big German looking lad with short cropped fair hair, another new rousty to the crew was a guy from Dundee his name was Terry Hughes, Terry had a few years experience working offshore, but was still new to the rig, this trip is going to be a nightmare, I thought as we boarded the chopper,

On the flight out to the rig, I was trying not to think about the 2 weeks ahead, it was time to reflect what I got up to when I was home, and what I was going to do different next time, you didn't need new year to make resolutions, these were made and broken on a 2 week basis, and always on the way back to the rig, I cant speak for anybody else, but me, I was always full of the best of intentions, I knew I was drinking and gambling too much, and as usual promised myself that next time home would be different, I would promise myself that things would change for the better, I used to joke, that when I was home, I went on a drinking diet, and that I lost 5 days in a fortnight, in all honesty it was no joke, some days were lost to me altogether through drink, but each trip offshore, I would make the best laid plans for when I'm home again, but you know how the saying goes, don't you?

On the rig they were drilling the next section of the well, so my first week was spent running around like a blue arse fly, trying to rotate the jobs for the roustys so as not to piss them off doing the same thing day in, day out, Terry was on the flow line this day shovelling away, when the derrick/man called me to get a hand with a chemical mix, I was busy with Phil working with the crane, so I took Mark down to the mixing hoppers and explained what he was supposed to do, the derrick man wanted 2 pallets of lime put into the hopper, that would be about 40 sacks, I drove a pallet of lime up to the hopper with the forklift, explained the need for the protective working gear, goggles, rubber gloves, rubber apron, and so on to Mark, and told him to empty one sack at a time into the hopper, when the pallet was finished he was to give me a phone, and I would change out the pallet, then I left him to it. 20 minutes later, I was called to the pushers office, Dennis was there along with the rig medic, a guy named Henry, they wanted to know why I had left an inexperienced man on his own without supervision, Mark got some lime in his eye when the hopper blew back on him, oh he had his goggles on ok, it was when he took them off to see, that the lime dust got in his eye, I told Dennis and Henry exactly what I thought of this witch hunt, how many fucking guys to you think I've got here, I said? you are the ones that sanction new guys to come out here and as long as the job is getting done, none of you give a fuck, its only when something like this happens that you lot start asking questions, trying to explain that I thought giving Mark a simple task of mixing sacks, was better than exposing him to the dangers of working the deck with the crane, or really knock the heart out of him by putting him on the flow line,, I told them we are very busy out there, and I don't have time to nursemaid a new guy, but I was wasting my breath, they wanted a written statement of what happened, and any witnesses involved, a load of fucking bollocks. but that's the story everywhere you go in this industry, as long as things are going fine nobody bothers, but as soon as something goes wrong, you had better watch your arse because the office wallahs will have you, Mark was ok in a couple of days, and was soon back at work, I don't expect that he'll forget his first day offshore in a hurry

.Wednesday morning of our second week, I was surprised to find a birthday cake waiting in the tea/shack for me, I remember saying to one of the stewards the trip before, that I would be spending another birthday offshore, but I never for a moment thought anybody would bother, I was well chuffed, I can tell you, everybody singing happy birthday, to you, left me with a lump in my throat, some were asking if Dennis had left me a present, like a written warning, all wrapped with xmas paper, it made it a special day for me, it was beginning to become a habit spending not only my birthday offshore, but Xmas and new year as well, but like all highs, there is always a low, and this one was as low as they come, that day December 21st 1988 the Pan American flight 103 from Frankfurt heading for New York via London was blown up over Lockerbie killing 259 people on board and 11 people on the ground, this was another cowardly act of terrorism which reflects mans inhumanity to man, this is another date that I will always remember for all the wrong reasons, not just because its my birthday.

Xmas day was just like any other day for drilling, the other contractors got most of the day off but drilling were kept out all shift, (what happened to the one big family?) we weren't all sitting round the fucking dinner table that's for sure, it used to really piss the guys off when, everywhere you looked there was Xmas decorations hanging from the roof, our reasoning was, we knew it was Xmas and if we weren't getting any time off to celebrate it, then don't ram it up us by reminding us about it, It wasn't a case of bah humbug or anything like that, it was like if the powers that be wanted us to treat it like any other day, then that's exactly what we did, we would celebrate Xmas when we got home, the first Xmas I spent offshore set the trend for me, I have never had an Xmas dinner offshore since.

As I said earlier, people were leaving this rig on a regular basis, I remember one guy who once he had his induction, and had seen round the place, refused to come out to work, no amount of persuading would get this guy to change his mind, I'm not working on this fucking shite house, you don't seriously expect me to sleep in there do you? Was all he'd say, I didn't know where he was talking about, until later. Just get me on the next chopper out of here, he said. But the powers that be kept him on for 2 days, saying there were no available seats for him, but I know they were secretly hoping he'd change his mind. But give that guy his due he stuck to his guns and stayed in the accommodation until they got him a flight,

There was a rumour going about the rig that Dan Smedvig was losing the contract and that was the start of a mass exodus, people were leaving in the hope of picking something up elsewhere, it was a catch 22 situation, if you stayed till the end of the contract, and Smedvig had nothing else for you, you might find that all the jobs going elsewhere were taken, then again, if you left to go elsewhere, you could find that Smedvig had places elsewhere for everybody, so it was an individual decision as to what to do for the best. There was only about 2 trips left to do before the drilling programme was finished and as there were people leaving all the time, Smedvig offered a £25 a day loyalty bonus to entice the crews to stay and see out the contract, some did, some didn't, I was one of the ones who did, but not without some reservations, 2 days before my trip was up the Tool pusher asked me if I would do an extra week roustabouting, none of the other guys wanted to stay on, and the crew coming out were 2 men short, I thought about it for a while, then asked if on top of the time and a third they were paying for overtime, would I get the extra £25 a day on top, when he said yes, I told him I would do it, on crew change day, I was told to report to heli/admin to be given a room change, I had to change rooms as my back to back would be going into the rousty pushers cabin, and I was going into a roustabouts cabin, this was no big deal, after all, a rooms a room isn't' it or so I thought ! the guy in charge of heli/admin was Henry the medic, this was also part of his duties, now, I'd not forgotten how he tried to stitch me up with the lime incident, so when I went up to see him I just asked for my new room number so I could put my gear into it before starting shift again, he told me the number of the room, and away I went looking for it, I searched on levels 2,3,4,looking for this room, but the numbers didn't correspond, I was on my way back to see him when I bumped into one of the roughnecks, after explaining what I was doing he told me the room I was looking for was outside in the annex. No way I thought, the annex is condemned theirs nobody allowed on top of it during the night, in case they fall through the roof, but the roughneck was right, in this what looked like a rat infested, cockroach ridden den of inequity was my room, one look was enough for me, it was cold, damp, and dirty, the musky smell lingered everywhere, there were curtains hanging from the steel bunk beds that you wouldn't hang in your garden shed, the linoleum on the floor was in tatters, the shower and toilet facilities were appalling, how anyone could stay in here was remarkable to say the least, and I certainly wasn't staying here, not through choice anyway. I had been on this rig for a few months by now and never thought for a moment that the roughnecks and roustys stayed in here, I always thought they stayed in the main accommodation with the rest of us, back I went to see Henry and told him, either I stay in the main accommodation or I'm off on my regular crew change. He was wondering what all fuss was about, it's only a room, he said! Well he obviously hadn't been to see it, in the end they said that there was no rooms available in the main accommodation, so I went off with the crew.

Back on the beach again I thought I had it sussed with the customs, if you only had your cigarette or tobacco allowance in your bag they let you through without any hassle, so I started to tape packets of tobacco to my body, I would get as much as 10 packets strapped round my waist, and another 4 strapped to each leg, I would use elasticated bandages for the legs, but sometimes I had to use divers tape for my legs and waist if I couldn't find any electrical, or forgotten the bandages, now if you have ever used divers tape to secure anything to your body you will know how fucking painful it is to remove, I always remember sitting in the taxi on the way to the railway station trying to pull this tape off, without doing myself a serious injury, there was hardly a hair left on my legs or torso, and to make matters worse I usually ended up giving most of it away to guys in the pub, this smuggling run soon came to a halt when the guys I was giving it to for nothing, started asking me as soon as I got into the pub, (have you got my tobacco ?) I thought right, you cheeky bastards are getting nothing, when I told them that I couldn't get it anymore you should have seen their faces, it was as if I was doing them out of something that was theirs, Liz and I decided that they were taking the piss, and if I was going to get into trouble for smuggling contraband then it should be for our own use, that's when I stopped taking it for other people, it also gave my hairs a chance to grow in again, another thing Liz brought to my attention was the number of people who thought that because I was working on the rigs, I was a soft touch for a loan, I suppose that was my fault in a way because I was always flush with money, they would see me with a wad of notes buying drink and putting bets on thinking nothing of it if the bet got beat, the loans were small to begin with a 5 here or a 10 there and if I got it back that was fine, if I didn't then it was a small price to pay to get rid of them, you really need a hard neck, to tap someone you already owe money too. In the end I stopped giving out loans, what made me stop was some of the people I had given loans to knew I was back home again, but instead of coming to me and explaining that they couldn't pay it back at that time, they would drink elsewhere, and even avoid you in the street, it made me feel as if it was me who was in the wrong, but the crunch came when one of my so called mates asked me for a loan of 100, now this guy had been on the dole for as long as I knew him, and I had a sneaky feeling the money was for drink or gambling, it certainly wasn't for the house, when I told him there was no way he could afford the 20 a fortnight he offered to pay back off his dole cheque, and that I would either be a soft touch for giving it to him, knowing I wouldn't see it again, or an arsehole for saying no, that's when he started telling me it was alright for me, you've got a job working on the rigs, home every 2 weeks with plenty of money to spend and not a care in the world, that's when I stopped the conversation, it was going nowhere, if I had given him the money, I would have been a great guy, but because I said no, I was an arsehole, now that's what I call a no win, all lose, situation, there's no quicker way to lose friends than to lend them money.

The next trip went by without any hassle and by February I was on my last trip I was beginning to feel like a Jonah because on all the rigs I've been on so far, they have either had the drilling contractor changed, or they've shut down drilling until the next program. We were down to the die/hards on the crews now, the roughnecks had changed so much I hardly knew any of them, Phil, and Mark were gone, it was only Terry, me, and 2 new guys, that were left on deck, I was past giving a fuck by this time, Dennis was running around like a headless chicken trying to motivate people, (As if screaming at folk would motivate them) he was on a hiding to nothing, and I think he knew it, but try as he might he never broke our spirit, he would come through the rear entrance of the tea/shack and walk to the other, all the time looking at us, then at his watch, as if to say, it's time you lot were out of here, now rather than just come out and say, you've been in here long enough, he would look at you hoping to intimidate you into leaving, but it wasn't working, I remember sitting in the tea/shack one night with the rig welder a guy called Rab Dick, Rab came from the west coast somewhere, Hamilton, I think, a right comedian was Rab, anyway, Rab and me were sitting bullshitting away in the tea/shack when Dennis came in and started his nightly ritual of looking at us, then at his watch, just as he was passing us Rab said to him, is that a new watch you've been getting for Xmas Dennis, Dennis in his usual man/management skilled manner replied, uh, Rab once again said, that must be a nice new watch you've got because you keep on fucking looking at it, I was in stitches, but Dennis went red in the gills, Rab was in the same frame of mind as myself, we didn't give a fuck now, the job was finished, and we were just counting the days until the end of the our trip, but Dennis, he walked away grunting like an angry bear that just found out that somebody stole his porridge.

The second week was much the same as the first, only it was nearer to going home, we found out through rumour control on the rig, that one of the stewards had helped himself to some of the home made brew, that was secretly hidden away for the new year, he kept it hidden in his locker and one night decided to have a blow out, that was fine in itself if he had taken the drink then slept it off, but the guy needed a shit and when he went to the toilet he was shall we say a wee bit unsteady on his feet, I can picture him now pulling his pants down, then reaching behind himself to pull down the spring loaded seat to sit on, that's when he must have slipped and sat on the seat with his fingers stuck underneath because that's where his room mate found him, drunk as a cunt and fast asleep with a couple of dislocated fingers, that was all supposed to be kept quiet, but you can't keep things like that quiet, not on a place as small as a rig.

Its these little things that keep everybody going on the rigs, the friendly rivalry, the fun and the banter, in a nutshell you need a bit of crack, if it wasn't for these things happening, people would go stir crazy, oh don't get me wrong there are some people out there that thrive on misery, these are the guys that are as glum the day they go off the rig, as they were the day they came on, you soon find out that these people all stick together, all standing in heli/admin, moaning that its that time to go home again, fuck knows what kind of lifestyle they have at home, but it can't be pleasant, I was fooled one day when I thought I saw one of them smile at me when I passed him, only to find out, he was just passing wind. Yes you know who I'm on about? the production guys, it never ceases to amaze me and I suppose that I should be used to their attitude by now, but in the off chance of at least a one or two of them being civil I still nodded and waved, in the vain hope of a response, but the responses were very few and far between, I used to wonder if when they checked in at Aberdeen, were they then taken to a secret place and had a full frontal lobotomy before going offshore, personally speaking, I would rather have a full bottle in front of me.

The ever faithful John Smith met us at the heli/port £50 and cheque in hand, John reckoned that Smedvig had jobs for everybody, but they still hadn't decided who was going where, it was a case of wait and see, I wasn't to bothered about leaving the Heather, but if there was nowhere else to go, I suppose it was better than no job at all, it was the usual case of waiting on a phone call, after 3 weeks had past with still no word from the office, I had resigned myself to signing on the dole again, I thought about giving the office a phone but decided against that, for two reasons, one was, if they had somewhere for me to go they would have phoned me, secondly, I really didn't want to hear that they had nowhere else to send me, so I waited, hoping for the phone to ring.

Two days later a call from the office had me smiling and packing my bag again, I was off to the North West Hutton again as Roustabout/pusher. I think Liz was as relieved as me that I was going away again, money was becoming a bit tight, she was used to having me home for only two weeks and she budgeted the spending money to last that long, now it was near enough three and a half weeks and my lifestyle hadn't changed, I was spending just as much a day, well Liz was anyway, she was still buying the drink and putting the bets on even though I shouldn't have been at home, Oh I wasn't always putting on losing bets, when I did get a line up I would give Liz half, but like any gambler does, I only remembered the winners. Things are definitely going to change next time I'm home.

6

North West Hutton

The check in for the Hutton was at 6 am on either Wednesday or Friday as there were 2 crews working both derricks at any one time; I was on the Wednesday crew change and was told to be at Bond helicopters in Dyce on the 6th of April 89. at that time Dan Smedvig put us up in digs at the boarding house they used in Bon Accord street, and on Tuesday night, that was where I met Jim(Smiddy) Smith from Kirkcaldy, Jim was the crane operator on the crew I was going to be working with, and he made it clear to me that as I was going out as rousty pusher, I was also the assistant crane-operator, this was news to me as no one from the office said anything about that, don't get me wrong I was chuffed to fuck, to think that only a few months ago I had set my sights on being a crane-op, now here was my chance, Jim told me he would teach me everything there was to know about operating the crane, and I was only too willing to learn. That night Smiddy and I went for a drink and I was glad to find that he liked a drink as much as I did, we were fucking steamboats by the time we got back to the digs, as far as I can remember I had just put my head on the pillow when the alarm clock went off, trying to wake Smiddy was like waking the dead, I don't know if you've ever had that feeling of waking up and still felt drunk, if you have then you'll know how I felt that morning, I finally got Smiddy up and with the taxi waiting we made our check/in with about 5 minutes to spare.

On the platform itself were two derricks both in operation, rig1 and rig2 I was assigned to rig 2. at any one time there would be about 60 people all employed by Smedvig working on this platform, both rigs working on a different operation, or different sections of the wells, the pipe deck itself was not any larger than normal, considering we needed double of everything, but the sack/ store was massive, I suppose it had to be to accommodate double lots of chemicals, but there was only one forklift so you

101

can imagine the carry on when both derrick/men were needing a mix at the same time,

The inductions on here were carried out by one of the drill crew so a bit of time was taken to familiarize people new to the platform, after being shown round the place I felt comfortable with the surroundings, the rooms were quite spacious with only two bunks, so I had a room to myself, my relief being on shift, between my room and the one next door was a toilet, shower, and two wash hand basins, quite cosy, infact the only downside was there was no television, and when you turned the room lights off, and the guy next door had his on, it shone through the gaps in the walls, which were also paper thin, apart from that the rooms were fine, the galley was quite spacious, as was the smoking tea/shack, I suppose it had to be to accommodate the amount of people on board, the food was edible and there was plenty of it, the catering staff as with most rigs were a friendly bunch and their was no hassle of having to do your own laundry, even the drilling crews overalls were washed for them

Most of the tool/pushers I worked with on here were Dutch-men, they were a clannish lot, the saying on the platform was " if your not Dutch your not much" there was Hans Van Dijk, Hans Van Berg, Pete Dirks, Jan Collingberg, Reiks Botter, there was also Andy Young from the Star of Markinch (fife) Russell, and Dennis, "from the Heather", Keith Douglas, Jim Kennedy, Tommy Boyle, Most of the company men were yanks, the only good one out the lot of them was an old guy called Nathan, The driller on our crew was also a yank called Hank Bruinsma (Hank the Yank) he was so stressed out that when he went for a smoke, he used to smoke two fags at once so he didn't burn his lips, Bert Wokke was working as driller on rig I, he was still the same easy going guy as he was down on the West Intrepid in Lincoln.

Big Stevie Mackay was the assistant driller, he'd done well on the promotion ladder, Mark Riggall, Big Jake, John Smith, his fa-ther was the Smedvig courier, and another couple of guys Harry Malins, Stan Philips and John Greig made up the crew on the rig floor, the roustys on deck were Phil Robertson from the Heather, Jimmy Pratt, a guy called Lennie and me.

On here we were working the 12 to 12 shift again so the first day we started at 12 noon finished at 8pm off till 4 am then on again until 12, that was us on nights for the first week, days the second. The crane operators that I remember being on the rig with were Rab Mac, John M. Sutherland, Jamie Wright, and Tommy Chalmers, all on rig 1 and Colin Prentice, Jim Brydon, Jim Smith, Kenny Milne and later on Colin Watt on rig 2, as both rigs were working there was always two crane op's on shift at a time, Smiddy took me under his wing and any time we were not busy he had me up the crane for some tuition, he soon noticed that I wasn't as green at operating the crane as he first thought, I told him that I had had a few shots of the crane on the T.L.P. but by listening to him I was learning from scratch, Smiddy was keen to learn me the crane, but not as keen as I was to learn, He had another job in mind and wanted to get me experienced enough to take his place, I was what Smiddy would say, a natural, you either have it or you don't, he said, and you have it, Smiddy wanted to get me through my stage 2 that allowed me to do lifts about the deck unsupervised, and to get that, I had to attend a 5 day course at Sparrows Training Centre, but that was a long way off, first I had to prove I was competent at doing basic deck lifts,

My first couple of trips on there were fine, Amoco, the operator we were drilling for, had Smedvig put us through all sorts of courses, first was the fork lift truck course, which was done on the rig, then they sent the crew on a 3 day helicopter fire fighting course, in Montrose, and as we were the heli/deck team, our job was to re/fuel the choppers, disembark and embark the passengers, and their baggage, with 2 crews on shift at a time, manpower was no problem, as I was the assistant crane op I had to go on an Helicopter Landing Officers,(H,L,O,) course, that lasted 3 days, to compliment that I had to go on a re/fuelling course the trip after, also for 3 days, doing all these courses didn't bother me, these had to be done if I was going to be the crane op because they all complimented the other duties that came with that role,

We were always busy doing something on the rig, if we weren't busy with the crane and the rig floor, we were busy elsewhere either, scrubbing and cleaning, painting, mixing chemicals, or generally sorting out the deck cargo for the next boat, but time was always made for smoke breaks, Smiddy made sure of that, I was spending a lot of time in the crane, thanks to the efforts of Phil, Jimmy and Lennie working the deck between them, and it wasn't long before I was ready to go through stage 2 at Sparrows Training Centre.

With the amount of drilling guys on board, it was inevitable that some had problems at home, you always knew when that happened, if a guy is usually full of crack and then all of a sudden he goes quiet for no reason, then you knew there was something wrong, there's nothing worse than being on an oil rig and having family problems, you have to go home to sort them out, and it's not as if you can just jump on a bus and go home, get it sorted and then get the next bus back out, getting home takes time, and all you have on the rig is time on your hands to dwell on whatever the problem is, and believe me when I tell you 2 weeks out there with something eating away at you is like a month, if the problem has started before you go offshore, and its marital then your never going to sort it out on the rig, not on the phone anyway, it's too easy for both sides to hang up. the guys I've seen walking the corridors after shift because they can't eat or sleep through worry, is not real, you can sense their pain, their anger, or sorrow, and all you can do is become a sympathetic ear to their worries, I blame the companies for not being understanding in times like these, if a man, or woman for that matter, is not physically fit then their not allowed offshore, but what about the people who are not mentally fit, the people who are not focused on the job and could be a danger to themselves and others around them, I've witnessed it, In fact I've been there, and I'll tell you about that later on, but as far as I'm concerned the companies don't take this into consideration, if you have a bereavement in the family your allowed 3 days compassionate leave, any more than that is up to the rig managers discretion, the companies will pull out all the stops to get you home as soon as possible in the event of you having death in the family, but how do you go to your manager and tell him, I've fallen out with the wife or partner, or one of the kids is ill, or the C.S.A. (child support agency) has just had my wages arrested, can I get some time off to sort things out, everybody knows the answer, "yes without pay", and that only adds to the pressure you already have, teashacks on rigs the whole north sea over, are filled daily with guys with problems, some bottle them up and keep them to themselves, others are not so good at hiding them, everybody working offshore will experience a dilemma at some time or other in there personal life, you only hope that when your listening to someone else's problems, They never become yours.

A classic example of someone with a problem was when some of the fire extinguisher boxes around the rig were found to have the glass window in them broken, whether this was an act of pure vandalism or not, whoever did this was certainly not firing on all cylinders, he was definitely needing off, my thinking being, if he was capable of doing something as stupid as this, what else is he capable of doing.

On Jamie Wrights crew on rig 1, one of the roustys was sent down to the sack/store to do a small painting job, 10 minutes later he was back in the tea/shack with a cut finger, he did this with a screwdriver while opening the tin, after some minor first aid he was back in the sack/store where he phoned Jamie to tell him the paint was to thick, Jamie told him to thin it down a bit, meaning use thinners, but the guy used the high pressure cleaning gun with 500psi to try and get some water into the paint tin, fuck knows what he was thinking about, but there was yellow paint everywhere apart from the area he was supposed to paint, the inside of the tin was fucking spotless, but he and everything else was covered, as you can imagine there was a stewards enquiry into what happened, the guys defence, was his mind was elsewhere, his granny was ill and he was worried about her, it was only natural as she had brought him up since he was a kid, now you might think that's funny and I suppose it is in a way, but its also sad to think this young lads mind was at home with his granny, instead of being on the job, as I said before, this drilling game is dangerous, and if your not focussed in what your doing, then an accident is just waiting to happen, trust me!

The crack on the rig was good at times, the usual banter between the different contractors, Dan Smedvig, Wood Group, and Atlantic Power and Gas, (A.P.G.) being the main ones, there were also various others at certain times. even some of the Production guys were up for a laugh, after shift if we didn't take in a movie or watched T.V. we would congregate in the lounge and play the electric organ or make use of the guitars, others would play or record off the various tapes and discs that were available all paid for by the donations by the various contract workers on the platform, one thing the lads grudged paying for was the £5 phone card, this only gave you 30 minutes at best so if you were in the habit of phoning home on a regular basis you could find yourself out £20 or more depending on how often you phoned, this money was supposed to go to charity but the consensus of opinion was that we should be getting free phone calls, and that the various charities did well out of the other fund raising events that were held, my big mate J.M. Sutherland came up with the idea of using our own phone so one trip he brought one out with him, all we had to do was disconnect the one in the phone booth and plug in our own, it worked a treat and as it was also free we would call up the sex chat lines at night and get them to talk dirty to us, one time we got through to this woman and after talking to her for about 5 minutes she told us in no uncertain terms she wasn't going to talk dirty, so we asked her if their was anybody else there that would, we obviously dialled the wrong number. it was funny at times as there would be up to 4 guys cramming into this telephone booth all trying to listen to some stranger oohing and aahing over the phone.

The highlight of the week was a game called cabin bingo, most guys wouldn't be seen dead in a bingo hall at home, but out here it broke the monotony and most guys looked forward to it, me included. It was the same as ordinary bingo with the winner being the one with lowest numbers off, for a single line, then the same for a full house, One week Big Mackay and me had a single line in 21 numbers, that was generally not too bad, but the APG lads had a line in 19 numbers, they thought they were onto a winner, and so they were, until MacKay told them that we had a line in 18 numbers, So the APG guys to our astonishment binned their ticket, and we won with 21 numbers, you should have fucking heard them when they found out, they were ranting and raving, calling us a pair of cheating lying bastards, Mackay and me were just laughing at them, telling them to fuck off and that they shouldn't have binned their ticket or believed what we told them. One guy was going over the score in the way he was carrying on, until Mackay told him in no uncertain terms that if he didn't shut the fuck up, he was going to give him three rapid in the ribs. He quietened down after that, Imagine, all that carry on for £30, but it was worth it to see their faces when we won the single line with more numbers than they had.

When we were at home on leave, Smiddy would come up to my local in Glenrothes and me and him would go on the drink, the big man liked his drink as I said, he had, like me, a very understanding wife, she would drop him off at the pub, and Liz and me would take him back to Kirkcaldy at the end of play that day.

One time when I was at home, Liz found out that her daughter Nicky wanted to come and stay with us permanently, so arrangements were made and her father put her on a plane from down south, and we picked her up at Edinburgh airport and took her home to our house, she was only 12 and had had enough of moving from pillar to post, hopefully she would settle down with us, It would be about year later, when one night I phoned home and Liz told me that out that her son David was being sent to a boys home, if there was nowhere else for him to go, obviously there was problems with his father and his new wife, but that wasn't my concern, there was no question about it, the boy would come and stay with us and his sister. Thankfully they and Kaiser got on well.

It was on my leave in October of 89, that I was sent on the Sparrows 5 day stage 2 crane course, I started it on the 16th and successfully passed with merit on the 20th, I was over the moon, in just 6 months on here I had succeeded in at least achieving one of the goals I had set myself, all I had to do now was gain experience in offloading and back/loading the supply boats, Smiddy wasn't allowed to let me have a go at the supply boats, until I had completed my stage 2, but that didn't stop him having me up the crane when he was working them, I watched his every move and was certain that I would manage to do as good a job as him, Given time, Smiddy only stayed two more trips after I passed my stage 2 and I was promoted to Crane Operator/ Deck Foreman, I had come on leaps and bounds since my first trip offshore on the Tartan, Seldom was right about the promotion prospects, in just over 18 months, I shot right up the ladder.(EXCUSE THE PUN) But I don't mind telling you, my arse was twitching the first time I worked the boat on my own, before Smiddy left, Smedvig sent out a trainer/ assessor from the beach, to test me on my ability to work boats competently, and to my delight he passed me, that was me a fully qualified stage 3 crane-operator, allowed to work on my own, Phil became my assistant and a new guy joined the crew as rousty.

Things ticked along nicely on the platform with both rigs 1 and 2 having a full drilling program, which meant if everything went well it could last until 1992, that was a bonus in itself as most rigs worked on a 1 maybe 2 well program, this settled the crews with the knowledge that they had work for at least 2 years.

One thing that did piss the crews off was the ritual of having the weekly boat drill on Sunday morning at 7am, with us working 12 to 12 it was inevitable that two crews would be woken up for the drill, then one Saturday night at 22-30hrs, the crews were up mingling about and getting ready for nightshift, when the fire alarm was sounded, we all mustered at our dedicated points, silently enjoying the fact that the rest of the platform who were working 7am to 7pm had to get out of bed to muster, the alarm was soon silenced and we were told that it had been a spurious alarm, meaning the alarm went off for no apparent reason, but that we would be carrying on with the drill, we weren't giving a fuck about it being a spurious alarm, all it meant to us was the dayshift drill crews would get a long lie on Sunday morning, the following week it happened again the alarm going off at the same time 10 30pm again for no apparent reason, once again we mustered at night, but someone smelled a rat, because the two weeks we were off, there were no spurious alarms so they pinpointed the cause to the 2 crews that were on shift at the time, on our first week back the alarm went off again at about the same time on the Saturday night, but some of the production guys were posted at certain points on the platform to keep watch, one of the prody guys saw a rousty run out of the sack/store just after the alarm was sounded, and he was pulled in for questioning, the outcome was the rousty pusher had put this guy up to loosening the screws holding the glass front on the fire alarm with an allen key, then as the alarm went off, he quickly tightened them up again, that's why they couldn't find the cause of the alarms going off, the rousty pusher lost his job, and the other guy was moved to another rig. Oh well, back to getting up early on a Sunday morning, no rest for the wicked as they say.

There was always something happening on one rig or another but something that happened to both rigs one time, was when Smedvig called for both crews going ashore on the Wednesday and Friday to attend a drug screening test at the medical centre in Aberdeen, someone reckoned that the smells of deep heat, ralgex and other spray liniments in the corridors, were not to soothe aching bones, they were used to hide something more sinister, like people having a smoke, and we're not talking Golden Virginia here. you were allowed to smoke in the rooms on here and that was one of the pluses about the place, I personally never witnessed anyone smoking anything other than tobacco, and the test held no fears for me, although those that refused to take the test were NRB'd, I did notice one or two new faces the following trip but that could have meant anything, people moving on for example. I remember one time going home on the train when I was given a smoke of the (weird stuff) for the first time, the next thing I remember was, when I got off the train, and the train started moving again, I started running after it shouting for it to stop, because I thought I had left my leather jacket on it, then I heard Liz shouting to me that I had it on. That was really weird, Liz said I looked like I was running in slow motion, (how the fuck do you run in slow motion) I woke up the next morning with a bastard of a headache, that was my pot smoking days finished, they say smoking it makes you mellow, well it made me fucking ill.

Dougie (the blade) Steele was rousty pusher on rig1 and as the rig crews were the heli/deck team, him and one of his rousty's teamed up with two of mine when the chopper came in so that there was always somebody left on the deck to cover the rig floors needs, it was common practice for the lads to cross on to the heli/ deck via the rig floor, also it was easier than walking down three levels then up another three levels to the heli/deck. The only thing was, you had to climb over some handrails and step over a void about 2 feet wide but there was also about a 30 foot drop to the deck if you slipped, there was never a problem with this practice until one day when the roughnecks had just finished painting the handrails. Dougie had left his glove prints and boot prints on the fresh paint, instead of just taking a bollocking from the driller, Dougie in his wisdom told him to fuck off, bad move, the driller reported him and Dougie was NRB'd for breaching safety, It was also to make an example of him, as he was the immediate supervisor. The other guys were given warnings, but I thought it a bit hard on Dougie, as I said earlier the least wee thing like speaking back, or your face not fitting, could cost you your job.

Accidents happen in every industry and nobody starts the day intending to have one, but when they do, they try to learn from their mistakes so the same thing doesn't happen again. The thought of having to fill in the endless forms and attend an enquiry when something does happen makes most people stop and think about what their doing, if someone sprains an ankle, wrist, or twists his back, or does some injury to themselves that they will recover from, they think twice before attempting to do the job they were doing the same way. This can be said after the tragic accident to Martin Pead who was killed on the rig floor in the summer of 91. The operation that was going on at the time was looked at, and new measures were put into place on the rig floor after that, If it is any consolation to Martins family, that type of tragic accident can never be repeated, making it a safer place for all to work "lessons were learned that tragic day."

With the Blade gone, a very good mate of mine, Alex Robertson, (Sooty) from Glenrothes Fife, was brought in from the Fulmar platform to take his place, Sooty soon settled in, as he was an experienced guy and good at his job, but that counted for nothing 9 months later when a chain of events befell him, Travelling to Aberdeen one September Friday morning in his car, to check/in with the driller and a roughneck as passengers, the car broke down on the A90 a few miles south of Aberdeen, the driller and roughneck thumbed a lift the rest of the way, but Alex stayed with the car until it was sorted, when that was done, he travelled home again and phoned the office who gave him another check/in time for the following day, unfortunately Alex's wife Gina, was rushed into hospital that night after becoming unwell, again Alex phoned the office where they gave him a third check/in time, tragically Gina died from a blood clot the following day, to pour salt in the wound Alex was sacked for missing three check/ins in a row, my pleas for compassion fell on deaf ears on the rig, no matter how much I and others on the rig tried to get the Dutch pusher to examine the circumstances, he wouldn't budge, saying it was out of his hands because he missed three check/ins, the mans just lost his wife for fucks sake, I told him, how the fuck do you expect him to come to work?, but I was wasting my breath, I asked Alex to take them to a tribunal, but their attitude knocked the heart out of him, he said that he didn't want to work for a company that treated their workforce so terribly, Alex never worked offshore again after that, the boys on the platform collected nearly £800 to help him and his young daughter Dianne, Alex was very grateful when I took it home to him. How many times have you heard the saying, your only a name and number! Well this was a classic example.

I asked myself where was the personnel department, or human resources for that matter, Where was the compassion from the hierarchy? "Where indeed"?

Feelings were running high on the rig for the way Alex was treated and it was a few trips before things settled down, but I was seeing the management in a different light.

Jim Brydon was promoted to platform deck foreman, so a place became available on here for Con Masterson, Con had been floating about various rigs so I was glad when he was given a permanent slot here, but Con was older than the rest of the crane op's and not as agile, so when the new rig manager Eammon

Coyle wanted the hands on approach from the crane op's Con expressed his concern, we knew he wasn't fit enough to run around like the rest of us, but even though we told him to say nothing, Con told the rig manager that he wasn't prepared to change his ways, he said that Smedvig had employed him as a crane operator, and that's only what he was prepared to do, The inevitable happened, Con was moved to a rig that was shutting down and the old system of last one in, first one out, came into force. Con had told me in confidence that he had been diagnosed with terminal cancer, and had possibly less than a year to live, so he wasn't too bothered. Con died the following year but not before Liz and I got the chance to go and visit him and his family in Enniskillen, where we were treated like family ourselves for the whole week/end. I was so sorry I didn't make his funeral. But later the lads collected a £1000 which Liz and I duly delivered to his wife; we still have photos of him, his family and his grave to remind us of the loss of a very dear friend.

Hank the driller moved on and Bryan Cannon from Seaham in Sunderland took his place, Bryan was fine to work with and Liz and me spent the week/ end with him and his family, but Bryan was another casualty of the management system, his back to back Brian (Robbo) Robinson had phoned the office a week prior to going offshore informing them that he wouldn't be there, the day before Bryan was due home, the management told him he must stay the compulsory one day to cover for his relief, Bryan told them they could fuck off, they had plenty of time to organize a relief for him and they were just taking the piss, the company insisted he stay but Bryan went home on his regular crew change, the end result was he was sacked, then re/instated and moved to a rig working in Italy, the next time I saw him he was as brown as a berry, and said it was the best move he ever made. At least that one worked out ok.

Things at home weren't working out so well though, it seemed that every time I was home something was going wrong, they say bad news comes in three's, well the first was when Kaiser my ever faithful friend who I could always depend on (to bite somebody that is) did just that to the postman, the poor guy needed thirteen stitches to the back of his leg, I was given a letter off the post office informing me that if I didn't keep my dog under control then I would have to pick up my mail from the post office myself, I tried to deny that it was my dog that did it, but deep down, I knew it was, I could tell by that look on the fuckers face it was him, and by the way his head went down and his ears went back, when I told scolded him for taking off his muzzle.

The second involved Kaiser again, I had just filled the bath one morning when he started barking, someone was at the door, and when I answered it, I found it was one of the guys from my local boozer delivering a shower unit I had ordered off him, the guy left and I put the unit upstairs in one of the bedrooms and jumped in the bath, a few minutes later I heard a commotion downstairs, and Liz shouting on me, I wrapped a towel around myself and ran downstairs to the living room and found two guys sitting on the couch one of them had his trousers round his ankles and he was holding the back of his leg, the dog was snarling and barking at them and I couldn't hear a fucking thing they were saying, I told Liz to put him in the bedroom out the way and asked these two guys what the fuck was going on, It turned out they were the C.I.D.and said that they had reason to believe that I had just taken possession of a video recorder a few moments ago, they had obviously been watching the guy who dropped off the shower unit, when I told them that the only video I had was the one they could see in front of them, and that I was one smart cookie to have it up and running with the clock set at the right time in only a few minutes, but the weren't having any, Liz at this time was dabbing stuff on the guys leg trying to ease his pain, he was howling worse than the dog, I was hoping it was Vortex bleach she was using and not disinfectant, the other fellow was going on about getting a search warrant to find this so called video, I told them they could fuck off and do what they liked, the guy with the sore leg said, he was charging me with keeping a dangerous dog, I told him he's a guard dog and that there were signs on both gates to warn people, also they had no right to be in my house, they said your wife let us in, I said I'm not married, and she's the housekeeper with no authority to let anyone in, things were getting out of hand and I didn't want them searching my house as their was things I didn't want them to see, so I reluctantly told them that what I received that morning was a shower unit not the fucking video recorder they were looking for, after inspecting the shower "still in its original box by the way" one of them said he was going to check his records when he got back to the station and if he found that any shower units had been reported stolen he was coming back for it, well you better bring a fucking plumber with you, I told him, because it's going on the bathroom wall this morning, the saga ended with me and the dog appearing at the local magistrates, I was fined £20 and the dog let off with a caution, the shower was still in the bathroom 5 years later, until I replaced it with a new one.

The third was a good sign that I was on track to accomplish one of my dreams, because that's when I signed the papers to take out a mortgage and start the first of the 25 year payments, the way I worked it out then was I was paying less for the mortgage than I was paying in rent, all I had to do now was keep up the payments.

I had to look twice this day when I saw who the new driller was, it was Bob the Dog, and he started grinning like a fucking Cheshire cat when he saw me, we bullshitted for a while, then I asked him what happened down in Lincoln? He told me that when he woke up that Sunday, he felt like shit, and as there was only a day or two of the job left down there, he decided to go home, Bob stayed for a couple of trips then went elsewhere, I really liked Bob. So if your reading this mate, all the very best!

One thing about this rig was, if we brought the well in on time, and under budget we qualified for a well bonus. This could be from £100 to £500 per man, as the rig were drilling 3 or possibly 4 wells a year this was a big boost to the wages if we qualified, and it gave the lads a bit of incentive, rewarding guys with tee-shirts, jackets with a picture of a rig sewn onto it, or pats on the back, just doesn't work, were only out there for one thing, and that's the money. Getting well-done boys, from the management, doesn't pay the mortgage.

One thing Smiddy never taught me was, think first, before saying anything over the radio, about what you see from the crane, and I learned that to my dismay, I was working the boat one day when I spotted something in the water, I spoke to the skipper of the boat informing him that there was, what I thought, a turtle in the water. I knew straight away I should have kept my mouth shut, because a short while later, when I was lifting a container from the boat to the pipe-deck, I was slewing the crane back onto the platform and as the pipe-deck came into view, There sitting on a Sampson post (Bay divider) was a plastic bucket with a pole sticking through it and a pair of gloves stuck on each end, on the top of it was a hard hat, looking awfully like a turtle, I didn't rise to the banter that was coming over the radio, I was getting instructions like ok Johnotello down on your line, or your certainly coming out your shell, but the icing on the cake was when I went to eat, written on the menu board in the galley was lesser spotted turtle soup, it took months for the ribbing to stop, but in my defence I saw something that day, now if I see anything, I keep it to myself.

The cranes on here were restricted to work up to a wind speed of 40 knots. Anything above that, and they were put to bed, so to speak, while working days I worked with the crane op on rig 1 a guy named Tommy Chalmers, and while on nights it was with Rab, Rab was an accomplished guitarist and we spent many a winters night when the cranes were down singing and making up songs, I took the guitar that Liz bought me for Xmas, offshore to learn to play it, but I was never any good, although the secret compartment in the case was handy for smuggling fags, one of the songs we made up was sung to the tune of the camp town races, it went something like this, The wind is up and the cranes are down, doo dah, doo dah, we'll just have to sit around, all doo dah day. Crazy I know, but it passed the time, Rab would sometimes travel to Fife, and I would meet him in Andy Young's the Tool pushers house, where we would party the night away, but Rab was fond of the ladies, and this was his downfall, because sitting at the heli/port one day waiting on his chopper arriving, were two ladies, one was Rabs wife, the other his girlfriend, just picture the scene, two woman sitting together talking, I'm waiting on the Hutton flight, my husbands on it, says one, what a coincidence says the other, my boyfriend is on that flight, I wonder if they work together, then as Rab appears through the swing doors they both make a beeline for him, that's got to be your worse nightmare isn't it, I'll let you figure out what happened. But Rab never came back to the Hutton again, years later, I heard he was back working offshore again, but I haven't bumped into him. (Yet) I've a lot to ask him when I do.

1991 was the year of the Gulf War it also saw big changes for both rigs, the platform deck foremen were changed out. Jim Brydon left, and his back to back George Wylie moved to another rig, the platform drilling manager moved on and Andy Harper took his place, Jamie Wright from Glasgow, took Rabs place, there was talk on the rig about a shut down coming in early 92, and that unsettled everybody, John Frosdyke took over as driller on our crew, Russell and Reiks Botter, were changed out, and Paul

Richman and Keith Douglas taking their places, the roughnecks were changing out all the time, and it was difficult to find a settled crew. But I was fine; I had gained enough experience and confidence to see me through and if it came to moving elsewhere, I didn't foresee any problems.

One thing the drill crews hate the whole Industry over is being told that they will be getting a reward for doing a specific operation then find out they get nothing. (This is called blowing smoke up your arse) This happened when we were planning to do something they had never done on here before. A 13 and 3/8ths casing milling job, there was over 2000 metres of steel pipe to be milled out of the hole and sent back to the beach in skips, the job took over a week to set up, what with having to erect a steel chute, supported by scaffolding, leading down to the skid deck from just below the rig floor where the brillo pad like cuttings (swarf) were raked into the skips positioned below the chute, the lads involved in this operation were promised by the rig manager the scrap value of the steel when the job was complete, I personally back/loaded over 20 full skips weighing just under 6 ton each, and they still had the same amount again to go by the time we went off the platform, this was not an easy job by any means and only the thought of the bonus at the end kept the guys going hard at it. The job took just under 5 weeks to complete and everyone was speculating about how much scrap we had back/loaded and the value of it, we were looking for at least a couple of hundred quid for each crew, but as usual when it came down to paying it out, we got fuck-all, we got every fucking excuse you could think of, but at the end of the day we were all humphy backet with all the pats on the back we got for doing such a tricky, tiresome, thankless fucking job.

John Lee was our regular platform safety man and there was never any problem when he was required for anything, John was so easy going and approachable, that everybody felt comfortable in going to him with a safety matter, the same can't be said about the guy who was standing in for him when he was off sick. I remember a few occasions when I went to him, after getting no satisfaction about a couple of safety issues from the new platform deck foreman, and I was fobbed off with one excuse after another. Then one day one of the crew on the supply boat the Stirling Albion which I was working that day got some bad news at home and they were deciding whether to bring him onto the platform or not, to get the crew change helicopter home, after discussions between Fran the rig medic, the O.I.M. and the boat skipper, it was decided to bring the guy off the boat and send him home by helicopter. To do this we had to use the safety man- riding basket, called a Billy Pugh. This was a rope- made configuration attached to a round rubber base, measuring about 10 feet across, and when fully extended was about 30 feet high, once the metal ring at the top of the Billy Pugh was attached to the hook another safety line was also attached just above it just to make doubly sure it wouldn't become detached in error. The rope configuration was spliced into squares and the whole idea was to stand on the rubber ring on the outside and loop your arms together through the squares, you weren't allowed to stand inside the Billy Pugh for the obvious reason that if it ended up in the water you would be trapped inside. Baggage was the only thing allowed inside, anyway, we were all set to pick the guy up from the boat, 2 of my guys dressed in their flight suits and wearing life jackets, were going down with the Billy Pugh to help the guy hold on, we had just finished checking that everything was in place and that the guys were comfortable with what they had to do, when this safety guy appeared, Tommy the rig 1 crane op and me watched him from the crane for a few minutes talking to the guys, then he called me down to the deck, I could sense the bad atmosphere as soon as I reach him and the guys, he had a right bad attitude and that pissed people off, have you done this before? He asked in a condescending matter, yes I said; have these men any experience doing this? Yes I said. Have you got another driver in the crane with you? Yes I said, I was standing there answering these questions for about 10 minutes, and he was really getting on my fucking nerves with the way he was speaking to the guys and me. Then he asked, what's the name of the boat? I need to contact him. The Partick Thistle, I said, and then stood to the side, he then started talking into his radio, Partick Thistle, Partick Thistle, this is the North West Hutton safety officer here, call back please, the radio was silent, then he repeated it again, still silence, I was doubled up by this time, so was the rest of the guys, the safety guy kept changing channels on his radio, and repeating his transmission, it must have been about the 5th time of asking. That the skipper of the boat called back on the radio saying, I don't know who the Partick Thistle supporter is, but if Stirling Albion will do, then we hear you! That was fucking priceless, you should have seen that little pricks face, it was a picture, Eventually we successfully got the guy off the boat, and a short time later, he was on his way home, that was the only trip that safety guy spent on the Hutton. Thank fuck.

One of the constant nightshift Mechanics on here, was a guy called Hamish Muirhead who lived in Glenrothes and used to visit my local pub when we were both home at the same time, Hamish was a no nonsense didn't give a fuck for management sort of a guy, and a laugh a minute, and what he didn't know about the mechanical side of things wasn't worth knowing, he used to joke that if a thing is working, why sort it. But this attitude used to piss off his immediate supervisor who in turn tried to piss Hamish off by padlocking all the brand new tools away in the cabinets when he went off shift, this didn't put Hamish up nor down because Hamish was an accomplished lock picker, at night if there was a job on he went through the locked cabinets until he found the tools he needed. used them, then locked them up again, it used to annoy his boss when he found out that someone had been into the cabinets during the night because all the tools were not in there proper places, he couldn't understand how anyone had got in, these were supposed to be the best tamper proof padlocks you could buy, anyway he ordered new combination padlocks and when they arrived he fitted them to the cabinets, happy in the knowledge that only he had the combination, but you should have seen his face the next day when he tried to open them, unknown to him, Hamish had cracked the combination on them all, emptied the cabinets, changed the combinations on the padlocks and put them back on. Eventually he went and got a set of bolt cutters, cut the padlocks, only to find the cabinets empty. That was the last time padlocks were put on the cabinets. Hamish shot a video of the Hutton; I've still got a copy and sometimes look at it to remind me of the guys I worked with out there

Things at home were becoming quite volatile at times, after being away for 2 weeks at a time, I was beginning to feel like a lodger in my own home, it was good for the first couple of days until the novelty of having me home again began to wear off, while I was away Liz would be left to make any decisions on my behalf, she would pay the bills, do the chores, see to any problems that sort of thing, but when I got home again I would generally take over. The kids were getting older and obviously had minds of their own, they didn't like the idea of someone who wasn't their maternal father chastising them. I didn't like the noise of the stereo blasting out first thing in the morning, and I wasn't used to being given cheek. This started to cause friction between Liz and me; understandably Liz would take her children's side in most arguments. Like any rebellious teenager Nicky was staying off school, going around with people older than herself, and smoking cigarettes, the final straw was when she wouldn't come home at the time agreed on, I could sense the strain it was having on Liz and me, but I would put it out of my head hoping that things would get better, I was drinking just as much as before, and was glad to get away from it all for 2 weeks at a time,

2 weeks at home sounds a lot, but let me tell you there's not enough time to do anything, especially if you have courses to do, hardly a trip went by but we were on one course or another, I had a three day survival refresher course in January 91, I could hardly believe it was 3 years already since the first time, and my offshore medical the following month, these things fairly eat into your time off and before you know it your back on that chopper again deciding what's going to change next time your home

Out on the rig Smedvig Management gave us a visit, they were explaining how they were doing away with the trip pay and that it would be easier to pay us monthly(Easier for who?) this was the start of the offshore workforce being ripped off. As we were working 2 on 2 off we usually got our wages at the heliport, (this was called trip pay as we were paid after every trip) we would get this 13 times a year because we were doing 13 x 2 week trips a year. Now they wanted to pay us 12 times a year, but still work 13 trips. This looked as if they had given us a pay rise but in reality they put 13 wages into 12 pay packets, they said it worked itself out at the end of the year, what they didn't take into consideration was that some workers lived on a trip to trip basis, we all had to send in our bank details so that they could start paying us through the bank on the 28th of the month, the men were kicking up fuck but the decision had been made, because they were paying us monthly it didn't necessarily mean you qualified for a full months wage that first time, even after working 2 weeks, it was broke down into 28 th's, whatever date in the month you went offshore reflected on how many 28ths you got, I know of some people who only got 1 weeks pay after working 2 weeks, there was hell on, this caused a lot of arguments in a lot of households, but management in their wisdom said that any money owed would be given back when you left the company, A load of fucking bollocks.

Things were ticking away nicely on the rig, I was training up Phil in the crane and he was coming along nicely, as were the other assistant crane/ops. But Saturday night 14th of march 1992 was another to be imprinted in my head, it was then that the shuttle helicopter taking 17 passengers and crew from the Cormorant Alpha to the accommodation barge the Safe Supporter crashed into the sea leaving 11 dead and 6 survivors, the weather conditions were so bad that it was a miracle that any survivors were found at all, with the cranes down it was my crews job to be on the heli/deck to re/fuel the search and rescue (SAR's) helicopters when they needed it, one of the helicopters dropped off a number of body/bags to be used if needed. That was one job I and the crew didn't relish, it was the early hours of Sunday morning when the news of the survivors filtered through, and although there was some joy in that news, it was also tinged with sadness at the loss of the others, later Shell, B.P. And most of the other Oil operators alongside the helicopter operators reduced the weather limitations that allowed the helicopters to fly, hopefully preventing a similar tragedy. Now most heli/decks are closed at 60-knot winds and the sea state must be below 7 metres before helicopter operations resume.

Smedvig arranged for the supervisors on the rig who were at home on leave to attend a 3 day man/management seminar in April 92 at the Ardoe House hotel, Aberdeen, I didn't really fancy going to this but I had no option, when I arrived from the railway station by taxi, I thought I was getting the five star treatment, because as I climbed the stairs to the hotel carrying my holdall, this piper started playing a tune on his bagpipes, I stood watching him for a minute or two thinking, nice one mate, that's what I call a welcome, I was feeling in my pocket for some change, when I noticed the bride and groom coming down the corridor of the hotel.(ah well, just for a minute there.) This place was not one of your £10 a night bed and breakfast shots, this was the real McCoy, This was class, the en-suite rooms were massive, with a 26 inch colour television, and also with king size beds in them, and the meals were something else, the only thing was, with their being about twenty people on the seminar we were all seated at the one big table, and you weren't served your second course until everyone had finished their first, the meal took forever to end, (to much

119

talk and not enough eating) by the Norwegians, but this was just a useless ploy to keep us out of the bar, The course itself was just a brain washing session as far as I was concerned, and big MacKay and me spent the three days listening to two Norwegians going on about how we were in so many words, a useless bunch of cunts, and with this so called team building session this would all change, the money these fuckers were getting for this session, would have been better off going to charity, for all the attention we were paying, what a right pair of boring bastards these two turned out to be, at night after the meal,(we tried to order a bar lunch but our manager wouldn't allow that) it was just a drinking session with MacKay and me the last two out the bar, these norskies made it known to us, that they didn't mind us having a few after dinner refreshments, but they wanted us in bed early so we were fresh the next morning, on our last night there MacKay and me were heading up to our rooms at about 3 in the morning and as we past the reception desk I noticed a jar of sugar almonds sitting on the desk, also some leather bound menus, one was a price list for food, and the other drink, MacKay noticed that the glass tray with the cigars in it was open, so as he helped himself to the cigars, I had my hand stuck in the almond jar, I was that drunk I was like a fucking monkey holding nuts, afraid to let go in case I lost them, that's how we climbed the stairs, me holding the menus in one hand, and the other stuck in the almond jar, MacKay was laughing his head off at the amount of cigars he had, we just turned the corner on our level, when we literally bumped into one of the Norwegians knocking him on his arse, the looks we got the next morning told it all, MacKay and me were split up into different groups, but later in the day we got back together again that's how bad it was, we were naughty boys so they were punishing us like kids by keeping us apart, as the day wore on I remembered about the menus, and that afternoon in the room packing to go home, I found them stuck together in the trouser press machine, we were all asked to take back the knowledge we had gained at the seminar, to the guys lucky enough not to have been there, the only thing I took back was myself and loads of sugar almonds.

It was only the following trip that Management came out to the rig again to allay fears that the drilling program was coming to an end. Rig 1 had already shut down with the crews going else-where, so when our rig manager came out to tell us that we were the best crews in the drilling industry, and that we would never be idle again. He also told us it was standard procedure to send out the redundancy letters and that we were not to put to much emphasis on them, I treated it with scorn, as with all management visits, they only tell you what you want to hear, so it was no surprise when a couple of trips later the rig was shut down. For drilling purposes anyway,

I had built up a nice curriculum vitae (C.V.) and had already sent some out to prospective employers. Smedvig couldn't guarantee work for everybody, but I still thought they would have kept some of the experienced crane operators; after all, the platform was still working, even if drilling had stopped. But due to a decision reached by possibly some accountant, it was deemed cheaper to keep on the assistants and pay off the crane/ops,

The day that our crew came off the platform we were invited by management to the Thistle Hotel for a drink, and to talk about the new project of The Bruce platform for B.P. some of the lads that had been told that they were being sent on this project, went, but I didn't bother, Liz had already told me on the phone that my wage slip and P45 were waiting for me at home, so I didn't see any point. Although at the Airport I did speak to Andy Harper who was supervising part of the Bruce project down in Methil dockyard in Fife, and he said that he would do his best for me. I thought to myself as I watched the guys getting into their taxis to go home, so much for us being the best in the industry and that we would never be idle again, Now that's what I call blowing smoke up your arse.

Smedvig Offshore Leaders Seminar
Ardoe House 28 April – 1 May 1992

back row (l to r)
**John Sutherland, Steve Mackay, Howard Tringham,
Geoff Clark, Eamon Coyle, George Creighton**

third row (l to r)
**Eddie Slater, Mark Reed, Tom Fyfe, John Frosdick,
Graham Croll**

second row (l to r)
**Lynne Forbes, John Ramsay, Jim Hindhaugh, Tom Macken,
Bob Galbraith, Mike Slater**

front row (l to r)
**Rieks Botter, Alex McLean, Geoff Hogarth, Colin Finnie,
Harry Davidson**

Bristows Helicopter

North West Hutton

7

The West Omikron

It was the near the end of June 92 and most of the £2000 I got as wages and redundancy, had a big hole in it, things were not looking to good on the work front either, all the replies I got from the drilling companies that I sent my C.V. too you could have counted on one hand and even then they were all negative. Thank you for your interest in our company but at this moment in time we regret to inform you that due to the downturn in activities blah, blah, blah. But some of the agencies I contacted at least said they would keep my C.V. on file, and if anything came up they would be in touch. I needed to find something and quick. All the intentions I had of working offshore for a few years, save some money, buy my house and set up a wee business, were not working out as I expected. I had worked offshore for over 4 years now and at 39 years of age I wasn't getting any younger. Things were definitely going to have to change as soon as I was working full time again. Then one Friday in early July Smedvig phoned me to see if I would do a weeks work on the West Omikron in Denmark as the regular crane/op Simon Donaldson, from Aberdeen, was off sick, no problem I said, and got my joining instructions over the phone that day, I had just signed the dole the day before, so a weeks work would do just fine, I should be home in time to sign on again, if everything went ok. Liz dropped me off at Edinburgh Airport at 7 am on Tuesday the 7th where I picked up my travel tickets and met up with the crew going out with me, the Tool Pushers name was Jeff Hogarth and I introduced myself to him, the crew were all in the bar having a last drink before going away for three weeks, but I thought it was a bad idea me having one, as one leads to two and so on, so I didn't bother. The flight was a fixed wing special charter and within a couple of hours of checking/in we had landed at Esberg airport and straight away boarded the chopper out to the rig.

The rig itself was a Jack/up something I had no experience of before, all the other rigs I was on were fixed platforms, this was a mobile rig just like a semi-submersible, once it was finished doing its work it could be towed to another location, so this was a new experience for me. The lads on here were a fine bunch to work with, some of the ones I remember are Dave Saldias, (night tool/pusher) Billy Meldrum, (driller) Ernie Mackintosh, (Chief Mechanic) Mick Gower,(mechanic) Tommy Rattray, (Chief Electrician) Alex Bolton, (Crane/Op) John Manley (rousty pusher) and Alan Yule (Bresh) one of the roustys, As I was only on there for one week its hard to remember everyone's name, but working with them was a pleasure. I can't say the same about working the cranes; they were a fucking nightmare to get used to. (Marathon Le Tourney) cranes, that's what they were, (electric- hydraulic) when sitting at the controls in the cab, it didn't matter what way you wanted to face, the swivel seat you were sitting in faced a different way, my back was in fucking agony trying to fight with this seat, all three cranes were the same, at one time or other during the shift the crane you were working in would shut down for no apparent reason, and you would have to climb inside the pedestal and re-set the fucking thing talk about doing your head in no wonder the other crane/op was off sick.

On my second day Wednesday, I was enquiring about how to get an outside line, so I could phone Liz and let her know how I was getting on, sitting in the tea/shack Mick Gower the mechanic told me that on here as they were working 3 weeks on 3 weeks off, you accumulated 3 minutes of phone time only after you did your first week, I thought he was at the wind up, but some of the other guys re/iterated what he was saying was true. Well I was going to find out for myself, Up in heli/admin I spoke to the woman who gave me my tee/card and room number on arrival, and asked her to shed some light on the phoning arrangements on here, she said it worked on 3 minute phone call to the beach for every week worked on the rig, this was monitored by the radio/op. When I told her I needed to phone home to let the wife know where I was, she checked her records and said that I hadn't been on long enough to accrue any phone time and that I would have to wait till next Tuesday to qualify for 3 minutes, I was trying my best not to swear but this fucking nonsense was getting out of order. It was like something out of the dark ages, I couldn't believe that in 1992 while working away from home for three weeks at a time in another country, that you had to work a week to earn 3 minutes on the phone, somebody somewhere is seriously taking the piss. It was only when I went to the tool/pusher and told him, I'm not going back in that fucking crane, and until I get to use a phone and let my missus know that I'm ok. Eventually I was given a ship to shore line to the beach by the radio/op who all the time was watching the clock, to see how long I was taking, but before I went on the phone I told him I wouldn't be long, so don't even think about cutting me off, I suppose I was looked at as a bit of a trouble maker after that escapade. but there was no way I was spending a week without phoning home, also I couldn't believe the guys were putting up with that sort of Victorian attitude, I told Liz what was going on, and explained that I would phone again when I landed in Esberg on Tuesday, and let her know my flight time into Edinburgh. Talk about civil liberties, "your treated better in jail"

It was on my 4th shift Friday (I was on dayshift for the week working 12am to 12pm) at about 1-30 pm when I was sitting in the crane watching this helicopter circling the rig and listening to the personal announcement system (P.A.) persistently calling for the H.L.O. to call the radio room on line 3 immediately. I wonder where the fuck he is? I thought to myself, just then the PA system called for the crane/op to call line 3, there were phones in the cranes so I called line 3 and spoke to the radio/op on the other end, he said, where are you? The chopper pilot is calling for clearance to land. I said, it's ok by me mate, the cranes are not moving. What he was trying to tell me was, the pilot was waiting for clearance from me, as I was the H.L.O. now lets not fuck about here, you would think that someone on the rig would have told me that being the H.L.O was part of my duties, but take it from me they didn't, I hurried from the crane to the radio room and picked up the VHF radio and the radio /op asked me not to forget to put the mail bag on the chopper, don't worry I said, and hurried off!. By the time I got to the heli/deck the rest of the deck crew were up there waiting for me. thank fuck John Manley had done the fuel sample, at least someone knew what was going on, everything was going smoothly after the initial cock/up, with the passengers and bags being successfully changed out. Then with the chopper re/fuelled and on its way back to the beach, I was heading down to the radio room to return the V.H.F. radio, when I spotted the mail bag, sitting on the stairs where I left it, when I told the radio/op about the bag, and suggested it go on the next chopper, he said there wasn't one till the following week, and the mail had to go on this one, so back came the chopper to get the mail bag and I was beginning to wish, I was going on the fucking thing as well. There were only 2 flights a week out to this rig, so roll on the next one, it's mine.

The two man cabins on here were clean enough and had an adjoining shower and toilet. The regular crane ops also had their own portable T.V. but the reception on the rig was terrible, so I suppose that's why they also had a video recorder in the room so they could watch videos after shift, if you could get one from the baker that wasn't covered in flour that is. I remember one of the rousty's Nobby; (The Sheep) was his nickname. (I'll let you work out why) he was the Dennis Norden of the rig, a right film buff. It was a big mistake to let him see the title of the film you had picked to watch. Because he was hell bent on telling you, the start, middle, and end of it, It was hard to fall out with this guy, because he was a likeable cunt, but when he started on about the film I had chosen, I nearly lost it a couple of times, he just would not shut the fuck up. I wanted to watch it, not listen to his rendition of it.

The week went by quick enough and I learned before I left, that once the well they were working on was finished, (this would take about another 2 or 3days), then the rig was getting towed back to Methil in Fife to wait for another contract. But the crews would be ok, the rig manager told them they were the best in the world and that they would never be idle again. "Now where have I heard that wee porky pie before?" I wasn't too fussed that they didn't ask me to stay on for the trip back to Methil, because for some reason I didn't feel comfortable on here, that built in sixth sense that everybody has was niggling away at me, apart from that the regular crane op was coming out anyway

Liz picked me up at Edinburgh airport on the Tuesday and she said she could tell by the look on my face that I was glad to be home, she was right I was never so glad to get off a rig as I was to get off of this one, that night when we got home I phoned everybody I knew, just to get back into the swing of things of using the phone again, she thought I was kidding about the 3 minute curfew but I managed to convince her it was all true.

Thursday morning found me down at the dole office signing on and confessing everything I'd done over the last fortnight, the young teenage girl behind the desk told me that I must keep a record of all jobs applied for, and show them evidence if asked, of what I was doing to search for work. Failure to do this could result in my benefit being reduced. Considering the dole never helped me get a job in the last 14 years and in that time I was only idle twice, and that was only for a couple of weeks at a time. I thought it was a bit cheeky of them to ask what I was doing. I thought it was their fucking job to find me work. The look on her face when I said I was looking for a job that paid £600 a week with 2 weeks holiday a month was priceless.

Sitting watching the news on the Saturday my attention was drawn to the name West Omikron, seemingly it was on tow from Bergen to Methil on the Firth of Forth when it got into difficulties when one of the three tugs towing it broke its tow line and it started listing in bad weather just off the coast of Fraserburgh in the North East of Scotland, The coast guard was alerted and all non essential were air lifted off by Sea King Helicopter to Fraserburgh leaving a compliment of 8 guys left on board. The first thing to go through my head was how long did the radio operator spend on the phone, calling the coast guard, I hoped he didn't take longer than the allocated 3 minutes. But seriously, I was glad to hear that the rig eventually made it safely to Methil. One thing that news bulletin brought home to me was "never ignoring that sixth sense"

Wednesday morning 22nd July saw me getting ready to go to the pub when the phone rang, it was a guy called Alan Small who ran an agency in Crown Street, Aberdeen called Inter-services, he had my C.V. in front of him and wanted to know if I would be interested in a short term contract that could possibly lead to full time employment.? Very interested I said, and arrangements were made for me to go up that afternoon for an interview. Liz and I drove up and we arrived at 2pm, in his office I met Alan and a guy I remembered as being an instructor at Sparrows Training Centre his name was Richard Keiler, after the initial introductions and a review of what experience I had crane operating, and what type of cranes I had operated, Alan told me the contract was for Stenna and it was a specialist job requiring 2 experienced crane/ops for approximately 3 weeks working on a satellite rig (unmanned oil or gas producing platform) down in the Southern sector of the North Sea. He asked that if I was successful with the interview, would I be able to travel at short notice? No problem I said, just give me a phone if you need me. On the way home I told Liz that although I thought the interview went ok, they still had a couple of guys to see. So we would have to wait and see what happens. But deep down I felt quietly confident that I had the job.

Semi - Submersibles in heavy weather

Calm before the storm

Semi - Submersible

Supply boat battling heavy weather

Supply boats battling heavy weather

Supply boat battling heavy weather

8

The Stenna Seawell

Over a week had past with still no word from Inter-services, it was Thursday now and I had decided to go up to Aberdeen the following Monday and spend a few days going round the drilling companies and the agencies, the money I had was becoming a bit tight because I was still drinking as much and living the lifestyle that came with working offshore, even though I wasn't earning the money, Liz had taken on a part-time job delivering meals on wheels for the local council and it wouldn't be till later on that I found out she did this to subsidize the housekeeping money, unknown to me I was obviously spending more than I was earning, but like always, she never complained, she always made sure that I was alright,

On Saturday morning August 1st I was out cutting the grass when Liz called me to the phone, it was Alan Small from Interservices asking if I was still interested in the job down South. Well you know the answer to that, of course I was. But when he said I had to be at the quay side of a dock in Grimsby at 3pm that afternoon to join the Diving Support Vessel (D.S.V.) Stenna Seawell, I had to tell him there was no way I could get ready and travel down there for that time, it was 11.30 am already, and you were looking at,at least a 5 hour journey depending on traffic. He said if I was prepared to try, he would send a car for me in half an hour, ok then I said, and got his mobile phone number off him, to keep him posted of my progress.

I was standing at my back door, rig bag in hand, with £150 in my pocket, looking at the half cut grass, when this taxi pulled up looking for me. I couldn't believe he sent a taxi, and the driver couldn't believe he was going to Grimsby. All he was told was to pick me up and take me wherever I was going. It turned out that Alan Small had a relative who ran a taxi business in Perth (Fife) and this is who he phoned to try and get me down to Grimsby in 4 hours. (no chance) the journey down there was just as you would

134

expect on a Saturday afternoon, the traffic on parts of the A1 to
Newcastle alone, was horrendous, what with trying to overtake
articulated lorries and cars towing caravans out for week-end
jolly, then carrying on the A1M. it took us 6 hours just to get to
Grimsby, then another half an hour to find the dock, inevitably
the boat had sailed at 3pm according to the harbour master.
There was nothing left for me to do but phone up Alan Small and
put him in the picture, when I did eventually get him he said to
make my way to a place called Mablethorpe in Lincolnshire, book
myself into digs, then phone him when I got there, I can tell you
now I was getting a wee bit pissed off by this time, and so was
Tam the taxi driver, I only hoped he wasn't expecting me to pay
for the hire, once we got the map out to find out where Mablethorpe was, we headed for there arriving at about 8.00pm. Tam and
me booked into a guest house for the night, giving the landlady
the £15 each for bed and breakfast, later in the bar I phoned Alan
again and told him where we were booked into and gave him the
phone number so he could call me back, I was fed up calling his
mobile, using my own money. When he did phone back, I wanted
re-assurance that I would be getting paid a days wage for all the
fucking about, and the dig money I just paid out. He allayed my
fears by saying that he would see me all right, and that he would
phone me the next day with instructions of what to do next. Tam
and me spent the next 3 hours in the bar, and when I got up the
next morning he was gone, I hung about the digs most of the
morning waiting on Alan phoning me and when he did, he gave
me instructions to report to Strubby airport (a Conoco airfield
outside Mablethorpe) at 7am on Monday morning to check/in for
the flight to the Seawell, that meant spending the whole of Sunday walking about Mablethorpe seeing the sights, and believe me
when I tell you there was nothing to see, Mablethorpe is a small
holiday town in the middle of nowhere on the east coast of the
country, it had a fairground but most of it was closed on a Sunday, a couple of pubs and clubs, a bookies, some shops and guest
houses one or two hotels that was it. There wasn't much to do
except sit in the pub. What I did do was phone and order a taxi for
6 30am on Monday and asked him if they knew where Strubby
airport was ?, when the guy said yes, I was a wee bit more at ease,
as I found it hard to believe that this small town with fuck all else
in it. Had an airport. I wandered about most of the day trying to
kill time, the digs were only bed and breakfast, so it was a meal

out of the chip-shop for my tea, later that night in the bar of the digs I met up with a guy who was doing a ventriloquist act in one of the clubs, we were getting rat arsed with the drink and he went up to his room and brought down this stuffed bear, that's how we ended the night, me, him and the bear, holding a three way conversation, it was fucking hilarious, I can't remember the last time I laughed so long and loud. But unknown to me It would be a while before I would laugh again.

The next morning soon had me wishing I hadn't stayed up so late or drunk as much as I did, because in the taxi on the way to the airfield I felt fucking ill, it was only a 10 minute ride there, but it felt like an hour, I was glad to get out of the taxi to get some air, I must have looked rough because I certainly felt it, I joined another lot of guys in the waiting room at the airport and when they went to check/in I followed on, when it was my turn to check/in the guy told me the flight was full and I would have to come back tomorrow and try again, I couldn't believe it, what's this I asked the security guy? a lucky dip to see if you could get a flight or not, he said there was only one flight a day, out to the Conoco loggs field, and today's was full, when I told him I was going to the Stenna Seawell, he said that the Loggs field chopper was the one I would be on, but not today. I can tell you now; I was not a happy chappie. I phoned for the taxi to come back and get me, and was back in the digs before breakfast had started.

9 00am couldn't come quick enough, I was trying to calm down before I phoned Alan Small, this was like a bad dream, I had spent three days on the go, spending my own money, also I still wasn't convinced I wasn't going to be out of pocket. When I got through to Small's office and he asked me where I was, I thought I was going to blow a gasket, I'm still in fucking Mablethorpe I said, because there was no seat available on the chopper for me, he told me to stay in the guest house, and he would phone me back with news of what's happening. Once again he told me I would be reimbursed any out of pocket expenses, when I told him; I was running short of cash. I only had about £80 left; it would be less if I had to pay another night's dig money. He phoned back about 10 am and assured me I was on the Tuesday flight, check/in same as Monday. Another day wandering about from pub to pub, and a short spell at the fair ground saw out Monday, another fucking day wasted. I phoned Liz to tell her what was going on, and that

I felt like coming home, only the thought of 3 weeks work made me stay

If there had been any problems of getting on the chopper on Tuesday, I'm certain I would have went home, but there wasn't, Not until we landed on the Loggs rig itself that is, I was sitting at the back of the chopper and could hardly make out what the pilot was saying over the tannoy system, so when we landed on the rig and the HLO motioned for everybody to get off, I got off as well, I knew this wasn't my stop, but thought that maybe they were going to re/fuel the chopper, when they do that its common practice for everybody to get off for safety reasons, so I followed everybody else into the platforms heli/admin area, and sat waiting to be called back to the chopper, I sat and sat and when everybody else had disappeared away to their rooms, I was still fucking sitting there, the heli/admin guy asked me who I was,? And what I was doing there? I told him I was going to join the Stenna Seawell and that it wasn't my idea to get off the chopper, I was only following the H.L.O.'s instructions, by this time the chopper had left without me, you would have thought the fucking pilot would have noticed that I was missing, so they had to call it back. I landed on this Satellite about 8.00am on the Tuesday morning, The HLO on here I found out later, was one of the riggers, he motioned me to the stairs leading down from the heli/deck where I waited and watched the chopper take off, then he took me down and introduced me to the O.I.M of this platform, he said they were expecting me a couple of days ago and I explained to him what had happened. On this normally un-manned platform was him and about a 8 riggers all waiting on me, the nightshift crane/op was taken off at seven in the morning, along with the nightshift crew, by the shuttle chopper that came in twice a day to change the crews out. I was working dayshift and after we had a cup of coffee and a fag the OIM showed me round the place, there was basically nothing to see, it only had 3 levels on it and the wells were closed in so the construction work could go on. Back on the top deck I spotted the crane, it was a Liebherr crane without the cab, when the OIM asked me if I had operated this type before. I said yes, but I also said someone's forgot to put a cab on this one, he just looked at me with a blank expression, that didn't go down to well I thought to myself. Most of the riggers were standing on the top deck looking up at us as the O.I.M. and me climbed the ladder to the crane, he was coming up with me to make sure I was competent at operating it Now as any crane operator will tell you, the basic function of a crane when it's working is, up's up and down's down, that's the basic rule of thumb. Getting the crane started is another matter, I entered the pedestal to have a look around and found the floor was covered in hydraulic oil, there was plenty in the holding tank so this wasn't a problem. Then I entered the engine room and found it was a diesel-driven engine with an air start, and hydraulic operated controls, it seemed simple enough. Once I found the air valve and turned it on, I pressed the starter button, but nothing happened, then I spotted 2 keys inserted into this dash board, I turned both keys to the first of 3 settings and tried again, to my delight the engine burst into life, when I came out of the engine room this OIM was standing outside, everything ok he asked? Sure I said, won't be long now, I'm just letting the hydraulic oil circulate for a while. As I said, there was no cab on this crane, so the only thing that was protecting the console with the override buttons, the lower/ hoist and slew/boom levers from natures elements, was a metal cover held in place by 2 big rubber lug like handles on either side that slotted into groves on the cover to make it watertight, as I attempted to remove this cover I got one of the handles off, boy it was tight, but as I wrestled with the other one, my hand slipped and I cut my fucking thumb, there was blood dripping everywhere, I went into the engine room and got myself a rag to stop the bleeding, I wrapped it round my thumb, then grabbed another rag and pretended to clean the console with it, the engine was running on full throttle, so you can imagine my surprise when the crane didn't move when I pulled back the boom hoist lever to take it out of the rest, all this time the riggers are standing on the top deck looking up at me. Once again I passed this O.I.M. on my way to the engine room, and he asked, is everything ok? Oh Yes, I said, I'm just waiting on the hydraulic oil heating up. What I really wanted to say was why don't you just fuck off and leave me in peace to get this heap of shit out of the rest and in the air. Back in the engine room I was completely baffled, I didn't know what else to try, here I was the specialist crane operator they had been waiting 3 days for, and I can't get the fucking thing out of the rest. I had another look at the 2 keys in the dashboard they were still at the first setting, so I turned them both to the second setting and went back up to the control levers, come up you bastard, I was silently praying, but nothing happened, as I past the O.I.M. on the way back into the engine room, I told him, won't be long now mate, I'm just checking the pressures in here, I don't know what he was thinking, but I was wanting to go home, I had had enough of this shite, I had resigned myself to getting run off the job, even before I had done a lift, in desperation I turned the 2 keys to the third and last setting then went back out to concede defeat, I looked down at the riggers looking up at me, and just shrugged my shoulders, then I pulled the boom hoist lever back and fuck me, up she came, rising in the air like something out of a Captain Nemo film, the look on my face must have said it all because the cheers and whistles that came from the riggers was music to my ears, even the OIM gave a wry smile, after showing him and the riggers that I could operate the crane competently, he told me to follow him and we would get my thumb looked at.

My duties on here were to do lifts for the riggers when and if required, the rest of the time was my own and I spent most of it sunbathing in the brilliant sunshine, the Stenna Seawell was sitting as close to this Satellite as possible and it was in easy reach of the crane so that was how we received our meals, I would lower a basket onto the deck of the ship, one of the stewards would put our meals into it, and I would lift it back up, this was done daily, if the sea was too rough for the ship to come close enough then we would use the ample cans of soup and Irish stew that was kept on there, but those days were few and far between, every day just before 7am and again at 7pm the shuttle chopper would arrive and the 2 crews would change out, the accommodation on the ship was fine, I had a room to myself, the food was good, I was earning a wage, all in all the job was fine, one thing that did bother me was, if the chopper came in twice a day from Strubby, why was I not on it on the Sunday, or even the Monday for that matter.

The job I was doing on here was to lift hollow pipes weighing about a ton and a quarter from the Satellite deck and lower them to the sea bed where the divers from the Seawell would join them together, the only set back was the strong currents where we were working restricted the work to a few hours in the morning and the same again at night, this didn't bother me, the longer it took the longer I was in a job, but like all good things they come to an end.

.The first time that I got really speaking to my relief was when the job was finished and we were waiting to find out where the ship was sailing to next, and where we were getting off. We had only exchanged courtesies at the change over on the heli/deck, now we got talking for the first time, he came from Leven in (Fife) only a couple of miles from where I lived, the conversation got round to how we ended up here, and that's when I found out that he was told about this job from Inter-services on the Thursday, so he had plenty of time to travel to Grimsby for the Saturday, he also said that another guy was supposed to travel with him, but he cried off at the last minute. I was beginning to understand now, why Inter-Services waited until the last minute before they phoned me, I wasn't their first choice, in/fact I don't even think I was their second choice, if I was, they would surely have phoned me on the Friday, No, it was looking to me like I was their last resort and I felt a wee bit bitter at that, All the fucking about I had getting here, all the bullshit about this being a specialist contract that could lead to bigger and better things was a con, one good thing about meeting the guy from Leven was I got some spare time sheets off him.

The rumours on the ship were that we were sailing either down into Great Yarmouth where if we wanted to we could get off, that would have suited me as I had relatives down there that I hadn't seen for years. I would have spent a day or two there, borrowed some money for my fair home, with the intention of returning it when I got my wages. Another was sailing up to Peterhead to pick up equipment, that wouldn't have suited me at all, yet another was us sailing up into Edinburgh, that would certainly have suited me if it happened. We also had the choice of getting the chopper back into Strubby airfield and make our way home from Mablethorpe I certainly didn't fancy that, if I never went to Mablethorpe again it wouldn't have put me up nor down. So my fingers were crossed for Edinburgh, and lady luck must have been looking down on me, because the decision had been made, Edinburgh here we come.

Exactly 13 days after I left home I was now only 45 minutes away from Glenrothes, berthed at the quay side of Edinburgh Leith docks, I could see Liz waiving to me from the pier, she was looking a wee bit anxious, but we had to wait until we were given the all clear to disembark from the captain, I had already told the guy from Leven that we would drop him off there, and on the drive home we polished off the 6 cans of beer that Liz had brought with her, she expressed her concerns about the friendly manner of the guys she had asked directions from. The way they were wanting to give her more than directions to Leith docks had taken her aback. I suppose I should have told her what the night life was like down that way after dark.

On Saturday morning I phoned Alan Small to let him know that the job for Stenna was finished, and that I was back home again, I also told him that all the receipts that I kept for expenses were in the post along with my time sheet. The guy running the job did me proud, he told me to mark down 14 hours a day for the 11 days that I was on the ship, and I had filled in 36 hours for the fucking about I had from the Saturday till I arrived on the Seawell on the Tuesday, I told Alan about the hours I had accumulated 190 and asked if there was going to be a problem getting paid for these and my expenses. He told me there wouldn't be a problem and true to his word on the Wednesday I received a check and a pay slip from them for over a £1100, when I saw it, the first thing to go through my head was, there's been a mistake here somewhere. After all they didn't have my p45. The dole still had that, so I should have paid emergency tax. The reason the dole still had my P45 was, I had asked Liz to phone them on the 13th the day I was due to sign on and tell them some excuse and I would come down on the Monday, and get six of the belt, and a lecture for not turning up on my signing on day.

On Sunday 16th august I got a phone call from my old rig manager Andy Harper, he asked me if I was still interested in a job on the Bruce contract, and if I was could I report to Methil docks on Monday at 7 30am to take over from the crane operator who was down there, I couldn't believe my luck, I remembered Andy saying to me after the North West Hutton fiasco that he would do his best for me, well he certainly meant it, so I accepted his offer. I filled in the signing off card that I had from the dole, telling them that as from Monday 17th August I would no longer be signing on for unemployment benefit, "I had a job, hopefully for a while anyway"

9

The Bruce P.U.Q.

On Monday morning 17 august1992, I reported to the security gate at Methil docks and from there directed to the BP offices on the site, there I met the project manager who went through some safety issues with me and also to answer any queries or concerns that I might have had, I didn't. So after donning my working gear he took me down to the section of the yard where the top side Process, Utilities and Quarters "P.U.Q." module of the Bruce was being fabricated. He introduced me to the Smedvig Crane/Mechanic a guy called Sandy Bruce and the operator I was relieving Brian Sharman from Sunderland. After initial introductions Brian took me up the crane to familiarize me with the start, stop procedures, and all the other basic functions, I was quite familiar with this type of crane it was a Stothert and Pitt OS200 a type I had worked before, so it only took about 1 hour to show me round then Brian was off to catch his train home to start his 2 weeks leave. That left Sandy, me and a Stothert and Pitt engineer on our own to discuss the job itself, the hours I would be working, and how long the job would last. Basically it was a 12 hour dayshift job 7am till 7pm but we would finish when nobody else needed any lifts, which was usually about 4pm in the afternoon, There was no nightshift being worked except for 2 security guards acting as night/watchmen as the job itself was near completion with possibly under 3 weeks work left at the dock, before it was placed on a floating barge and towed out to its location in the North Sea.

Working at Methil brought back memories to me of the time I worked at the Scott Lithgow shipyard in Greenock in the late sixties early seventies before moving to Glenrothes, My father, some uncles and cousins all worked in one shipyard or another on the Clyde at some time in their lives so Methil was just another stepping stone in my working career, it was just as I remembered, a hive of industry, from the crane looking down, the people walking to and fro looked just like worker ants busily working away. And there were lots of them.

Sandy and me got on well, he was operating the South crane while I did all the lifts required with the North crane, the day past by quickly enough, what with us going to the yard canteen at 12noon and not starting again until we were needed, it gave us time to bullshit about things in general. I found out from Sandy that some of the guys I had worked offshore with were on other locations working on different modules of the Bruce Contract. My mate Jamie Wright, Joe Rochester, Simon Donaldson the guy whom I stood in for because he was off sick on the Omikron, Paul McCabe "Crane Mechanic" Derek Dunn "Chief Mechanic" were all working in Marseilles,(France) on the drilling Module. While Steve Ritchie, Brian, Sandy and myself were down here.

Other modules of the project were being fabricated in different parts of Europe and once they were all completed they would be towed out on barges to the location and pieced together like a giant jigsaw puzzle, the module I was working on was one of the last pieces to go on and that was only a couple of weeks away.

Andy Harper the drilling rig manager for Smedvig appeared at the site the next morning with a couple of BP guys for a tour of the module, it was after dinner before I got speaking to him to ask the question of whether or not I was getting a full time job again, once the platform was on location, one thing about Andy was, he didn't blow smoke up your arse and tell you what you wanted to hear. He told me straight that at the moment I was on a temporary basis and would be paid weekly. "Hopefully not too weakly" But as soon as he could give me a definite answer to my question he would. That was good enough for me, for all the rig managers I had worked with in the past, very few spoke without fork tongue and Andy was one of them.

The job itself was a piece of piss, it was the middle of summer and the weather couldn't have been any better. I was home in the pub every night getting paid 12 hours a day for working 9, sometimes on a Saturday and Sunday I would be in the pub before the official opening hours. You couldn't buy a job like this and like all good things that surely come to an end. I was enjoying it before that happened

Liz was still working at meals on wheels so as I didn't know what time of day I would be finished I would take our car to work and she would use her works van, then after going home to check on the kids and Kaiser to make sure they were ok. She would meet me in the pub at night to discuss those days' events. I was still drinking as much as ever, maybe more now that I was home every night, but not once did I sleep in or was late for work, ok sometimes I was a wee bit hung over in the morning, and if the truth be known there was more than one occasion when, if I was given the breathalyzer, I would have failed it miserably.

As the week went on the weather was beautiful, but it was getting hotter and hotter, not a cloud in the sky or a breath of wind to cool you down. Sandy and me stopped going to the canteen at dinner time as it was too much of a chore coming all the way down from the top of the module and walk the 500 odd yards there and back, so we started to bring pack lunches with us and had them in the Smedvig porto/cabin. But if we knew we were going to be busy in the afternoon then we wouldn't bother coming down at all and we would have our lunch in the crane. We were doing just that on my first Friday afternoon.

The banks/man I was taking my instructions from informed me just before he went for lunch that the Electricians needed to be lifted in a man. /riding basket to work on some electrical equipment, it could take an hour or longer he said, but didn't know for sure. Now Friday was usually a legitimate 3pm finish day so I didn't want to be kept later than could be helped. The lift was with the North crane so there was no need for Sandy to stay back. He lived outside Aberdeen but was staying in digs in Burntisland (Fife). Sandy left just after dinner time and I was left waiting on the banks/man and the Electricians. They turned up just after 1pm and I had them in the basket and lifted up to the place they were working a few minutes later. It was red hot in the crane even though the air conditioning was on full blast with the door and all the windows open, I was sitting in the chair stripped to the waist with just my jeans and boots on sweating like Fuck, Periodically I was called on the radio to lower the electricians a few feet, they would finish what they were doing and I would lower them a bit more, I couldn't see what was happening as I was lifting blind, only obeying the banks/man's instructions. then about 2pm I was told that they would be finished by half past so I started to put my flask and sandwich box in my bag ready for the off, that's when I found a can of orange juice inside the bag, "it was still cool from lying in the shade of the crane cab", I opened the can and took a swig out of it to quench my thirst, leaving plenty left. The electricians were needing to be lowered some more so on Instruction I lowered them using only my right hand on the control lever, with my left hand I reached for the can to get another swig of juice and just as I got the can to my mouth all the time watching the hoist/ lower line and feeling the rotation indicator to make sure I was going slowly enough I noticed a big Fucking wasp sitting on the rim of the can, suddenly it flew off the rim and landed on my nose, well fuck me, with the fright I got I dropped the can into my lap spilling the contents all over me, automatically my hand came off the control lever which stopped lowering the electricians with a sudden jolt, then I swatted the wasp with my right hand and felt the bastard sting me, it landed on the floor and I jumped out the seat and ground the big bastard into the rubber matting with my size 9 boot calling it every fucking name in the book of swear words, there was juice everywhere, my jeans were soaked and it looked as if I'd pissed myself, my nose was a little sore but not too bad that I couldn't carry on working, it didn't really matter anyway, because the electricians had had enough for one day especially after the sudden stop they just had, I think they were wanting to change their trousers too "but for different reasons" if you know what I mean.

By the time I lowered them to the ground, had the basket un-hooked and put the crane in its rest, it was about 3 pm, still early enough considering I was getting paid till 7pm, shortly I was in the car driving to the security gate where on stopping to show the security guys my pass, I caught a glimpse of one of the security guys having a wee snigger to himself, now this one in particular was normally a bit of a sour puss, so it puzzled me as to why he was grinning like he was, "or maybe he was just trying to pass wind."

On the drive home my nose was getting sorer as time went on, but I didn't pay any attention to it other than to rub it now and again, but by the time I got to the pub I was a bit more anxious as it felt like twice its normal size, but things came to a head (ex-cuse the pun) as soon as I walked into the pub, because everyone started laughing and asking me, what's that on your fucking nose Big Man ?, I headed straight for the toilet where in the mirror I could see what they were talking about, my nose had swollen to double proportions, normally I have what's called a roman nose but this one was roaming all over my fucking face, it was all red and angry looking with the wasps barbed sting still hanging from

145

it, no wonder mister sour puss security guy was laughing, I must have really made that Fuckers day. By the time I pulled out the sting, it was to late to do anything with the swelling or the coloring for that matter, so I just had to laugh it off and believe me I didn't feel like fucking laughing, I swear I could sit up in bed at night with the light out and still read a book or daily paper from the glow coming from my nose. I took a bit of ribbing the next morning off of Sandy and for the next couple of days I looked like a Jimmy Durrante double, I was taking antibiotic tablets for 2 weeks after that, "that fucking wasp had a lot to answer for" I still have a mark on my nose to this day thanks to that bastard.

Sandy faxed in the time and expenses sheets for the previous week on Monday morning 24th, I had already sent my p45 to Smedvig the previous Wednesday 19th so it was a case of wait and see how much they were going to pay me, it ended up, that as I started on the Monday and the weekly time sheets started on the Saturday and finished Friday, it meant I had only 5 days pay to collect for that week, past experience of being ripped off made me very aware of what could happen here, so I took careful note of all the days I worked and kept signed copies of the time sheets, In the end it didn't really matter because I was eventually paid everything I was due, plus extra.

The following week flew in, Sandy and me were sunbathing on the top of the module for most of the time, periodically doing the odd lifts here and there for whoever needed them, Then on Thursday morning Andy appeared again at the yard with the news that everything involving the cranes were to be sea-fastened down as they were planning to put the module on the barge over the week-end and get ready to sail (ASAP) after that, that put a bit of a dampener on things for me, I was hoping for at least another week out of this, but as I said before, "all good things." Feeling a bit dejected I watched Andy and Sandy walk away towards our porto-cabin when Andy stopped and shouted to me, "Oh by the way Johnnie"!, I've got your new contract in my car!, come to the porto-cabin in an hour and we'll discuss it, Ok, Right at that moment I could have fucking hugged him, but I just shouted back, Ok Andy,! I'll be there.

In the porto-cabin Andy gave me the new contract and explained that the usual 3 month trial period terms were included, but he told me to sign it dated Tuesday 1st of September and send it off to the Aberdeen office, I would still be paid for the

146

days worked at the shipyard, but in effect I would not officially be employed again by Smedvig until the 1st of September 1992. That suited me just fine.

The rest of the week Sandy and me were busy securing everything that could move involving the cranes, the rest of the sea-fastening jobs on the module was done by the yard workers, the last thing we had to do was fill up drums of diesel and we put half a dozen 25 gallon drums onto each crane outside the engine room and secured them to the handrails with fibre strops and rope we also made sure the cranes were fully fuelled up before we left the yard on Saturday morning. That was us finished down there but we still went in on Sunday for a few hours just to check everything was still secure and also to be seen so we could justify 12 hours pay for that day. There was nothing for us to do because the crane booms were sea/fastened in their rests, ready for the outward journey on the barge in the next day or two. all we had to do now was fill in the time and expenses sheets, Sandy was taking them into the office in Aberdeen on Monday, then saying our farewells to each-other hoping to meet up again in the near future out in the North Sea somewhere on The Bruce. We went our separate ways.

I was sitting in the pub later on that Sunday afternoon, when a phone call from Liz gave me some concern, she said that Andy Harper was just on the phone looking for me and could I give him a ring back, I would have done, if I'd had his number, but I didn't, and this was long before you could dial 1471 on your telephone to get the last callers number. There was nothing I could do except wait and hope he called back, I was in two minds whether to go home and wait, or just ask Liz to give him the pub number, I decided to go home and that was the right decision because 5 minutes after getting in, the phone rang, it was Andy, he wanted to know if I could check in on Tuesday at Bristows Helicopters at 6am and fly out to the Micoperi 7000, "M7000" a lifting barge to wait on the Bruce "P.U.Q." module being towed out there, well you can imagine my answer "yes" in all honesty I couldn't get him off the phone quick enough before he started asking awkward questions like why I was home so early. My parting words to him were, don't you worry Andy, I'll be there mate. "And thanks again."

Liz and I went back to the pub to celebrate the good news, some of the guys that were mates of mine and were home on leave from offshore were in there, Jim Pitcairn, Seldom, Alex Robertson, Jim Macgregor, my best mate Ian Macleod and a few others made up the company, we didn't really need an excuse to go on the rattle, "so to speak", but if an excuse was needed then my good news was it.

The next morning I phoned Smedvig's office to confirm they had arranged digs for me that night?, they had, I was staying at the regular place in Bon Accord Street, I didn't know what I was going to be doing on this lifting barge so I took it easy on the drink on the Monday night, Tuesday morning the taxi arrived to pick me up and took me to Bristows where I checked in at 6am, while looking around to see if I recognized anyone who was going to the same place, I was met with a wall of unfamiliar faces, so I stayed on my own until we were called through the security gate to suit up and watch the pre-flight video, 20 minutes later we were sat on the chopper all 15 of us and I settled down for the 2 hour journey out to the barge. As I keep saying, there's nothing to do on the chopper but read, sleep or sit and stare out the window, "if you have a window seat that is," the chopper usually flies at about 3000 feet so there's not really much to see, That's when your mind starts to wander again about things in general, especially what's happened at home, I always get a knot in my stomach when going offshore, its been there since the T.L.P. days, and it was there again today just like clockwork, I don't imagine now after all these years that it will ever go away. I'm alright after the flight and I'm on the rig, its just before and during that's the problem. That's one of the reasons I don't sleep on the flight and it gave me time to reflect on what had happened since I was paid off the North West Hutton, since that happened in June I had only really been idle for about 3 weeks between then and now, not to bad considering it could have been longer. My intention now was to try and kid myself on, that I was starting afresh in the Oil Industry, what I told myself was, lets forget the last 5 years, lets have a whole new look at things and put them into perspective, I was psyching myself up to go for the goals that I initially set myself, after all, if everything went well on the Bruce it could mean a drilling contract for at least 3 or possibly 5 years and as Smedvig also had the crane contract that would hopefully run parallel to the drilling contract surely that was more than enough time to get myself sorted out and get back on track.

New safety measures were put in place regarding flights off-shore, it was now compulsory that a few minutes before we took off or landed on any oil installation to pull the hood of your survival suit over your head and make sure the suit was fully zipped up to make a watertight seal incase the chopper had to ditch for some reason, it didn't give me any cause for concern, it was just another safety procedure as far as I was concerned, the only thing was it was as uncomfortable as fuck, you could hardly turn your head from one side to the other, and if you kept the hood up for too long you were in danger of getting a crick in your neck, that's why as soon as possible everybody unzipped their suits and took off the hoods.

We were all in the process of doing just this as we walked from the chopper down to the heli/admin on this barge, all I can say is, the first thought to go through my head was, this is like a floating shipyard, it was MASSIVE, I didn't get a good look at it from the chopper but now that I was on it I was Impressed. How this thing floated was beyond belief. That was still the foremost thought in my head as I checked-in and made my way down to my allocated cabin. There I met my mate Jamie Wright; he had been on here a fortnight already and was looking forward to going home,

After shooting the shit for a while, him telling me about his escapades working Overseas in the Far East and France, and me reciting mine, he took me on a tour of this Monster of a lifting barge, I honestly can't emphasis enough the enormity of this place everything was huge, it was one of the largest lifting barges in the world, others I can name are The Balder, The Hermod, and The Thialf all part of the Hereema Marine Contractors fleet. There were two massive cranes, one port, one starboard, each could lift 7000 tons hence the name M7000, later known as the Seipen, the deck itself was the size of Hampden football park, there were smaller mobile cranes moving about, there were tractors, forklift trucks and the deck seemed to be swarming with men, later on I found out that there was only about 2 dozen English speaking people on here, the rest of the workforce was made up from Orientals and Europeans, there were Brazilians, Porto Ricans, Mexicans, Portuguese, Italians and Spanish, the Ships Officers and crew were of different nationalities as well, you name it they were there. We were lucky in a way by having a room to ourselves because most of the workforces were sharing 3 and 4 to a room. Our job on here was to wait on the last of the modules for the PUQ to arrive and then we would be busy, but until then, the time was our own.

Looking over the side I could see that the drilling module was already installed, that was the one Jamie and the other lads were working on in France, he said the Jacket for the module was already in place and pile driven into the hard rock below the sea bed before he got there, then the module support frame was installed ready for the top/side module arriving from France, A few days prior to me going out there Jamie told me he was on the floating barge carrying the drilling top/side module when both the M7000 cranes lifted it off and placed it onto the support frame and slotted the huge locating pins into the holes before the welders welded it secure, now this was something I wished I had seen, and a few days later I was going to get my wish, its not every day you get to see one of the worlds largest lifting barges at work.

Jamie and me spent our day wandering about the accommodation we were not allowed out on the deck of the barge basically because of the constant activity going on, and the movement of the various mobile plant continuously on the go, that didn't stop us from watching what was going on from one of the observation decks below the wheelhouse, we were both in awe at the size of the cranes and hoped that at some point before we left here, we would get to have a look round them, from where we were standing, we could see the crane operators cab and just below where the 2 air driven winch operators stood. Seemingly, when the crane was lifting a load, these 2 winches were attached to either side of the load to keep a constant tension on it, to stop it swinging back and forth, the crane operator would stop the load himself if it was swinging from side to side, we were led to believe the cranes were mostly computerized and state of the art, so we were desperate to have a look for ourselves.

Wandering about the floors of the accommodation we went into the galley, this place was the size of Blackpools Tower Ballroom, the tables each seated 6 comfortably, the choice of menu was variable to suit the different nationalities, but what struck me was there was always rice with everything, with your Tacos, chilies, curries or anything else that was on, watching the men queuing at the galley counter, every one of them had a separate bowl of rice irrespective of what else he was having. (Obviously some sort of a culture thing). At one side of the door leading out of the galley were case upon case of cans of different kinds of soft drinks, lemonade, orange, coke, ginger beer, Irn- Bru and also bottles of mineral water, these were there for the taking as the drinking water on here was much to be desired. On the other side were boxes of chocolate bars, mars bars, bounty bars, twix bars, aero's, it was help yourself time to these and Jamie and me did just that. Leaving the galley we went looking for the Bonded store so I could buy fags, it took us a while to find the guy in charge and when we finally did, it took him about 5 minutes to take the several padlocks off the door so we could get in "obviously not a very trusting guy with his fellow shipmates" he sounded to me like a Mexican "not that I speak Mexican" it was the way he kept on calling me Senor that gave me the idea, but in his broken English I got the gist of what he was wanting off me, (my passport), if you can picture me standing there asking this guy in my Sunday best Greenock accent for a carton of cigarettes, cigarillos, smoke's, tobacco for fuck sake, "this Fucker was either taking the piss or he genuinely didn't know what I was talking about" It was only when I started miming smoking a fag that he finally got the message, then he said in his best Mexican accent, ahhh senor, cigarillos, you give me passport, I give you cigarillos, Now there was no way in the world I was giving this fucker a look at my passport, never mind letting him keep it as collateral for a carton of fags, I said no passport Pedro, I will pay you cash, no Senor, he said again, I need passport, I turned to Jamie and said, I don't believe this fucker's going to take no for an answer!, then turning back to this guy I said, forget it Pedro, I will go and see the EL Capitano and see what he say's about this, this seemed to jolt him a wee bit, because he then said Ok Senor, I will take cash, in the end I ended up with a carton of French Gaullose cigarettes for £8 from this Mexican Bandit, Please believe me when I tell you, if you ever want to give up smoking, try smoking a carton of these, "Their Fucking Rotten."

Walking about the Barge was tiring so I had an early night, there was no television in the room so it was lights out and bed, there was no need to get up early in the morning so I slept right through till 8am, when I got up I headed down to the galley to find Jamie, for some reason the galley was closed at that time, strange time to shut, I thought?, so I wandered about until I found him sitting in one of the lounges watching the guys off shift playing what at first glance was dominoes but it was really a Chinese game of Mahjongg. This was a big thing on here and they were adamant they didn't play for money and to support this statement there was no visible sign of coins or notes on the table, they played with plastic tokens, later we were told gambling was strictly forbidden on here and to highlight this, there were signs posted reflecting this rule on the walls of each lounge, also any offenders caught gambling were sacked on the spot, a bit harsh I thought, but when I realized that these workers were on here for at least 3 months at a time, sometimes 6 months if they were doing extra time, "so much for doing an extra week" it doesn't bare thinking about that you could lose all your wages playing cards while working away from home for that length of time, still I'm not totally convinced that they weren't gambling.

The reason being by the way some of them were carrying on at times when the last of the dominoes were being played, there were too many fists being clenched and waived and to many raised angry voices for them to be just having a game of Happy Fucking Families.

Jamie and I left them to it and sat at the counter of the Espresso bar complete with high stools at the counter, this was obviously an after thought in the design of the lounge because it looked nearly new, the steward behind the counter couldn't speak a word of English but you wouldn't know that with the greeting he gave you "espresso sir" he asked looking at me,? Yes thank you I replied, as he prepared my drink, I asked him. How's your day been mate? Trying to strike up a conversation with him, He ignored me and turned to Jamie and asked him "espresso sir" Jamie just nodded as if to say yes. I thought that maybe he didn't hear me, so I tried again and said, your not very busy in here to-day are you mate? "The place was empty apart from him, Jamie and me". Espresso sir, he asked me again? No thanks I said, I've not finished this one yet, I thought to myself, this fuckers deaf or just an ignorant cunt, then Jamie told me that I was wasting my time talking to him, because he couldn't understand a word I was saying, the only English he knew was "espresso sir"

Sitting with our coffee, I asked Jamie about the galley being closed at 8am in the morning, he said it didn't open until 11am but there was a breakfast lounge open from 5am till 9am next to the galley, I obviously missed this place as there were so many doors to go through it was quite easy to get lost, Jamie said we would visit it the next morning, The rest of that day we wandered about the decks again, if we had stayed in the main accommodation and looked out the windows we could have kidded ourselves on that we were on a world cruise, but when we ventured outside onto one of the observation decks we were soon brought back to reality with the hustle and bustle that was going on out on the massive deck below,

That second afternoon we were introduced to the Chief Electrician working for BP on the Bruce project his name was Andy Mclaren, he put us in the picture of what was going to be happening in the next couple of days but until then we were to relax and enjoy the scenery. Andy let us use the phone in his office on the barge and I called Liz to let her know that I was Ok and also to find out if she posted my new contract to Smedvig which she had, I told her I didn't know how long I would be out here but said that Jamie had already done 2 weeks and there was no sign of a relief for him, so I would just play it by ear and periodically phone home to keep her informed.

Time was beginning to drag a bit now and being cooped up on the barge was beginning to become a bit monotonous, it was the third day now and we still weren't allowed out onto the barges deck, from the observation deck we could see the accommodation barge the "Polyconfidence" far away in the distance, this was due to arrive early on the Friday morning and be hooked up to the drilling module sometime over the week-end, the barges carrying the last two modules for the P.U.Q. were still nowhere to be seen so it looked like another day of sitting around twiddling our thumbs.

The one and only time I went for breakfast was a stroke of luck because later on sitting across from Jamie and me was an English speaking Chief Mechanical Fitter working on the barge. Jamie and I got talking to this guy telling him that it would have been nice to have had a look round the cranes and deck of the Lifting Barge at least once before we left to stay on the Poly, he told us what we already knew, "we weren't allowed on deck by ourselves" but if we waited 30 minutes he would give us a guided tour himself. Jamie and I were sitting in the tea/shack leading out onto the main deck in 10 minutes flat, working gear on and ready to go when this guy turned up as promised the 3 of us went walkabout,

When I said the deck looked massive looking down from the observation deck I wasn't exaggerating, but from the deck looking up, it looked even bigger, the three of us looked like dwarfs against the giant machinery around us, laying horizontally on one side of the deck was the flare tower which was easily 300 feet in length, on the other was the bridge section which would straddle the drilling module and the P.U.Q. This itself was a little shorter than the flare tower, but not by much, taking us around the perimeter of the cranes was like walking around one of those big gas or oil tanks you see in the oil and gas refineries and when we had a look inside of one of the crane pedestals there was only what I can describe as a workshop, not a little workshop with a bench, and a couple of vices, a tool/box and some spanners lying about, I mean a fully equipped workshop with lathes, welding plant, burning plant, everything you could think of that would be needed in a fully functioning mechanical workshop. The other crane was identical, although we weren't allowed inside the crane operators cab from through the windows we could see the console he sat at and the small television screens, which portrayed the information relayed back from the computerized system built into the crane itself, I cannot emphasis enough that these cranes truly were magnificent. And I'd like to say thanks again, to the guy who showed us round.

The reason for my one and only time having breakfast in the breakfast lounge on here was because on Thursday morning I ventured in there at about 8 -15am and there standing behind the counter was this deformed dwarf, all 6 feet 6 inches of him, black as coal he was too, this guy wouldn't have looked out of place playing basketball for the Harlem Globetrotters. I gave him a friendly nod and said good morning to him, all the response I got was a vacant look as he stood staring at me. "I thought fuck me here we go again" could I have some bacon and eggs please? I asked, he mumbled something in his native tongue and walked away. there were about 4 or 5 other people sitting in the lounge looking at me as I stood like a cunt at the counter, wondering if he was coming back again or not, then a few minutes later he appeared with a full plate of half cooked bacon and under cooked eggs all floating on a puddle of grease, I looked at this guy and then at the plate as he held it out to me from behind the counter, I tried to hold the plate steady to stop the grease from running off it, thinking to myself as I looked at him, you certainly won't scald yourself with the hot fat, "you cunt." Looking around for an empty table, near a bucket, "because that's where this muck was going" as soon as this big fucker stopped watching me, finding one, I sat down with my back to him and started playing with the eggs with my fork, watching the uncooked clear gel of the yolk slowly mix in with the grease, the bacon looked revolting too, even if it had been cooked, it was still all fat round the edges with a bit of ham in the middle, I was glad when Jamie came in and sat down opposite me, keep your eye on the big man behind the counter,! I said, as soon as he disappears this lots going in that fucking bucket, and as soon as he did, that's where it went, we were having some toast when the fitter arrived and we got speaking to him. But that was the reason I never went for breakfast again,

Friday morning, and the polyconfidence was much nearer the drilling module, but the weather was steadily becoming worse, that meant it wouldn't be able to tie up to the module until at least Saturday, the bad weather also meant a delay with the P.U.Q. modules that were due on Saturday morning, Word filtered down to Jamie and me that the 2 floating barges would be here early Saturday night, so we could be required at any time over the week-end.

With the arrival of the polyconfidence and the accompanying anchor handlers, it gave us a change of scenery to look at from the lifting barge. Friday and Saturday found Jamie and me going from watching the men playing mahjongg in the games lounge, to the espresso bar," for a quick chat with the waiter" then to one of the television lounges in the hope of finding one with a British programme on, normally we couldn't understand a fucking word that was said on the TV, it was all spoken in a foreign language, one time we went into the cinema and the film "Gone with the Wind" with Clark Gable and Maureen O'Hara was on, everybody in there were laughing their heads off, I turned to Jamie and said I've seen this film and there's fuck all funny about it, "maybe they dubbed the sound with different words" from there we would go to the galley for lunch have a wee siesta in the afternoon then repeat the whole routine over again, sounds boring I know, but it passed the time away. Before I turned in for the night I could see the barges with the modules in the distance, it looked as if we would be busy in the following days to come,

On Sunday morning Jamie and I were wakened at 7am with the news that we were to attend a meeting in the smoking tea/ shack at 8 am, washed, dressed and in there at 7 30 am we met with Andy Mclaren the chief Electrician and some other BP guys who briefed us with what was happening, during the night the barge had lifted the top/side accommodation module onto the P.U.Q. and now was in the process of lifting the top/side of the Utilities module into place, once this was completed we were going over to the module itself to get the cranes working and start lifting the personnel who would be transferred from the M7000 to one of the anchor handlers and lift them aboard the P.U.Q. with the Billy- Pugh. All we had to do now was wait, in the meantime we watched the cranes do their business in lifting the Utilities module into place, it was hanging in the air supported by huge wire slings hooked onto both cranes as the floating barge was towed away from underneath, then the M7000 slowly moved forwards towards the platform to a pre/determined distance so the module could be lowered and slotted into place by the huge cone like locating pins and then welded secure.

Jamie and me were in awe of what was going on, we didn't speak a word as we watched the lift being done, we just stood and watched, happy in the knowledge that we had witnessed something very few people will ever see in their working life, that includes many offshore workers, right then I was wishing I had brought my camera with me to capture the events for posterity.

We knew once the module was landed and the cranes un-hooked by the men already on the platform, that we were to get the cranes up and running, but Jamie and I never really gave much thought about how we were going to get onto the platform to do this. We had a couple of ideas, one was us being lifted on by the crane, another was being lowered on by helicopter, we didn't think there was any other way than these two, " but we were wrong." At 9.00am we were called to another meeting and told to bring our survival suits with us, on our way there I spoke to Jamie and said, see I told you it would be by helicopter why else would they want us in our survival suits, at the meeting we were told again what was required of us once we got onto the platform. Then we were told to suit up and put on a life/jacket as they were preparing to launch the Fast Rescue Craft, "F.R.C." Jamie and me looked at each other and simultaneously said Fast Rescue Craft, I thought the guy was joking but he wasn't, Jamie and me climbed into our suits and put the life/jackets on as instructed then followed the other 2 foreign lads going with us, outside on the deck waiting at the FRC was Andy the Electrician and the 2 men in charge of the craft, before we knew it we were in this fucking rubber dingy lifted over the side by one of the mobile cranes, and were on our way to the platform, we were all sitting in single file, the guy steering the dingy at the back and his mate at the front and us 5 in between, this thing was doing a fair rate of knots in the 2 to 3 metre swell, us hanging on like grim death every time the dingy gave a heave and came down again with a thump, it only took a few minutes to reach the platform but it felt longer, once we were along side this was when the fun and games started, if they had told us on the barge what was to happen once we got here, I'm pretty certain Jamie and me would have told them to shove it, but now that we were here we had to jump from the F.R.C. on to the steel ladder once it got close enough to the leg and start climbing to the top, well this thing was heaving like a bastard, "just like my stomach" one minute you were looking at the new steel of the ladder, the next second looking at seaweed clinging to the leg, the guy at the front of the boat was shouting on us to hurry up and take up our position ready to jump off as soon as the dingy reached the top of a wave, First to go was Andy, then one of the other guys, then it was my turn, the dingy was going back and forth bouncing off the leg, I was hanging on waiting on the dingy to reach its peak then I jumped and grabbed hold of the ladder, my heart was beating like a big base drum, I watched as the dingy fell away in the swell then came up again to meet me, I couldn't move, I was frozen to the ladder "fuck this for a game of soldiers I thought to myself" the shouts from the guy in the dingy gesturing with his arm for me to climb, brought me back to reality and I slowly started climbing gripping every rung as I went, finally I reached the top and climbed out of the hatch completely out of breath and waited with the first 2 on Jamie and the other guy, Jamie eventually appeared but the other fellow fell in the water and was pulled back into the F.R.C. and returned to the barge. Once we got our breath back we started the long climb up the stairwells to the top of the module where we were met by some of the lifting barge guys who were there to unhook the slings from the cranes, they obviously arrived the same way we did.

Andy and Jamie went together to find the compressors and generators and fire them up so we would have some power and air, my job was to make sure all the sea/fastenings were off the cranes and once there was enough air in the tanks start them up and start to bring the personnel off the anchor handler waiting nearby, Andy had brought a bag of radios with him and we shared them out so we could keep in contact with each other, after checking that both cranes were free from their fastenings all I could do was wait on Andy giving me air so I could start them up.

Over an hour later and several attempts at starting one of the cranes I finally got the North crane going and started to bring the men aboard 8 at a time, it was just turning 11am when I got the last of them onboard, I had done about 5 trips to the anchor handler so there was about 50 guys onboard, including the ones already here when we got on, at 12am I dropped the Billy-Pugh down to the anchor handler and brought up the pre-packed meals for the men, this routine would be followed for the next few days until the flare tower and the bridge section were installed giving access to both the drilling platform and the P.U.Q, changing out the crews at 6am and 6pm was the highlight of the day for Jamie and me, there were only some occasional lifts to be done outside of that, Jamie and I decided we would stick with our regular crew change he would go nights and I would stay days, he would lift me onto the platform and I would lift him off and vice versa. The men on here were mostly welders and labourers working round the clock welding the top/side modules to the bottom ones, watching from the barge at night you could see the bluey/white flashes from the welding rods as the men went about their work like ants.

Looking over towards the drilling platform I could see that the polyconfidence was moored alongside, the workforce on there were busy commissioning it, and I knew that some of the Smedvig drill crews were on there, but I had no contact with them, I would have to wait until the bridge section was in place before I could get across.

On Monday just before dinner time I could see from the North Crane that one of the Lifting barge cranes was busy lifting the triangular shaped flare tower from it's horizontal position on the deck, to a vertical one, there were no slings used this time, instead 2 hydraulic clamps closed around circular lifting points near the top of the flare tower, these clamps were then supported by a lifting bridle attached to the cranes hook, picking the tower up was a slow process, but foot by foot up it went until it was hanging in the air, on either side a winch wire rope was attached to stop it swinging back and forth also to stop it turning in mid-air then the barge moved slowly towards the platform just as it

158

did with the last 2 modules until it was close enough for the crane to lower the tower onto the 3 locating pins already in place as part of the top/side deck. once this was done and still being attached to the crane the flare towers 3 legs were welded secure by the welders, it took most of the day to do this and by early evening as the weather was starting to pick up again the barge wanted to pull away, but as they tried to release the hydraulic clamps still attached to the tower they failed to open, time and time again they tried but they didn't budge, after some consultation with the welding foreman everybody was taken off the job and moved away from the vicinity of the tower, the decision was made to get the men to unhook the bridle from the crane and when this was done then the barge slowly pulled away stretching and snapping the hydraulic hoses in the process, there was hydraulic oil everywhere, it was running down the flare tower covering the decks, the welders and labourers mostly Orientals now became cleaners, rushing about cleaning up the oil with oil soak pads and buckets of concentrated cleaning fluid so the welding could carry on, it was like watching the fucking Key Stone Cops in action, I was always waiting on Charlie Chaplin making an appearance, one thing about these oriental gaffers was, if they said jump, the workforce asked ho hi.

Tuesday was a wasted day, we still changed out as usual because Jamie was going home that day, Steve Ritchie was coming out to relieve him, but it was too rough for the barge to attempt putting the bridge section on so I spent the day doing the odd lift here and there and taking in the scenery.

Wednesday was a better day, the weather was a lot calmer and the barge crane already had the bridge section slung up in the morning when we crew changed, I did some lifts with the South crane then hurried over to the North where I had a birds-eye view of the bridge section being installed, looking down from the crane to the bridge section, then to the gap it was going to span between the two platforms, I thought to myself, this isn't going to fit, the bridge looked too small, even as it inched closer and the gap got smaller, I still wasn't convinced it would fit, and in the afternoon when it was on, true enough, there was a gap on either side, so steel plates had to be welded on, to bridge these, Oh it slotted into the locating pins ok and looked alright, but I'm not totally convinced those gaps should have been there, then again I'm just a crane operator, not an Engineer. Once the crane was unhooked it pulled away from the platform to change position then it came back to the north side of the P.U.Q to retrieve the lifting bridle and clamps still attached to the flare tower, The rest of the day was spent running hydraulic lines from the clamps back to the crane on the barge and once these were attached the barge came closer to try and retrieve the clamps. I watched as the deck hands climbed the tower to hook the lifting bridle onto the crane and then stand back, as the crane took the strain, a few minutes later there was an almighty bang as the clamps were finally released, they swung out towards the crane then back again hitting the flare tower, the guys still up there must have been shitting themselves, "well they all looked pretty yellow about the gills when they came down"

That was about it for the M7000, it had successfully done it's work and would no doubt soon be heading to another contract somewhere else in the world, when Steve came onboard that night with what was only a token workforce, "probably to make sure they hadn't left anything on board the P.U.Q." he had brought his personal belongings with him, he like me was going over to stay on the polyconfidence, once the lifting barge was finished, all it remained for me to do was collect my gear off the barge get Steve to lift me back onto the P.U.Q then make my way across the 2 bridges to the Poly and get settled on there.

The next morning the M7000 was nowhere in sight, for a barge its size it could move at a fair rate of knots, I can honestly say my stay on there was an experience I will always remember.

With the Poly hooked up to the Drilling Platform and the bridge joining that to the P.U.Q. it was time to bring out the construction workers, "THE BEARS" as there known Offshore, these are the men who will perform the HOOK-UP, Its exactly what it means, hooking everything up and getting things on line like, the power, the water, getting the heating and ventilation system going, basically they will do everything that needs to be done to get the platform up and running, the bears are a mixed workforce with Electricians, Instrument Technicians, Platers, Pipe-Fitters, Scaffolders, Riggers, Painters,etc,etc, and what happens is the job itself is flooded with these guys so everything can be completed in the shortest time possible, these hook up jobs are bread and butter jobs to these guys, so to speak, in the early days it used to take up to a year or more to complete a decent sized hook-up, but with most of the pre- fabricating now being done in the ship-

160

yards it only takes up to 4 or 6 months sometimes less, then the majority of these guys are idle again till the next job comes along, one thing about working with these guys is there's always one character or more in every squad so there's hardly a day goes by without a laugh at someone or something.

Staying on the Poly was like staying in a hotel, the room I shared with the Smedvig Electrician a German guy called Seigfried Timmerbrink "Ziggy" was a big double room fully carpeted with 2 large beds, a dressing table and chairs, a wall mounted T.V. and an en-suite bathroom with shower, the window in the room looked straight out onto the bridge that joined us to the platform and in the morning I used to look out the window to see if the bridge was up or down, if it was up then I knew I was going to work, if it was down, I went back to bed. Ziggy did the same; everything on here was on a large scale from the cinema to the galley. Everywhere you went there was always plenty of room to move, and considering there was over 700 men and woman on here that was saying something, at night after shift there was always something on, in the way of home entertainment, bingo, darts and dominoes tournaments, karaoke, or you could go to the gym or cinema or just watch TV in your room, at the week-end you had the Saturday football coupon to look forward too, what happened here was there were 25 teams and you had to predict the result whether it was a home win, away win, or draw, marking a 1, 2,or X for your selections, the one with the highest correct results took the pot, less 10% for charity. More than half the guys on the Poly had a go at this and with it costing £5 for three goes that amounted to a lot of cash, sometimes as much as £1500 or more.

There were 10 crane operators initially employed on the Bruce during the hook-up, 4 for each crane on dayshift and 2 for nightshift I knew them all personally, some I still keep in touch with to this day. There was John M Sutherland, Jamie Wright, Simon Donaldson, Kenny Milne, Joe Rochester, and Brian Sharman. Alex Bolton, Steve Ritchie, Alan Matthew, and me, the crane mechanics also did some operating to help us out during dinner breaks they were Paul McCabe, Sandy Bruce, Alistair Murray "pip", and Graham Barron,

My routine in the morning was rise at 5.30am have breakfast, watch a bit of news on T.V., then walk across the bridge to the drilling package, arriving there for 6.30am there I would normally meet the nightshift guy and have a blether with him for 5 minutes then I would make my way to the other bridge and cross over to the P.U.Q. where I would climb the 6 double stairwells levels to the top level of the module, then climb the ladder to the cranes and wait there completely out of breath till the Amec deck crew came on shift at 7.00am. Then I would do any lifts required with the North crane, "another crane-op did them with the South". Then at dinnertime I would make the long journey back to the Poly, and do the same journey again after dinner and the same again after shift, all in all I did this journey 4 times a day. For tea breaks I only had to come down from the crane, as there was tea/shack and some temporary toilets on the top deck and the decks below, but as we were allowed to smoke in the cranes at that time I usually didn't bother coming down at tea/ break time. I followed this routine daily until it was my time to go home on the Tuesday15th.

From September 92 to March 93 the work went on non-stop, all the different contractors doing their bit to ensure the success of the hook-up, but as with all big jobs there were bound to be one or two hic-up's, the weather factor was one of them, with it being the winter season and with the wind howling and the waves horrendous, the poly had to pull away from the platform on numerous occasions, one of these lasting 5 days on one of the trips that I was on, and there was hardly a trip went by without the bridge being lifted for some reason or another.

Another couple of days were lost when one morning I was asked to lift an empty basket down to the a third level area on the North side of the platform so two of the deck crew that I had worked with since the start of the hook-up could fill it with scaffolding clamps, clips and short poles, I had reached the spot near enough to where they would need me to be, and had stopped and sat waiting on them giving me instructions over the radio, about 5 minutes had passed when looking over towards the drilling platform I noticed a couple of scaffold boards floating in the water, then pip the mechanic who was operating one of the drilling cranes called me on the radio and said that 2 Scaffolders were in the water, my first reaction was to drop the basket down to the water so they could swim over to it, climb in, and I would bring them back up to the platform again, but the basket wasn't needed, they had swam over to one of the legs and climbed the ladder back up where they were taken away by the medic to be checked over in the sick bay back on the Poly, all activity on both platforms came to a halt and wouldn't resume until there was an investigation, This was standard procedure when an incident of this severity occurred. I was silently congratulating myself on my quick reaction, and once I had the basket removed from the crane hook I went to see how the two men were doing. But as they were still in the sick bay waiting on a helicopter coming to take them back to the beach I didn't get to speak to them. I didn't give it much more thought as I was told they seemed to be ok, but like all things that happen, if there doesn't seem to be a reasonable explanation for it, then the rumors start. One cause that was bandied about was that the crane operator knocked them into the water with the basket, I could picture the headlines in the daily papers "DRUG CRAZED CRANE-OP TRIES TO DROWN TWO SCAFFS" another was, the basket was foul hooked underneath the scaffolding and when the crane operator picked it up he pulled the scaffolding with him, toppling the two guys into the water, CRANE-OP TRIES TO DEMOLISH NORTH SEA PLATFORM, there was nothing I could do to stop these rumors, only the outcome of the investigation which took place when the Health and Safety Executive "H.S.E." came on board would do that, and that's exactly what happened, the outcome was, when the men were standing on the scaffolding platform getting ready to throw the fittings into the basket, the weight of the scaffolding boards, clips, and poles combined with the weight of the two men proved to much for the platform to take and subsequently it collapsed sending one of the guys straight into the sea with boards, poles and fittings dropping all around him, the other guy was left holding on for a while until he had no option but to drop into the sea as well. I had to attend the enquiry and was asked once or twice if I had foul hooked the platform or if I had swung the basket in a way that it might have knocked them into the water, or if I might have landed the basket onto the platform by mistake adding more weight to the platform, all these questions were answered by no, no, and no again. Finally they went and emptied the Mipeg, This is a computerized print out of the weight of the loads being lifted by the crane, and found that the weight indicator showed no fluctuation from the time I lifted the empty basket, until the guys were retrieved from the water. Later when the investigation was over and I was absolved from any blame by the Mipeg readout, my written account of what I saw and a written statement from the guys themselves, I still felt quite annoyed that the finger of blame was pointed in my direction albeit for a very short time through rumors, one thing I learned from that incident was, you can go from Hero to Arsehole in minutes, all because of a rumor.

The trips were going in fast and furious now and the hook-up was coming along, if it wasn't exactly on schedule as planned, it wasn't far behind. This was due to the dedication and hard work by the contractors even though many of them knew that once this job was finished, then so were they, until something else came up.

As I said before "The Bears" were mostly a happy go lucky bunch, always ready to play along in the entertainment venues that went on during the trip, If the barge had pulled off waiting on weather, and especially at the week-end you would find them playing Bingo, crib, dart and dominoes tournaments, even singing on the karaoke machine from time to time or betting on the horses at race-nights, all these venues were really good crack and the friendly banter between the various contractors only heightened the enjoyment. But you know what they say about an angry bear, "Stay clear"

What happened to upset the bears and everybody else on the Poly was this.

Every Saturday during the football season, a football coupon was run in the way I explained earlier, only this week there were 3 teams still to play on the Sunday, most of the correct results at the end of Saturdays games stood at 15, now the best that anyone could get was 18 and that was a pretty good result, but when the games had finished on Sunday and the ones who put claims in for 18 correct results found that the girl who was running the coupon had won it with 19 results, the pot for that week was well over £2500 a very nice lift indeed. But there were no cheers of congratulations or shouts of well done, the Bears smelt a rat and it stank to high heaven when they found out that she was going home the next day and wasn't coming back. Tongues began to wag and tempers were raised I can only imagine that they thought as I did that some jiggery pokery was involved here and that everything was not above board, they didn't exactly come out and shout foul but there were a lot of unhappy BEARS in the woods that day. I know I was one of them.

By the time December came round it was looking like I was going to spend both Xmas and New Year offshore and that's exactly what happened, on Dec 22nd the day after my birthday I was on my way out to the platform again for another 2 weeks, Liz and I were, well lets just say still together, things at home weren't getting any better, I was still drinking and gambling as much despite the promises I'd made to her and to myself for that matter that I would cut down, the arguments in the house were no worse than usual, in fact it was getting to the stage where we hardly spoke to each other at all and the long silences between us were becoming longer, Liz, like myself was a stubborn person, we both had the same nature, but once I got something in my head and an argument started, even though I knew I was in the wrong, nobody was going was going to change it, no matter what was said or done, Liz was the same. I was speaking more to Kaiser than to anyone else in the house. I think that was because he listened to every word, and didn't agree or disagree with anything I said.

On Xmas eve it was decided to get everybody back to the Poly at the end of shift only leaving a skeleton crew on the P.U.Q. because they wanted to move the accommodation barge from the West side of the drilling platform to the South side of the P.U.Q. the weather was picking up and they said it could be a while before the weather got good enough to tie up at the platform and for the anchor handlers to run out the anchors. Pip the Crane Mechanic was one of the 12 volunteers that stayed on the P.U.Q. and once enough bottled water and food rations etc, etc, were sent over for them, the Poly retrieved its anchors, pulled up the bridge and sailed under its own steam away from the platform to a safe distance to wait on better weather.

For the next 4 days we were tossed about the North Sea, some of the huge waves that hit us were frighteningly powerful, threatening to capsize the barge and send us all to a watery grave, that was how it felt when the barge gave an awkward pitch or roll and you could see the concern on some faces of whether it was going to stay upright or not, It was during this time that I met one of the Smedvig Tool-Pushers a guy called John Munn "Munster" he lived in a place called Law, on the outskirts of Glasgow. Munster "as he was know as" and I were on the same crew change and it was agreed that he would pick me up and drop me off in Dundee on crew change days, to save me staying overnight in Aberdeen.

This arrangement suited me well and unknown to me then, it would last for the next 7 years.

The festive activities carried on with the various contractors going to have their Xmas dinner at different times, as you can imagine with the amount of people onboard the barge it was impossible for everyone to eat at the same time, so as one lot went to eat, the rest played games or took the chance to wait in line for the one of the phones to become available so they could wish their loved ones all the best. As usual, I didn't bother with the Xmas meal; I would wait until the buffet at night before I ate; besides there was still plenty of chocolate in the room to finish off.

By the time we got back into working mode there was less than a week of my trip to do and this was spent with nothing out of the ordinary happening. The only thing that changed was I didn't have so far to walk to get to work as the Poly was now berthed at the P.U.Q. Oh I still had the stairwells to climb to get to the top level, but I only had one bridge to cross.

When crew change day 5th January1993 arrived, it was time to go home and celebrate the New Year, I had phoned Liz to tell her about the new travel arrangements and she was waiting at Dundee's railway station car park when Munster and me arrived, I think she got a bit of a shock when she found that I was sober, and after a quick introduction to Munster we said cheerio to him, promising to meet him back at the same place in 2 weeks time, on the journey home Liz told me that my Mother, Sadie and younger Sister Jane, were coming for a few days, so I was warned to be on my best behavior, this best behavior that I was on only lasted a couple of days, after all it was the New Year and I was partying like an animal, Liz had bought me a new hi-fi system for my Xmas and one night while full of the drink, dancing about in the living room like a fucking idiot, I fell against the wall knocking down Liz's favorite picture damaging the frame, there wasn't a lot said but you could have cut the atmosphere with a knife, I fucked off to bed hoping that all would be forgiven in the morning, but unknown to me then, that incident was the final straw. The rest of my leave was spent in stony silence, Liz only speaking when she had too, so I was glad when the time came, to go back offshore, Liz dropped me off at Dundee giving me a token kiss goodbye, then Munster drove the rest of the way to Aberdeen.

A lot of soul searching and New Years resolutions were made on the way out to the platform that day in the chopper, I started thinking about the things that would change the next time I get home, "and I promised myself" I'm going to stick to the changes this time.

We landed on the Poly as usual but this time we were directed to the accommodation on the P.U.Q. this is where all the crane-ops, the drill crews and most of the BP guys would be staying from now on, the heli/deck on here wasn't commissioned yet so until that was done we would still use the Poly's. It was ideal on here for me all I had to do in the morning was get the elevator to level 6 go through 2 the air-lock doors and I was on the top deck looking at the cranes, there was no more of that half marathon shit before getting to work. I was sharing a room with Simon Donaldson and as we were both dayshift we struck up a bit of a rapport between us, Simon was operating the crane on the drill-ing platform and at dinner times we would meet up and eat to-gether at night after shift we would shoot the shit with the rest of the dayshift operators and drill crew, Simon was a quiet guy not like me or the rest of the guys, he was also a good listener, and he needed to be for what happened the following trip.

Nothing out of the ordinary happened that trip, apart from some days lost due to the weather, when the Poly bridge was lifted and a halt was put to the progress being made, after all it was the end of January and the weather was pretty dismal to say the least, but all in all the Bears were still beavering away at the various tasks they had and were powering their way to complete the hook-up if not on time then it wouldn't be far away, there wasn't much they could do about the weather, and that was the only thing that was holding them up,

Crew change day came round again as slowly as it usually does, it was time to get home again and be quizzed by the various wags who never fucking tire of telling me, that's never two weeks you've been away, or ask me, when do you go back? So for all you people out there that ask me the same fucking questions every time you see me, let me tell you this, the only thing that goes quick out there, is the tea and dinner breaks, and the two weeks leave. Everything else drags.

Liz picked me up in Dundee where Munster dropped me off and she seemed her usual self on the 40 minute journey to Glen-rothes, there was no mention of my behavior or the damaged picture from the last time I was home, so I thought that I was forgiven, "once again" everything seemed normal if you could call living with me normal that is, but on reflection everything was far from normal, there were none of the petty arguments that we had quite frequently, the kids went out of their way to avoid confrontation and were on their best behavior, even Kaiser seemed strangely subdued, there was nothing said about how much I was drinking or gambling during the day, in fact, that trip home I could do no wrong, so I got to thinking everything's ok. Liz had an upset stomach the whole time I was home and it was worse on the drive back to Dundee on February 16th at the end of my leave. Then as Munster drove up we kissed and said cheerio to each other with my parting words, "phone you in a couple of days" then as Munster and me went one way, Liz went another and it would be 7 years before I saw her or the kids again.

Out on the Platform the crack was as good as ever, Simon and me were still sharing a room and as the lifts required were becoming fewer as the days went on, we would take turns at knocking off a wee bit earlier so we would beat the queues for the telephone, we had to use the phones on the poly as the telecommunications on the P.U.Q. still hadn't been connected, as normal I would phone home every 2nd night so on Thursday18 Feb. I slipped away early only to find the phone was engaged when I rang home, I thought Liz or the kids must be talking to someone so I waited till later and tried again, but it was still engaged, by this time the Bears were coming in from work and the Queues started to form, there were 5 phones on the barge but with the amount of people on board phone time was limited to 5 minutes, if you wanted to phone again you joined the end of the queue, twice that night I joined the queue only to find the same monotonous tone the phone engaged sound gives, I didn't let it bother me that much, although it seemed strange for the phone to be in use for that length of time, I thought maybe one of the kids hadn't put the receiver correctly into its cradle, or maybe there was a fault in the line. Anyway I went to bed that night without trying again, telling Simon about what had happened he was thinking the same as me, the line was faulty, or the receiver's not in its cradle properly. I'll try again tomorrow, I said, as I bedded down for the night.

The next morning after a restless night I told Simon that I would wait until dinnertime before trying to phone again, but I couldn't concentrate on what was happening so I told the Amec deck foreman that I was going over to the poly to use the phone,

Pip the crane Mechanic took over for me as we were unusually busy that morning, when I got to the Poly there was no problem finding an empty booth but when I dialed my number that fucking engaged tone was still there, by this time I knew that something was up, it didn't take a rocket scientist to work that fucker out, but I didn't know what, there was all sorts of scenarios going through my head but none of them made any sense, I didn't know what to do, I couldn't phone Macleod he would be at work till 4 00 pm, and then he would probably be in the pub, then it hit me, I couldn't remember Macleod's number or the fucking pub number for that matter. Any other time and I would have just dialed them both without even thinking about the numbers they would come just naturally, have you ever been in that situation where normally you would do something automatically but then find your minds a blank, If you have, then you'll know how I felt, my head was spinning I couldn't think straight, all the way back to the platform I kept asking myself, what are they numbers? What are they fucking numbers? I didn't come down from the crane at dinnertime I didn't have the stomach to eat so I stayed up there till 4-00pm then got Pip to relieve me again as I headed back to the Poly, the phones were being used by some of the nightshift guys before going on shift but I didn't have long to wait until one was free, I dialed my own number and the few seconds it took to connect seemed like hours then the engaged tone sounded again in my ear, I slammed down the phone then automatically dialed Macleod's number without even thinking what it was, a few seconds later he picked up and I put him in the picture with what was happening, then asked him to go round to my house and see what was wrong, "he always had a spare key to my house"

I told him I would phone him at my house in 10 minutes to give him time to walk the two hundred yards round there, and believe me waiting that 10 minutes was like waiting forever, I was in the phone booth dialing my number then hanging up as soon as the engaged tone sounded, I kept on trying until the ring tone sounded then I heard McLeod's voice. What's happened, I asked? Your not going to like this, he said, I've been upstairs and the bedrooms are near enough empty, the window in your room is broken and flapping about in the wind, most of the wardrobes and cupboards are bare, and the phone was left off the hook, it looks like Liz and the kids are gone, what about the dog I asked? He's gone too, ok I said, do what you can with the window and I'll be home as soon as I can, at that I hung up, I was gutted, what did she have to go and do that for? I kept asking myself, surely things weren't that bad between us that it came to this, and why did she wait till I went away before moving out. I wanted answers and I wasn't going to get them out here, I needed off and quickly.

I went to Hans Van Dijk the Toolpusher and told him I needed off A.S.A.P. I didn't go into any details I just said it was family problems, that was good enough for him and he arranged for me to be on the next available flight which was Saturday, I was beginning to think that things couldn't get any worse, all Friday night I tossed and turned in bed, sleep was definitely out of the question, my head was bursting, I had a knot in my stomach the size of a beach ball, I lay on top of the bed and chain smoked cigarettes all night, Simon's head must have been bursting too because I kept him up most of the night with my constant jabbering, I was asking him questions that he didn't have nor could have answers too. That was one of the longest nights I have ever spent. Simon and me looked like shit when we got out of bed the next morning, our eyes were all red and angry through lack of sleep, my throat was sore from smoking, my head was still splitting and the knot in my stomach felt worse, Simon pleaded with me to try and eat something so the two of us went to the galley for breakfast, I was only going to have some toast to put something in my stomach to ease the pain, but when I looked out the galley window I could have fucking screamed, for there in the distance was the Poly, she only fucking pulled off during the night because of the weather, didn't she, I left the galley and got the lift up to the top deck, then without any protective gear on "P.P.E." I crossed the deck to the handrail and looked towards the sea then my whole body just slumped, it was blowing a fucking gale and the waves were easily 7 metres high or more, there was no chance in hell of a chopper landing in this weather and even if one did get in, I was on the P.U.Q. and the heli-deck was on the Poly. In my frustration I looked up towards the sky and said, oh thank you very fucking much.

The weather didn't break until late Sunday night, the sea was still a bit rough and I didn't hold out much hope of getting off but by Monday afternoon I was on my way to Aberdeen where two mates of mine Alex Robertson and Jim Pitcairn were waiting to drive me home. When I left the Poly that day I remember Simon saying to me, I hope everything works out Johnnie! And to be fair he meant well, but secretly I think he was glad to see the back of me so he could have a decent nights sleep.

On the two-hour journey home I was asking the boys questions that they had no answers too, surely somebody knows something? I kept on asking, but as far as they were concerned it was as much a shock to them as it was to me, they kept on telling me not to worry, everything will get sorted out, but I wasn't so sure, Liz had a mind of her own and if she decided to do something then no will in the world would stop her, we would just have to wait and see what happens.

On arriving home I forced myself to look around the house, Macleod was there waiting for us to arrive looking at me with pity in his eyes, I couldn't speak to him as I robotically went from room to room taking in all that was left, all I could see were my own possessions, Liz had taken everything else, I didn't want to be alone right then, so we all got in the car and headed for the boozer where for as much as I had to drink, I couldn't get drunk, give the boys their due they were trying to get me to look on the bright side of things telling me things would seem better in the morning, but for the life of me all there was, was darkness.

That for me was the boot up the arse that I needed, I had a long look at my lifestyle and I was going to change the way things were even if it was only for my own sake, At first the anger I felt at being betrayed showed very potently in my attitude to the people who were trying to show me sympathy when they said, sorry to hear about you and Liz, some of my friends were genuinely concerned about me and I thanked them for that, but others were just being fucking nosey, and I gave them short thrift with, fuck off and mind your own fucking business, I had a lot to sort out and not a lot of time to do it before I was due back at work, so time was of the essence, I wrote down as many of the places that I would have to visit to make sure that at least the bills were paid, first the bank, then the building society, then the poll tax people, the list was never ending, but once I got round them all the damage wasn't as bad as I first had feared, there were one or two outstanding bills to pay, but I could deal with them, as long as I keep working then everything else will take it's course, that's what I kept telling myself, the last thing I did before I went back to work was I bought three of they electric timer switches so the lights would come on at different times in different parts of the house, hopefully giving the illusion that there was someone in, Macleod promised to check it every day but it was an additional deterrent I remember some of the local thieves saying to me, don't worry about the house when your away Big Man we'll keep an eye on it, I in turn said to them, keep your fucking eyes off my house when I'm away, I've got enough to worry about without worrying about getting broken into, and on that front I never had any problems. I phoned the Munster and told him the situation I was in and he started to pick me up and drop me off at home, when crew change days came round

The next couple of trips going offshore were going to be the hardest, I didn't want to become a recluse and withdraw into myself, keeping everything bottled up, on the other hand I didn't want to become another statistic where everyone gives you a sympathetic ear then after a while what they really want to say to you is Fuck off you Boring Bastard and tell someone else your worries, believe me after a while that's what happens, there were one or two good friends offshore that I did confide in but hopefully not to the extent that they were deliberately staying out of my way.

I was glad when the Drilling Platform started to get their drill crews sorted out and although I was quite happy working on the P.U.Q. when I was one of the Operators picked to run a crew I was quite relieved, I knew that that would keep me busy enough and keep my mind from thinking about other things, I would only be back on the P.U.Q. to eat, sleep, spend my 12 hours off and possibly do a spot of relief operating the rest of the time would be spent on the Drilling Platform.

10

The Bruce Drilling Platform

Munster phoned me to tell me that the drilling crew change would now be on a Thursday, that sounded ok to me as it meant an extra day at home, he said he would pick me up at 5am on the 4th March as the check/in time was 7-30am giving us more than enough time to make that, on the drive to Aberdeen Munster never asked any awkward questions and I was still a bit down in the mouth so I was glad of that, later on in the trip I would tell him what was going on but for now we travelled in near enough silence, we checked in at Bond as usual and after the all too familiar routine of the pre/flight brief we were soon on our way to the Bruce. But this time on the flight out I was thinking about how I was going to approach the situation I was in, I was making plans in my head that I knew that this time I would definitely have to stick too if for my own peace of mind, I knew the house would be safe and that Macleod would go round every night to check it, I had bought a couple of those electric timer switches so that the lights would come on at various times in different parts of the house to give the impression that someone was in there, so that at least was one worry out the way. What I had to do now was concentrate on the job; it was a new rig, new crew, and a new start for me.

Most of the drill crew were strangers to me, like Andy Kenyon (Driller) Duncan (Buster) McCruvie, (Derrick man) Stan (the man) Philip, (Pump-Man) the Roughnecks were, Ian Sturton and Mark Riggall, my big mate Steve Mackay was the (Assistant Driller) these were the initial guys on the rig floor but some would change crews as the years went on and others would take their place, the deck crew that I would be working with were Gordon (Gordy) Findlay,(Rousty Pusher) Nat Ritchie, Mick Casey and Jim Law, inevitably some of them would move on too, The Tool/Pushers were Hans Van Dijk, Paul Richmond, John Munn and

Dave Hutchinson, these were the guys that I would be directly accountable too.

The crane operators on here were J.M. Sutherland, Jamie Wright, Brian Sharman and myself, on the P.U.Q. were Alan Matthew and Steve Ritchie back to back with each other, the other crane op's that were there for the hook-up were placed elsewhere on other installations.

The operation that was ongoing on the rig was the connection of the wells already drilled on the seabed to the platform. Seemingly, long before the platform was installed, a semi-submersible rig called the John Shaw had pre-drilled 8 wells through a template on the seabed and capped them, waiting on the drilling rig which was us, to come along and tap into them and produce the oil and gas for export to the beach. this operation basically meant that we ran sections of casing reaching down from the platform to the seabed which screwed into the existing casing left by the John Shaw, then we ran a completion string of tubing inside the casing, connected that to the manifold and we were in business. This was a pretty straight forward operation for myself and the deck crew all we had to do was supply the rig floor with casing and tubing, to complete a pre-drilled well like this would take between 7 and 10 days where as normally it would take 3 months from start to finish. That was the main reason the Bruce produced first oil in early May of 1993.

With this being a brand new platform and possibly the flagship of the B.P. fleet of platforms. BP management made it compulsory for all employees when outside the accommodation to wear ear and eye protection, this was a non-negotional demand and failure to comply would be seen as a breach of the safety rules and could end up with disciplinary action being taken towards the offender. It wasn't as if there was a spate of people putting in claims for industrial deafness or a sudden upsurge in the eye injury department, this was a case of do as we say or you won't be here. My own personal view as with many others on the ear issue was, my granny always told me the only thing you should put in your ear is your elbow, now everybody knows you can't do that, but for someone to insist that up to at least 6 times a day you ram these foam fibre earplugs into your lughole is asking a bit much. And as for the wearing of plastic glasses which get scored and scratched and difficult to see out of when its raining or even worse when your looking up surrounded by bright floodlights in the dark, the trip hazard alone warranted common sense as to when to wear them. But the rules were carved in stone and must be obeyed.

These were just a couple of negative issues that bothered everybody, on the positive side we were to be included in the yearly Gain-share scheme being promoted by BP themselves, what this entailed was, if by the end of each year the platform had met the targets that were set, then a maximum payment of £2000 a man would be paid. This would be banked on a quarterly basis, but if for any reason one of the targets had not been met for that particular quarter then a proportion of the quarterly payment would be deducted. This £2000 maximum applied only to the contractors on the platform, the BP production guys were to get a percentage of their wages, a really big difference considering we were all supposed to be one big team. Some of the penalties came in the form of how many injuries the platform had, or if there was any damage done to the environment, like an oil spillage to the sea, oil and gas production also came into it as did the annual HSE report. You also had to be on the platform for a certain number of days during the year to qualify, But all in all it was a scheme we wouldn't have been in, if we hadn't been here, We thought all our Xmas's had come together when we found out that we would also get a well bonus, if we brought the well in under budget and on time, but were brought back to reality when told that any bonuses we earned on the wells would be deducted from the platform bonus. Still it was a really big boost to the morale on the drilling platform with everyone working together as a team should.

As the months went on there was still no sign or word from Liz, I contacted her family to see if they knew anything but the response I got was negative, nobody knew anything, that's what they told me anyway. My big mate Jim Pitcairn and myself bought a car between us, the idea was, as he was working back to back with me at the moment, he would use it when he was home and vice versa. This arrangement suited us both, I used it to drive around and see if I could find her, but when I went to her place of work nobody had even heard of her, you can imagine my frustration when an old guy, I saw waving to her anytime I drove her to work, denied even knowing her, he obviously didn't want involved, so rather than cause trouble I just left it at that, The car itself was a bit of a banger, but the £300 we paid for it was supposed to be an investment, because of the registration number,

ALS666, we thought that if we ran it into the ground then at least we could sell the number plates to some devil worshipping cult and possibly double our money, we couldn't go wrong, but things didn't work out that way because when the car was having some minor repairs done to it by one of our mates, some bastard stole it, it wasn't as if we could claim the insurance because we didn't have any, I suppose you will think that that was a bit irresponsible on our behalf, but as far as we were concerned it was a sort of devil may care attitude, anyway we never seen that car again or the number plates for that matter, although for months after that I was looking at every car that passed me, just to check its plates. (Talk about lucky white heather)

It would be at least 2 trips after we lost the car that when I got home my father Alex told me that Nicky had phoned the house asking for me, but when he told her I was away working, she just said she would phone back, but she never did.

I got into a routine of every time I went home I always bought something for the house, it might be new carpets one month then new bedding the next, but always something, I would slowly furnish the house with brand new gear, my father and sister Jane stayed there a couple of months till I got myself sorted, in that time I got a new bathroom suite and Jane's husband Billy tiled the bathroom for me, I also got some of the lads round to install a security alarm just to give me a greater piece of mind when I was away and the house lay empty, I wasn't drinking nearly as much and the gambling had all but stopped. I certainly reaped the benefits of this because one trip at the end of the year just before I went offshore, I arranged for the whole house to be double glazed and paid for it in cash, by the time I got home Jane had put drop blinds on all the windows and decorated all the bedrooms, it was like moving into a new house, I remember my sister saying she would like to come here and stay as she had everything in the house just the way she wanted it, but I liked my privacy when I was home and with Billy and her two kids Robert and Claire I wouldn't get much of that.

We had just finished the second of the 24 completed wells and work-overs that I would be involved in on here by the start of 1994, so a New Year was upon us and new challenges were to be met, we received a couple of drilling bonuses for the wells but the gain share produced nothing until 1995, I did another Survival refresher, and attended another medical examination, so that set me up for another 4 years on the Survival and 2 years on the medical, seemingly you have to attend a medical every 2 years if your over 40.and every year after that over 50. Hopefully I'd be out of here by the time I reach that age.

Things on the pipe-deck were as repetitive as ever, the only thing that was changing was the different size of Tubulars that we were working with, and like all wells, once we had finished drilling one to completion, we started all over again on the next one, operations happening on the pipe-deck were the same as all platforms that were in the drilling mode, deck space on here was just as sparse as any other rig despite it being a new platform, you would have thought that lessons would have been learned from previous designs of other installations and allocated more deck space, but that wasn't the case on here, we were always having to move things about to make room for the different sizes of pipe, Containers and baskets that came aboard, the pipe-deck was a very busy place and everybody had to have their wits about them especially when working with the crane.

We were told that we had at least 5 years work ahead of us and to tell that to drilling crews that were used to working from one well to the next, never knowing if they were going to be paid off the following trip or not, then that was an added bonus.

It was becoming apparent on here that as the crews were working a steady 2 on 2 off rotation, it was going to be the same crew that was working away from home at Xmas and New Year time, to combat this Smedvig Management came up with the idea of the crews doing a 3 week change over mid July, this would mean that only one crew would work over both the festive periods every 2 years, what this meant was, you did 3 weeks on first then 3 weeks off or vice versa, then back to a 2 on 2off rotation, this would put you on the complete opposite rotation that you had been working, this was ok until you tried to put in a request for your yearly 1 week holiday. Basically if your relief didn't cover for you, then if you really wanted a week off, you took it off losing a week's wage. Management told everyone that they should arrange their holidays on their 3 weeks off. Fine if you want to pay premium rates at the height of the holiday season, but not everyone wants to go on holiday in July. And so much for them being bothered about who was working over the festival, The only good thing on here was the platform had their annual planned shutdown usually from July to the middle of August which gave the lads up to 6 weeks off without loss of pay, but that was down to B.P. not Smedvig. The crane op's didn't get anytime off as they were needed for the shutdown, I wasn't too bothered as it made a change from the usual routine, we still worked days and nights but fell into line with the starting times the rest of the platform were working The work done during this time was work that could only be done when drilling had stopped and the production plant had shut down.

Nearly everyone worked 7 to 7 dayshift when this shutdown was on with only a few working nights, this gave me a chance to meet some of the guys working on the PUQ that I would normally have little contact with, guys like scaffolding Foreman John Barbour and scaffolders Philip (chung) Wilcox, Wee Loui, Maz, Big Lee McKenzie and Rab Smith all good guys.

The deck Foreman Bobby Booth and his crew Sandy, Jimmy, Robbie and Pedro. Were also very easy to get on with, Bobby's back to back was a guy called Frank Spence.

All these guys and many more were contractors who like myself, would stop and pass the time of day with you, but the atmosphere between most of the BP production guys and contractors was worse on here than anywhere else I had worked. I'm not taking sides and blaming one or the other but for me personally I was disgusted by a good few of the production guys and their attitude and ignorance by the way they would go out there way to look the other way or look at the ground rather than look you in the eye, or totally ignore my hello or good mornings, I expected better with this being a new platform and all the hype being showered on us from above that we were all one big happy family, in the end I ignored them, but I didn't feel right about doing that. The attitude they had adopted certainly didn't come from above, well certainly not from the first 2 O.I.M.'s that I had met, these 2 guys Peter Stewart and Ricky Walker were the salt of the earth, even though they held the position that they did, they still took time out to stop and chat to you, Peter had a habit of, if he didn't know your name the first time he spoke to you, he made a point of finding out what it was and called you by it the second time, other people of high profile were easy to speak to as well, there were the 2 General Services Supervisors (G.S.S.) Jim Hedges and Rab Gilbert I couldn't find fault with either of them, even though I didn't always see eye to eye with them, they spoke away to me and anyone else that was around without this serious air of authority that some seemed to think went with a pair of BP overalls.

This animosity was further fueled when one day everyone on the platform was called to the cinema for a discussion on a spate of minor accidents that had occurred recently, the meeting was in full swing with a lot of good positive points on safety working practices being made, the O.I.M. who was chairing the meeting was pointing to one guy after another that had his hand up offering him the chance to express his views, then when it came to one particular guy who just happened to work for BP he stood up and said, I suggest one way to stop these accidents is to pay off all the Contractors, this fucking idiot honestly believed that it was only Contractors who had accidents, the shouts of sit down and shut up you Prick, Arsehole, and Fucking Wanker said it all, the O.I.M. tried to quiet things down but I could see from his facial expression he wasn't happy with this cunt, even some of his workmates were cringing in embarrassment, but that gives you an idea of what was going on and what a small minority of the BP guys thought of us.

I'm a firm believer in every man to himself as long as it doesn't give me grief, and when I think back to some of the guys that were a treat to be associated with, guys like Gerry Nicholson, George Allan, Arthur Biggs, Chris Tyrell, those I mentioned previously and many more, if only BP could weed out these diehard antagonists who think all contractors are scum and replace them with guys like these, then their platforms would be a lot happier places to work on, and you know what they say about a happy workforce, don't you?

The drill crews came back again in late August and the drilling program commenced once again, it was a case of taking things slowly at first just to get the guys back into the swing of things again after their time off and let the new guys get settled into the routine, but it wouldn't be long until operations were back up to full speed again, Working on the deck demanded full concentration at all times, especially when the crane was involved. That was why I tried to keep the experienced guys on deck an send the less experienced to do other tasks, but operations don't always allow this, it was a case of make do with who you have,

It was when I was home on leave in August that I learned my big mate Jim Pitcairn had been medi-vaced from the rig Emerald Producer, seemingly as per procedure, a few minutes before the helicopter he was on made its approach to the installation, the passengers were told to pull on their survival hoods, while doing this he severely twisted his neck, he was given first aid immediately on arrival but a couple of days later it was evident his condition was getting worse, he was eventually returned to the beach where after weeks of physiotherapy it was decided an operation was required to sort out some problem in his neck, Jim never worked offshore again after that incident due to incapacity. To this day he still has pains in his neck; it just goes to show that you don't have to be working to injure yourself, who would have thought that an everyday task of putting on a hood would ruin you for life. It would be a few years later before this all in one type of survival suit was replaced by the more robust but much more comfortable type, with the hood neatly stored inside a pocket attached to one of the legs, ready for use if needed.

The passing of time was, as the saying goes, beginning to be a good healer, but although I was subsequently single again, I wasn't leading a bachelors life, when I was at home I would still go out during the day and have a few beers with the lads, but I would stay in at night and do the household chores, I was certainly becoming very domesticated what with learning how to iron my shirts without burning a hole in them, I was fed up having to wear a jumper because the shirt was all creased, I also found a way to put a crease in the legs of my black trousers without putting a shine on them that I could see my face in, I would now do lots of things that I normally had done for me, like cleaning the windows, hovering the carpets and polishing the furniture, doing the washing, changing the bedclothes, getting the messages and things like that, all the monthly bills were now paid by direct debit, the only things I had to pay cash for were for power cards and the monthly gas payment scheme, I was now doing all the things that I normally took for granted, because they were usually done for me, but now I was determined to be independent, I never wanted to rely on anyone again, that way I would not be disappointed, I would only have myself to blame if things went wrong. Before I went back offshore in September 94 I started one of those saving plans that promised to give you a better return for your money than any High street Bank or Building Society at the end of the plans term. After the first year's monthly payments the installments rose by 10% for each year after that, so after 11 years if I kept the plan going I would never be skint again, roll on the Year 2005.

Munster and me picked up another passenger to travel with us, his name was George Paterson, from Kirkcaldy, (Fife), George was one of the rig Electricians and as he only stayed 6 miles away from me, we decided that he might as well travel with us, it would save him money on train fares and digs and also give Munster a bit extra cash, I'll never forget the first time the 3 of us traveled together, It was late November and we were running about ¾ of an hour late as Munster had to dig the car out of the snow, by the time we arrived in Dundee it was 6.45am with a good 1 hours journey ahead of us to Aberdeen, the roads were fine, there was no snow up there, but it was pitch black and freezing cold as we hammered the wee Mini Metro "Munster called Betsy" up the duel carriageway trying to make the 7.30 am check/in, George was dozing in the back and I was listening to the radio when all of a sudden both lanes of the duel carriageway lit up, not once, but twice in quick succession, Munster turned to me and said, did you see that lightning Big Man?, I turned to look at him and said, I think you'll find that lightning was the fucking speed camera Munster, at that he hammered on the brakes to slow us down, I said, it's a bit late for that now Munster, don't you think? That's when he mumbled, what a stupid place to have a Fucking Speed camera.

We arrived at Bond Helicopters just as the last 2 guys were checking in so full marks to Munster and his driving he was worried about the Speed camera and getting a few penalty points on his license but he never heard anymore about it, obviously there was no tape in that particular camera.

Back on the rig again my back to back JM Sutherland told me that they were half way through drilling another well, so I knew we would have a reasonably busy trip and like after every shore leave, it doesn't take long to get back into the usual routine again because as soon as you set foot on the rig it feels as if you've never been away.

As with every platform that has drilling personnel onboard, there is always a bit of friendly banter with the other contractor's and the catering staff, on here was no different, The 2 catering supervisors (camp bosses as their called offshore) working back to back, were Alan Mitchell and Jim Howarth, I only saw Alan for a couple of days near the end of my trip, but saw Jimmy for the first 11 days, Jimmy was a die-hard Glasgow Celtic supporter who took great delight in rubbing my nose in the proverbial shit, if my team the Glasgow Rangers were not performing to well and when this happened one day Jim's sense of humor would be tested to the limit. The majority of the guys I worked with were Rangers men as well so if I was getting ribbed by him then so were they. Jim was like your original Glasgow Spiv, always immaculate in his dress, what hair he had left was brushed back and his wee black mustache neatly trimmed, everything about him was perfect and that reflected on his catering skills as well, he took great pride in the presentation of the food that was prepared but as usual all this hype was wasted on us, all we wanted was something quick and hot to eat, then it was back to work or off to bed. This particular day Jimmy was out mingling in the galley talking to the top table guys, the O.I.M, the G.S.S., the O.I.E. (Offshore Inspection Engineer) the O.O.E. (Offshore Operations Engineer) and a few other head bummers, we had just finished working nightshift so it was about 12 30pm, I had finished eating and had just stood up to take my plate back to the plate rack to get it washed when Jimmy asked me sarcastically, did you enjoy your meal sir? I turned to him and in a voice loud enough for the top table men to hear I said, Jimmy, I've always said that after a good days work, there's nothing like a good meal and that was Fucking nothing like a good meal. With that buzzing in his ear I fucked off, but I could still hear the laughter from some of the drill crew as I left the galley. Luckily everyone saw the funny side of it including Jimmy or I could have been in trouble. Maybe red carded for dissent, I wonder to this day if he and his partner still sit in the bath and drink a bottle of champagne on his first night home. (Jimmy you're a wee Toff).

The catering crew that were working near enough the same rota as myself were a fine bunch of people, ordinary punters like myself working towards the same goal that was, to get out there, do the job, and get home again as quickly as possible, everybody had their duties to perform, people like Gavin, Grant, Alex and Big Stewart were chefs and bakers, based in the galley itself, then there were the stewardesses Aggie, Martha, Annette, Christine, Grace, Sharon, Shirley and Cathy, Cathy used to make sure I got the weekly edition of the Racing and Football Outlook before it went missing, these women would make sure your rooms were always clean and tidy, they also delivered your clean laundry to outside your room door ready for you in the morning, As you can imagine with the number of guys on board, "usually about 170 or more", the language at times could be a little bit choice, that never bothered the women because they were all over eighteen and could give, as good as they got, so there was nobody more surprised than me when one trip as soon as we arrived on the platform, we were all called to the cinema for a meeting with the new O.I.M. After his initial speech and Informing us that we were well paid for the work we were doing, he then proceeded to tell us to curb our bad language in front of the stewardesses, fuck knows where they got this guy from but if he had been on a couple of trips previous he would have heard a stewardess "not one of the ones named above" recite her favorite saying, which was, there's nearly 6 mile of Fucking Pricks in the North Sea and I cannae get 6 Fucking inches on here. And unless he was walking about the accommodation with his ear plugs in he surely must have heard "one I have named above" telling guys, too get their Fucking dirty boots off my floor Ya Bastards, because she'd just washed it. Talking like this is normal on rigs, from both women and men and nobody really pays any attention to it, or takes offence, Don't get me wrong it's not like everybody walks about cursing and swearing all day just for the sake of it, I suppose the reasoning behind the cursing is, it's quicker to tell someone to Fuck off, than go into an explanation of why you want them to go away. So unless this guy gags everybody, he will have to get used to it.

The way the shift rota was turned around back in July, it meant that I was off the rig for both Xmas and the New Year. So it was January the 5th 1995 that we arrived back on the rig to be greeted by the news that the Gain-share payment for all contractors would be £1200 paid out in February, that sounded good to us, but when we were reminded that any bonuses earned from drilling would be deducted from that, we were, shall we say, disappointed, we had had a couple of bonuses from drilling which amounted to about £650 so deduct that from £1200 and we were left with £550, less tax of course. I must admit the drilling bonuses on here were pretty regular but not once in all the time spent on here did we ever receive the full £2000, there was always some reason or another that they deducted money from the pot, and a few people, myself included thought that BP were prone to moving the goalposts to suit themselves whenever it looked like the targets might just be met.

Munster, George and me were into a routine now, as soon as we hit the beach Munster would drive Wee Betsy to the nearest cash and carry, where either George or myself, depending on who's turn it was, would get out and buy the carryout usually 4 cans of beer each for the journey home, Munster would get sweeties and a couple of cans of juice, the cans would be finished by the time we reached my house so they would come in and use the toilet, giving me time to put my dirty washing into the machine and set it on a universal wash, then Munster would drop me off at my local before heading away to drop off George, on this particular day one of my mates Keith Roberts was in the pub, home from working down in Africa, the pub was in full swing, there was Pitcairn, Macleod, Rab Whyte, James T Kirk and a few others, all tanked up with the drink, I only intended having a quiet couple of pints but that didn't happen, 20 minutes after I got in we started drinking double vodkas and beer chasers, I was starving after about 2 hours and was ready for going home when one of the local lads said he was going to the chip-shop and asked did anybody want anything, I asked him to get me 2 single smoked sausages and a portion of chips and handed him £10, when he came back he gave me the parcel and £5,-20 pence change, I looked at him and asked, what did you get me?, he said a double sausage supper, but when I opened it up and looked sitting in the polystyrene tray was one and a half pieces of sausage and a small portion of chips, fuck this I thought, that cunt in the chip shop is taking the piss again with his short measures and I decided I was going up to see him, I wrapped up the parcel and left it on the table while I went to the toilet, on returning I picked it up and headed off to the chip-shop, by the time I got there the shop was mobbed, but I went straight to the front of the queue and demanded to know what the fuck he was playing at with his short measures, (a classic case of when the drinks in the wit is out) he was looking at me in bewilderment wondering what I was talking about, that's never a double sausage supper I told him and I want my fucking money back, I looked round and there was my big mate Pitcairn, he had followed me to make sure I didn't get into any trouble, on turning back to the counter the owner had unwrapped the parcel and there staring me in the face was about 10 chips and 2 wee bits of smoked sausage, seemingly while I was in the toilet the lads had helped themselves to my supper, but the damage was done, there was no backing down now, I still wanted my money back regardless, for all the short measures he had given me in the past, I could hear Jimmy arguing with this guy in the queue, the guy insisting he was an off duty policeman, Jimmy didn't believe him and told him so, (but he was) and when the guy tried to take hold of Jimmy he ended up with a sore face for his trouble, then all hell broke loose when some of the customers started to get involved, Jimmy and me were standing back to back like something out of the Fucking Alamo swinging punches at everything that moved but we were that drunk we were hitting air most of the time, we were still swinging when 2 police cars and a van arrived, Inevitably we were thrown into the back of the van and as we were being driven away I could see Macleod watching us from the pavement, I couldn't even wave to him as my hands like Jimmy's were handcuffed behind my back, after a night in the cells we were taken to court where through a court appointed lawyer we pled not guilty to all charges, we were then bailed to appear at a different date for trial, this went on for months, the Procurator Fiscal wanted to (lock us up) or as he put it, impose a custodial sentence for our crimes, the charges against us were, Breach of the Peace, Assault, Drunk and Disorderly, Racist Remarks, Malicious Damage to Property, Causing an affray and Resisting Arrest, just about every charge they can think of when you get arrested for being drunk, two of the dates that we were supposed to appear in court I was away working, so through our lawyer we got them postponed until a later date, finally through our lawyer we agreed to plead guilty to two charges of Breach of the Peace and Assault, with the promise of receiving a fine, but when we did eventually appear in court and the P.F. read out all the charges to the Magistrate, we couldn't believe it, this was the last thing we expected, we thought the only charges that would be mentioned was the ones we were pleading guilty too.

We both stood in the dock looking pretty sheepish until the Judge asked Jimmy if he had called the owner of the chip shop a black bastard. Jimmy replied, Oh no your honor, what I said was, the sausage was black ya bastard. Just then I thought I was going to burst a gut, it took me all my time not to laugh but it was a struggle I can tell you. I'm sure the Judge would have sent both of us across the water to Saughton Prison in Edinburgh if I had. In the end he fined us both £250 and sent us on our way. That was the dearest smoked sausage supper I never had. As you can imagine we both took some stick from the guys in the pub for a long time afterwards.

The Roughnecks on my crew were a great bunch of lads, it always seemed that I was working with the best crew on the rig, but I suppose every crew thought that they were the best, what I can say is, there was never a dull moment with these lads they would get up to all sorts as a crew an as individuals, one guy who seemed to have seen and done everything in life, was a guy called Jimmy the Witness, he got this nickname because if anything happened in the place that Jimmy was in at the time, he saw it, you couldn't come right out and call Jimmy a liar, that would be unfair, maybe a stranger to the truth would be more apt, when the crew met up again after our leave we would swap stories about what we had done in our 2 weeks off, everybody took a turn at this, and with all narrated stories a wee bit of exaggeration was bound to creep in, and that was accepted, just to make the story more interesting, but with Jimmy, it was different to say the least, he started off his stories with "you won't believe this but" and he would come out with some whoppers believe me, like when he was at home if he wasn't jamming on his guitar with Johnnie Cash or John Denver or some other celebrity that just happened to pop in to his local pub, then he was down in London touching up some priceless paintings for the National Art Gallery, failing that he would probably be putting the final touches to the latest fishing boat he was building, now you might think that us grown men would have fucked him off, but the entertainment value was priceless, one time on leave he told us he bought a Thunderbird 1000cc motorbike and went haring about the country side with it reaching speeds of up to 130-150 mph on the straights, one day he was going that fast he said that when he reached the bottom of this hill there standing in the middle of the road, was a cow. Jimmy said he knew couldn't stop in time, so he just kept going and cut the cow clean in half, I'll never forget the look on that cows face he said, "with a hint of sadness in his voice" as I went clean through it, the rest of us were doubled up with laughter, then there was the time he went on holiday to Florida, Jimmy re-called there was a typhoon blowing on his first night there, but he didn't hear anything after he closed the double glazed windows of the beach apartment he was staying in, so you can imagine his surprise when he woke the next morning and found a Great White shark covered in seaweed and chewing an empty 45 gallon oil drum thrashing about on his balcony, all these stories were taken with a pinch of salt, but as long as Jimmy narrated them, he would always have an audience, but Jimmy had a sort of death wish as far as his job went, he was always threatening to pack in, there wasn't a trip went by without Jimmy telling the Driller or Tool Pushers that he had had enough and was going home in the morning, but they usually humored him and told him not to be so stupid and get back to work, this was becoming a regular occurrence until one night when he told the Pusher he was going home the next day, the Pusher said, ok then come up to the office and sign your resignation letter and you can go home tomorrow, Jimmy should have backed down there and then, but he didn't, in the office his resignation was typed out and Jimmy signed it, then he went over to the P.U.Q. where obviously after some thought, he phoned the Pusher and tried to retract his resignation but it was too late, he had cried wolf too many times and the Pushers were sick of him, to rub salt into his wounds the weather closed in and Jimmy was fogged on for another 2 days and he was off the pay-role, all I can say is, for a man that had ballooned round the world in less days than it took Phileas Fogg, you would have thought that he would have checked the weather forecast before telling the Pusher to stick the job up his Arse.

Like all rigs the whole world over they run on a budget, this one was no different, everything was done at a price and usually when the suppliers find out that the equipment ordered was for an Oil platform the price seems to go sky high, not only that, the cost of transporting the equipment offshore is also highway robbery, This was all cascaded down to the Crane operators one day "although not in the way I've put it" after being summoned to one of the regular Logistics meetings held by the upper management on here, we were reminded of the cost of the Supply Boats while they were sitting alongside the platform and were encouraged to get them Offloaded and Back/loaded as quickly but safely as possible, because once they were away from our Installation they were being paid for out of some other rigs budget, The other crane operators and myself took this speech with a pinch of salt, we were working the boats as quickly as possible and as far as BP logistics on the beach were concerned this platform had the quickest turn around of Supply Boats in the whole BP fleet of platforms in the North Sea, to show their appreciation for this and the way we managed the lifting equipment they awarded each of the operators and the crane mechanics £250 for our efforts, We were over the moon by this gesture, but after this latest meeting on the platform we were all pissed off, the reason was, Management on here wanted an extra 5 ton an hour on top of the average tonnage we were giving them which was about 25 ton an hour excluding Tubulars, their reckoning was, the boat cost £12 a minute while it was working alongside, that worked out at £720 an hour, "not too bad if you own the boat" and every hour saved on working time was £720 saved on the budget. They also wanted us to think of ways to speed up the operation and give them feed back as to how, I never really gave it much thought, until one night while we were waiting on the boat finishing at the P.U.Q. so we could start working it on the Drilling Platform, my big mate Alan Matthew called me on the radio to tell me he had one more lift to go down to the boat then he was finished with it, I expected the boat to be alongside me in about 10 minutes and informed Gordy to get the guys ready for then, but an hour later I was still sitting in the crane waiting, I called Alan on the radio to see what the problem was, and what he told me blew the whole logistics thing out the fucking water. What he said was he was waiting on the skipper of the boat to send up the money for the cigarettes that were sent down to him and his crew. I couldn't fucking believe it, Firstly, how could they justify the boat waiting alongside doing nothing, Secondly, they obviously didn't trust the Drilling guys to look after whatever money was in the envelope, and Thirdly, why didn't they send the boat round to the Drilling Platform and send one of the P.U.Q. deck crew over to pick up the bag with the money in it saving an hours work and £720, The feedback I gave them was, somebody's needing their Arse kicked here, and it isn't one of us for a change. I can honestly say that didn't go down too well, but as the saying goes, "the truth always hurts".

As the age old saying goes, if its not a feast it's a famine, this could be said about what was happening on here, there wasn't many rigs that could boast about a 5 year drilling contact like we could, but that fact didn't reflect what was happening on the wages front, it seemed to be that as soon as the wage rise subject reared its ugly head management came up with excuse after excuse as to why they couldn't give us one, favorite ones were, the downturn in the drilling industry, or, to remain competitive we must blah, blah, blah. This was all very well but we hadn't had a wage rise for the last 3 years, and if that wasn't bad enough they actually stopped some of the perks that made up the wages structure, for instance they stopped paying for taxis taking the men to their digs and the airport, I suppose there was some sense in doing that because they stopped paying for the digs as well, to soften the blow they came up with an allowance to help pay towards your outlay, but it still came up short of what people were actually paying out in expenses, hence you were even worse off at the end of the month but trying to get management to accept this was hopeless, over the years the offshore worker especially in the drilling sector, has lost out in terms of monetary value in the sense that wages have not risen to combat inflation, if you consider that now there's no extra payment for bank or public holidays, or for attending the weekly boat drills, or the safety meetings that can drag on for an hour or more it's no wonder people get pissed off especially when its compulsory that you do attend,

I remember having an argument with the rig manager about having to attend the pre-tour tool box talk, what this involved was spending 15 minutes a day of your own time before shift discussing the planned events for that day. My gripe was that after doing this for 2 weeks then adding it up over the 13 trips I done offshore a year I was working 45 hours a year for nothing. That's like someone on the beach working a week for their employer and not get paid for it, I was told that it was compulsory for me to attend these meetings and basically if I didn't then I would be looking for another job, I knew the choice was mine and relented, but it would be interesting to see how an industrial tribunal would look at it. Wages for working offshore were good in the early days but as the years have gone on the wages have remained stagnant, that's why you'll find that the majority of people who leave the Offshore Oil industry and finds a job on the beach will not be drawn back to the offshore game, they know they will not be much worse off at the end of the month, and at least they will be home every night. The only thing that draws people to the offshore game now is the time off; it's certainly not the money.

By the time the crews done their 3 week change over it was August and there was talk on the platform that another module was being planned for the following year 1996 this was to be joined to the drilling package by a bridge and was going to enhance the Oil and Gas production from the Platform itself, the whole project was going to impact on the drilling program by over 6 months that meant that the crews would be off the rig for more than half the year, it wasn't going to affect the crane operators as we would be needed to lift the various sizes of pipes into place for the riggers, but that was a long way off there was still over a year of drilling to go yet.

Safety is paramount on all Offshore installations and this one was no exception, we were always told that no job is so important that time can't be taken to do it safely. This was all very well until things turned to rat shit and the pushers were getting hassle from upstairs, and you know what happens then? The shit starts to run downhill doesn't it, I've seen it happen time and time again, people running around like headless chickens trying to put right whatever went wrong, but getting nowhere fast, that's when the accidents happen and when they do, the first people on the scene is usually the medic, Davy Wilson was relief medic and a proper gent then there was the two regular guys Tom and Dick I don't remember their ever being a Harry but there might have been after I left, Tom was an easy going guy with a big bushy mustache, there was nothing he wouldn't do for you and anytime I had cause to visit him I was treated like a patient not a contractor. But Dick on the other hand was a BP man through and through, he didn't like being called Dick, he liked being called Richard but he deserved the name so that's why we called him it, I remember on one occasion I had to visit him when I had a sore throat, I asked him for some lozenges to ease it, I just can't give you lozenges without first examining you, was his reply, and at that I was sat in the chair as he pressed down my tongue with one of those lollypop sticks and looking down my throat, telling me to say ahhh, then he asked me if I smoked, I told him yes thanks, I'll have an embassy regal if you've got one, this didn't seem to go down to well as he ushered me out the door telling me to gargle with salt water, another time I was looking for a bottle of Benolyn off him to help me sleep, but was told there was none, I couldn't argue so I left, but while I was sitting having a cigarette I noticed a BP guy coming out of Dick's surgery holding a bottle of the stuff that he didn't have, I thought you Bastard, I sat there seething until I said to myself Fuck it, and went back to confront him, when I told him what I'd seen, and that as there was no supply boat alongside or that I didn't hear the helicopter landing bringing him fresh supplies, I just wondered if he was showing a wee bit of favoritism to the BP guy's over the Contractors and if he was, I would be interested to hear what the OIM had to say about it, that

190

seemed to do the trick I got my bottle of Benolyn, albeit a small one. These to me were all pretty petty things, but the one that cost Jamie Wright his job was more serious, what happened was, Jamie went to see the Medic on his crew change day just before the chopper arrived, he was wanting some medicine for the cold he had, he was given some Codeine Linctus and sent on his way, but Jamie was going for his medical the next day and the Codeine Linctus he had taken showed up in his urine sample as a banned substance, they didn't tell him it was Codeine Linctus they just said he had taken a banned substance. Jamie insisted he took nothing, not even mentioning the Linctus until later, The trouble that caused was unreal, when they did check up the medic hadn't recorded giving Jamie anything so denied it, and Jamie couldn't prove he had, it was only when Jamie went to his own doctor to try and make some sense out of it all, that it came to light, for a man that didn't smoke, drink tea or coffee, that bottle of Linctus caused a whole load of grief, Jamie was eventually re-instated but it just goes to show you how things can happen.

Safety Training Observation Programme (STOP) was a system introduced on here in 1995, it was a system to be used by the workforce to help make our workplace a safer place to be, at first it was used to highlight problem areas where people were being forgetful in their approach to their duties, to explain in layman's terms it worked like this, if you saw someone working or acting in an unsafe manner, then you would approach them and hold a discussion until both parties agreed that the were happy and that the offender had seen the error of his ways and wouldn't do what he was doing wrong again, this was fine to start with then some people would take offence at being STOP carded and would go out of their way to STOP card you back, it was all seen as good fun until the Management decided that everybody must use the system, what was at first a way of making the place safer to work in and some lessons being learned, was now becoming a number's game, people were told to put in at least 2 STOP cards a trip making a mockery of what the system was all about, what was happening was people were now making up incidents and re-cording them as actual events, so once management looked these over on the beach they were not getting a true account of events highlighted as possible high risk potential accidents, some of the favorites recorded were people not wearing glasses or gloves, people running down stairs or not holding onto the handrail, nobody could prove that these events happened because the system was a no name no blame system, but on the beach management thought that everyone was running around the rig without gloves or glasses on because that's what most of the cards had highlighted, I blame them for abusing a system that could have worked, but for the fact they wanted quantity in the cards, not quality.

Throughout this book you will have noticed that I mention that a pat on the back does nothing for the guys and once again I bring it up, for the past 4 years the crew I've worked with have not had an accident or Lost Time Incident (L.T.I.) this is a major achievement anywhere, never mind on a rig that's in full swing, but the reward for this milestone came in the form of a fire-blanket, that's not much better than the first aid kit we got the year before, but its certainly better than the 2 years before that when we got Fuck All, but we could always rely on the management to send out the letter of praise telling us what good guys we were and to keep up the good work, now we all know that nobody wants to see anybody being hurt, and we also know that a good safety record will go a long way to retaining and winning contracts for the company, but I ask you, to give first aid kits to people who haven't had an accident for 3 years is like giving a gallon of petrol to someone who has a diesel car.

1995 went out as quick as it came in with only a few changes to personnel and some more wells being drilled, some people were promoted and some just left, the changes to the Maintenance team had the most impact, Sandy Bruce and Paul McCabe were made Chief Mechanics being replaced by Jim Brown and Dave Cartwright as the Crane Mechanics, Alistair (PIP) Murray moved on, Paul was later replaced by Callum Stewart when he moved to an office job on the beach, the rest of the Mechanics were Bruce Fraser, Davy Taylor and Frank McPherson, the sparkys were Ziggy, Marcus Ross, Alan Bleasdale and George Paterson, with the welders Neil Cowie, and Ernie Milne, being replaced by Ronnie Johnson when Ernie moved on, and on his own was Wee Mark McGill as the Instrument Tech. all a right motley crew if ever there was one.

The start of 96 saw a few changes with the Management as well, Andy Harper was replaced earlier by Eammon Coyle who himself would move on, and be replaced by a number of different Rig Managers, Hans Van Dijk left so Dave Hutchison took his place as Day Pusher back to back with Paul Richman, our Driller

Andy Kenyon went back to back with Munster as the Night Pushers, making way for a different number of drillers on our crew, but the biggest impact for me was when Wee Gordy Findlay left to work for the platform deck crew. Gordy had worked for Smedvig longer than I had, he was working on a different crew when we both worked on the North West Hutton so a more experienced hand you couldn't ask for Gordy knew every operation off by heart, he could tell the size of Elevators and Slips just by looking at them and I thought myself lucky to have him and Nat Ritchie working with me, but like everything else in the Drilling game if you blow smoke up people's arses for long enough then they'll get fed up and that's what happened here, Since the Hutton days Gordy was promised the next crane operator's job when it came up, he had been through his stage 1 and 2 and all he needed was experience on working the boats but that was never going to happen on here Management kept on stalling and Gordy got fed up, so when an opportunity arose and a vacancy became available for the deck crew Gordy applied and became successful, ever since that day Gordy never looked back, overnight he was given a £5,000 a year pay rise plus a pension, all I can say is the Drilling Company lost a loyal employee that was sadly missed all because they dangled the carrot for too long.

The run up too July saw a lot of changes on the crew, the only regular guy was Wee Nat, the roustys were made up from Agency hands or guys from other rigs working overtime, Nat should have been made up to Rousty Pusher but they brought in a more experienced guy called Ronnie Cussiter, Ronnie had worked as Jim Pitcairn's back to back on the Fulmar Platform so he knew the score, all in all I never knew who would be on the crew from one month to the next but we were all supposed to blend in and work as a team, but with this shutdown looming ahead nobody knew what was going to happen, there was talk about the rig being shutdown for a year or more so they could concentrate on the planned extension, people were beginning to wonder if it was time to move on, there was no way BP was going to keep 4 crews of guys on full wages while they sat idle on the beach, there were rumours about splitting the guys up and sending them elsewhere but that couldn't be guaranteed, everyone was speculating and every week brought a new rumor, Management came out to the platform with their usual "don't worry boy's everything will be ok" attitude, but only the really naïve believed that, I think most wanted to believe there would be jobs for everyone but in the drilling game that never happens.

From the middle of June it was becoming apparent that the only guys staying on here from the drilling side during the shutdown was the maintenance guys and a couple of Tool Pushers along with 4 crane op's, 2 of these were the regular guys on the P.U.Q. that left 4 of us to fill 2 places and to determine who was staying, Management did an appraisal on the 4 of us, the outcome was that J.M. Sutherland and myself were picked to stay leaving Brian Sharman and Jamie out, and by the second week in July everyone who was going had gone, Brian found himself a job working in a local shipyard and Jamie found some Agency work.

With the whole of the pipe-deck cleared and the rig floor empty of all tubulars "these were sent back to the beach for inspection" there was all the room in the world to start bringing on the baskets containing the various sizes of pipes that were going to be connected together from the top deck of the P.U.Q. all the way down the Module across the top of the bridge then around the North West side of the drilling platform to await connection to the new Compression and Reception Module (CR) being installed there, the modules jacket was already pile driven into place and the lifting barge the Thialf was going to lift the module into place when it arrived, this new module would be connected to the drilling platform by a bridge which already had sections of these pipes already secured on top of it awaiting connection to the others, this was all going to take time and manpower so it was no surprise when The Bears were brought back out, to do their thing so to speak.

J.M.and myself were working back to back with each other on dayshift 7 to 7 basically working with the riggers as required, sometimes I would sit for hours just holding onto a section of pipe while it was welded to another one and so on, it was really something to watch these riggers at work, to watch them move section after section of pipe from sometimes impossible positions where the crane couldn't reach like the top of the bridge for example, and get them into place by chain-hoist and snatch-block was an experience indeed, the 2 riggers I was mostly involved in working with were a guy from Glenrothes called Ian Fowler (Foxy) as he liked to be called and a guy from down South called Keith Johnson (Johna) what these 2 guy's didn't know about rigging wasn't worth knowing, there was none of the head scratch-

194

ing and shrugging of the shoulders with these 2 men that you normally find when a complicated rigging job comes up, these 2 had obviously been around and knew exactly what was what, 2 of the welders were Anton Desouza from Dundee and Steve Hands from Montrose, another guy I became very friendly with was a Plater from Inverness called Davie Ross, Wee Davie and I became the best of pals spending time in each others company Onshore as well as Offshore, to this day he's a regular visitor to my home, another operation ongoing at the same time was the destruct of the old drill cuttings system on the BOP deck and the installation of the new one, this was another big project and once finished would see the drill cuttings re-injected down another well instead of being left on the sea bed, another first for the Environment.

B.P. wanted to be seen as the frontrunner when it came to protecting the Environment and this was promoted on here in the form of segregation, in the past a waste skip was exactly that, everything that was considered waste went into it, but now there were skips for all kinds of waste, Plastic, Paper, Polystyrene, Wood, Metal, Glass, all were kept in different skips and everyone offshore took time to adhere to this policy, it just seemed a pity that when I was home I only had one rubbish bucket where everything but hot ashes went into, later the council gave me 2 buckets, one for paper and the other for everything else, but it still seems a pity when you see things that obviously could be recycled go into a landfill site.

J.M. and me didn't bother with the 3 week change over in July, we had decided that I would work Xmas and he would work New Year this suited him as he had a young family and I wasn't bothered either way, but it was still strange to get Xmas and Boxing Day off this would never have happened if the drill crews had still been on the rig, it was common practice for the other contractors to have both days off but never drilling, this used to piss the drilling guys off especially as the other contractors were paid extra for working what was classed as public holiday days, but that was the drilling way and nothing was going to change that, it was more important to make hole, as they say in the drilling game than to keep the men sweet by giving them time off. That would have been asking too much, as usual I didn't bother with Xmas lunch but still enjoyed the fact that I didn't have to go out to work. Some of the lads I was working with couldn't believe we didn't get time off, and when I told them that at meal breaks we weren't allowed to sit around the accommodation they thought I was taking the piss, I explained to them that the recreation room and the television lounge were out of bounds to drilling at these times, the rule was, once you have your meal and your on shift, you were required back on the drilling package to finish off your break. I remember one time when Jamie broke this rule, after he had finished his breakfast one morning while on nightshift he went to the snooker room at about 5-45 am he was playing a game of snooker with one of his roustys, watching them playing were 2 BP guys who went to complain to their supervisor that because 2 drilling guys were playing they couldn't get on, this was reported to the Tool-Pusher who hauled Jamie over the coals for his actions, now the question I asked myself then was, did these 2 BP guys finish early that day as they were working 7 till 7 and if they did were they reprimanded, or did they get up early to have a game of snooker before starting shift as you would normally do, (as if) or was it as I expect another dig at the contractor for being a contractor.

Things were taking shape and by March 97 some of the wire line crews were being mobilized to come out, this meant that a nightshift crane operator would be needed to do lifts as required, so JM and myself reverted onto nights with the crane Mechanics doing the lifts required for the platform during the day, the Installation of the new pipe work was over 2 thirds finished with only the new platform to be connected but here they hit a snag, there was nowhere to hang chain-blocks to transfer the pipes and the platform cranes couldn't reach, to combat this they welded an old mobile Telescopic Grove Crane to the deck at the North West end of the Drilling Platform sent us to Sparrows Yard in Aberdeen for a day to learn how to operate it and the operation commenced, it was around this time that there was talk of the crews coming back in June and I spoke to Paul Richman about my mate Jamie getting his job back when they did, all I wanted to do was plant the seed in his head when they started to recruit again, but things have a way of either working against you or for you and what happened worked out for me and Jamie, Alan Matthew the crane op on the PUQ injured himself while on leave, it seemed that he would be off work for quite some time, his relief didn't like doing over-time so it was left up to Smedvig to supply cover for him, JM and myself were asked to work a 3 on 1 off Rota until Alan was back but I didn't feel right and neither did J.M. about working overtime while one of us was on the dole, that's when I approached Paul again about Jamie and he said if we would cover for a trip then he would see about Jamie coming back. And that's what happened, Jamie was brought back and so was another guy I worked with before on the Omikron, a guy called John Manley, which was the 4 operators working on the Drilling package when the crews came back nearly a year after leaving.

Things soon got back to normal on the rig, with over a year of drilling time lost it was essential that the drilling program was started again and before long the new starts to the crews soon blended in and became a team, there were a couple of new guys on the rig floor Ian Sturton and Dave Skinner (Freaky) and on the deck were a couple of Agency guys Jimmy English and Jimmy Mustard I used to call them English Mustard. These guys were all experienced hands and could be left to work on their own which made my job much easier, Ian was a likeable loudmouthed guy who would shout rather than talk, I always thought he was deaf or maybe he thought that we were all deaf, the funniest thing about Ian was every Saturday after the Lottery was drawn he either had 4 winning numbers or 5 but he always stopped short of 5 and the bonus ball and never once got 6, we used to take bets on how many numbers he would have correct, don't get me wrong Ian would show us the numbers written in his wee book but they were written in pencil and would most certainly be the top or bottom line and we never got to see them until after the lottery was drawn, everyone would wind him up about this and he would go ballistic getting himself all worked up until he was so red in the face you thought his head was going to burst, another thing that got him going was someone sprinkling sugar in the coffee tray or used teabags left on the drip tray under the tea urn so people would do this deliberately to wind him up and believe me it worked. I must admit I used to wind him up just to see how long it took to get him 5000 feet in the air and back down again, but he got his own back when one trip I let my big mate Mackay cut my hair, I don't know what it is about working Offshore that makes your hair grow so fast maybe it's the salt air, anyway, I always got into the habit of getting my hair cut short at least once a month when I was at home, until one time I was too busy and went offshore badly needing one, sitting in the tea/shack before the end of shift we got talking about haircuts and one thing led to another, Mackay starting talking about the electric hair trimmer he had and if I really wanted a hair cut he would do it for me, you really can't go wrong with this trimmer he said, you just choose the setting and away you go, Fuck knows why I let myself get talked into this, but I did, in his room that night Mackay was all ready with towels on the floor to catch the hairs and the trimmer all charged up ready, I was soon seated in the chair and Mackay was going slowly with the trimmer at first, doing quite a good job as far as I could see, I was supposed to be having a number 3 setting of the hair cutting trimmer and everything was going ok until the trimmer started to drone a wee bit, I wasn't worried as Mackay said it always did that, the time I did become worried was when it stopped altogether and wouldn't fucking start again, still I thought everything was ok as I headed off for a shower, that's when I knew something was not right, in the shower there was tufts of hair falling off my scalp, when I looked in the mirror there wasn't a fucking square inch of hair the same length, going back to MacKay's room he was nowhere to be seen and neither was the trimmer, there was nothing left to do but wait until the trimmer was charged up again, so you can imagine the stick I took at work the next day sitting there looking like I had been stricken down with Alopecia over night, I went to see Brian (Robbo) Robinson who was the Driller on the opposite shift from us and he got his hair trimmer and cleaned up the mess Vee Door Mackay (as he was nicknamed after that) had made, I ended up looking like someone out of the film (The Hills Have Eyes) the only thing that was missing was the Banjo, and when I got home and visited my regular hairdresser asking if he could do anything with it he said yes, in about 8 weeks. There is a lesson to be learned here, and I'll let you work out what it is.

The shutdown in July 97 was only for 6 weeks so by the time the crews were mobilized again, it was the start of September, things ticked along nicely until the end of the year when there was a rumor of another big shutdown coming in the New Year, this didn't do much for the morale of the guys, they could see there wasn't a lot of activity in the North Sea, other drilling companies were either laying guys off because of lack of work, and the contracts that Smedvig had, were either fully manned or were themselves in shut-down mode, one bad sign for the Drilling companies is when Semi-Submersibles start to anchor off Invergordon and Methil that's a sure sign that the Operators have stopped Exploration for a while, and when that happens the knock on effect, affects everyone. So the rule of thumb when you see that happening is, if you have a job try and keep it.

I was never one for volunteering for courses only the ones I really needed, but if it was one that had to be done to keep my job then I had no choice but to attend, some of these courses were just nonsense stuff, I mean the content of some of these courses could be put over to you in a couple of hours not stretched to 1 day or sometimes 2 days out of your leave if you had an early morning start and you had to travel the day before, courses like Computer Based Rigging & Slinging, or Computer Based Manual Handling what's the fucking point of doing it on a computer, surely the whole idea should be, do the practical at work, not the theory on a computer, and the guy who came up with the Move-Smart Training Course should try a shift working on the rig floor when their tripping pipe for 12 hours, I would like to see how he goes about lifting the Slips or making the Tongs bite in the way he tells everyone to approach each job with bended knee and straight back. It's all very well in theory talking about it in a classroom, but to put it into practice is a different matter, just ask any roughneck.

The majority of these courses as far as I was concerned, were a sort of Arse covering exercise by the Management, it was their get out clause incase someone got hurt, for example if someone got Injured while slinging something up and they had done the Computer Based course then he was recorded as being competent in doing that job, so the guy himself was partly to blame, the same goes with the Manual Handling Course, Management use these courses to show to the Operator that they have Competent Personnel on their books and you can't fault them in that respect, because that sort of thing wins contracts, but in the drilling game there's no substitute for hands on experience and as far as I'm concerned you don't get that from passing an exam on a computer.

Getting back to the ones I really needed were my Survival Refresher which I completed in early 98 this time it was down to 1 day, the other was my Medical which I did a few days later, I was a wee bit apprehensive about the medical because it seemed to me that my eyesight was failing and possibly so was my hearing, I put the failing eyesight down to the fact that now I was 44 years of age and what with wearing the plastic glasses and reading in the artificial light thought that also contributed to it, but the hearing had to go down to the noise from the crane engine and the live plant about the platform itself, before I came off the rig I told my mate big Mackay that I was going for my medical that time home and expressed my concerns to him, he didn't make me feel any more at ease when he told me that at the Medical Centre they had a new type hearing test called an audiogram, this involved sitting you inside a closed cubicle with headphones over your ears, the nurse outside set the audiogram machine on and as soon as you heard beeping sound through either the left or right headphone, you pressed a button on the handset to acknowledge it, he told me that if I was having difficulty hearing anything, not to worry, all I had to do was look out the small window on the cubicle door look at the dial arrow on the machine outside, and as soon as the arrow moved that was my cue to press the button on the handset, he said every time the arrow moved, press the button, well as I sat there in the cubicle I couldn't hear anything apart from someone walking about on the wooden floor and the noise from the cars outside running over the stones in the gravel car-park so I remembered what Mackay had said and looked out the wee window, sure enough the arrow on the dial was periodically moving so every time I saw it move, I pressed the button, I was getting the hang of this when the door suddenly flew open and the nurse who was sitting outside monitoring the machine reached in and lifted one of the headphones off my ear and said, Mr. Sutherland, you can hear sounds even dogs can't hear, when you hear a sound please press the button, then she closed the door leaving me with my heart beating ten to the dozen, I was so fucking flustered I didn't know if I could hear anything or not, so periodically when I thought I did hear something I just pressed the button, I presumed it was all over when she came and let me out, and I waited on her telling me I was deaf, but I must have done ok because there was nothing said, well if there was, I didn't hear anything.

Sunday afternoons at 1pm on our first week, was usually when we had our safety meeting for the trip, this was always a pain as we had just finished nightshift and everybody wanted to get to bed, it wasn't as if there was going to be anything different about this one, all safety meetings are the same the whole industry over with the only difference being, most contractors have theirs while their on shift, not so with drilling, it was usually the same points being brought up and the same routine being followed that sent most of the guys to sleep, but this time was different, the reason being there was a new BP Drilling Company Man on board and when he stood up and started speaking everyone gave their full attention, not for what he was saying, but for his pronunciation, it was so lah di da and with him standing there in his corduroy trousers, shirt & cravat covered with a leather jacket we were all wondering where the Fuck did he come from, the last time I heard anyone talking that way was on University Challenge, but you know what they say about first impressions, well we were all wrong about this guy, he was the salt of the earth even with his posh voice, his name was James Kyrle Pope and if you can believe the rumors he was supposedly over a 100th in line to the throne, he certainly had the breeding for it, if only for the way he spoke, James (he didn't like being called Jimmy) was like a breath of fresh air to us, we weren't used to the Company Men joining us at the meetings, never mind having a laugh with us, he introduced spot prizes like golf balls, pen and pencil sets and Tee Shirts to be given out at the meetings to people as rewards for their efforts in their daily duties, and as a special reward if you were seen to be behaving or had done something over and above the call of duty as he called it, you were presented with a Fleece Jacket, I can tell you I was chuffed to Fuck the day I received one, all because he had watched me working the supply boat and thought I deserved a special mention even though I was only doing my job. It was things like this that had the crew morale back on a high, he certainly knew how to motivate men, even his stories had a funny and serious side to them, like when he was asking us to be alert at all times because things can happen in a split second as it did to a friend of his while he was working abroad, seemingly he and his friend were standing talking one day, taking in the scenery of the heavy mobile plant moving about the construction site they were at, when his friends mobile phone rang and he answered it, walking all the time he was talking and not noticing the road-roller until it was too late and he was crushed to death underneath, this was his way of putting over to us the need for us to never get too complacent about anything we are doing, and always keep our eyes on the ball, focus gents, was his favorite saying, always stay focused. This guy was a Toff in more ways than one.

My dad wasn't keeping too well from around February 98 and his visits to me were becoming less frequent, we still kept in touch by phone every trip but I could tell by his shortness of breath when we spoke that everything was not as well as he said it was, I traveled down to Greenock periodically with some of the lads from home, just to check on him and my mum, it also gave me a chance to see how my daughter Michelle and son Jason were doing, I could tell just by looking at my dad that it was more than just a chesty cough he had, and by the amount of weight he had lost since I last saw him indicated things were definitely not looking good, but as usual he scoffed at the idea that he was ill, things were going to get worse there was no doubt about that, and that was the topic of conversation all the way home in the car, as I had said I had taken along some mates of mine that my dad knew very well and from the looks of him, I was glad I did.

The next 5 months on the rig were routine, the rumors of another big shutdown were rife and in July they were rumors no more, they were fact, the crews were told it could be the end of the year before another drilling program would be implemented but until then the company would do it's best to retain as many of them as possible, in the end however there were only a couple from each crew kept on here for Wire-line purposes and some sent to other platforms like The Andrew, The Scott, The Harding, and The Forties Field, but others were finished up with the promise of a start again when things picked up, I did hear through the grapevine that Wee Nat Ritchie finally got the promotion he deserved by being promoted to Rousty Pusher on the Scott Platform. J.M. and myself were once again kept on, as were Alan and Steve on the PUQ, Jamie went to The Scott and John Manley went to America for a while. We wouldn't all be back together again until the near the end of October 98.

There wasn't really a lot of crane work going on, on the drilling platform during the day so J.M. and myself were put back to back on permanent nights, this suited us and the Tool-pushers because as we were nights we would share a room with them so they didn't have to share with someone else who was on the same shift, giving them a room to themselves, so to speak, as due to the high POB everyone was sharing a room.

As the months went on my dad was getting worse, he was diagnosed as having an Asbestoses form of cancer that he contracted while working in the shipyards and the steel foundries, the doctors only gave him a few months after an operation to cut out the tumor they found, and when a secondary illness in the form of septicemia was diagnosed there was nothing else they could do for him except try to make him comfortable, it was heartbreaking to see him waste away when Jim Pitcairn and I visited him in Hairmyers Hospital outside East Kilbride along with my brother Alex and his wife Hilary but still he never complained, after a short stay in hospital they allowed him home and it was a big surprise to me when one time when I phoned to see how he was I found out he was in Raigmore Hospital in Inverness, seemingly while on a day's excursion with my brother and his wife he took ill and was kept in there until he was well enough to travel home, wee Davy Ross and myself went to visit him up there and that was the last time I saw him alive, he didn't die up there, he was transferred home a few days later and was taken into the charity run Ardgowan Hospice where on the 7th of September 1998 he peacefully passed away, I was working at the time and every hour on the hour after midnight I spoke to one of the nurses who told me they had called my brother because my dad was failing fast, it must have been between 6am and 7am because when I phoned at 7am he was gone, I informed Paul Richman what had happened and he organized a seat on that mornings chopper for me, it doesn't take long for word of a compassionate to get around the rig and people were coming up to me to pay their respects, now I know that there's nothing anyone can say at a time like this except to say sorry for your loss, but I will never forget one guy on there at the time for his remarks, I know he didn't say it with malice and he possibly didn't get the full story, but when he approached me, stuck out his hand to shake mine and said, sorry to hear about your father John, I hope he gets better, I didn't know what to fucking say, I look back on it now and laugh, but at that time I was numb. Sitting on the chopper going home there was all sorts of weird things going through my head, I couldn't remember the last time I told my dad I loved him, and now it was too late, I would never see him again, I was sad and glad both at the same time, sad that I wasn't there when he died and scolded myself for not visiting him enough when he was well, and glad that he wasn't in any more pain even though I knew that the morphine injections he was getting in ever heavier doses was probably easing it, the day of the funeral I was glad to see some of my mates had made the journey down to Greenock to pay their last respects along with my family, Ian Macleod, Jim Pitcairn, Eddie McKnight, (RIP) Tom Adamson and my wee pal from Inverness Davy Ross thank you all, it meant a lot to me.

October saw the return of the drill crews again and also a lot of new faces among them, Paul (Wolfie) McWilliams (Driller) Alan (Jenky) Jenkinson (Assistant Driller) Chris Orwin, Davy Jones and Mark Rigall and a lad called Brian? making up the rig crew, but one that wasn't new to me was my big mate from the Hutton T.L.P. days John Stubbs, John was to be my new Roustabout Pusher and he was certainly up for the task, I promised to get him in the crane as soon as possible and get him trained up, there was also the added bonus of having Robbo as Day Pusher he was best mates with John and would do his utmost to push him forward, but fate has a certain way of upsetting the best laid plans, on the night of January 29th 1999 the day after we crew changed, John and Robbo left the Plains Farm Social Club in Sunderland and were involved in a hit and run accident, Robbo sustained some minor leg injuries but John was so badly injured it looked as if he wouldn't make it, for a long,long time he was in a critical condition and it was only through the skill of the doctors and surgeons along with his own determination and body strength that pulled him through, his injuries were so severe that he spent many,many months in hospital, to this day he still needs crutches to get about and as you can imagine his working life Offshore ended that night thanks to a mindless act on behalf of the person responsible, I still keep in touch with John and recently visited him in Sunderland but I'll tell you about that later on.

1999 certainly didn't get off to a good start for John or Seldom for that matter, because Seldom's wife Sheila died unexpectantly at home in February of that year, Seldom gave up working Offshore for a few years so he could spend more time looking after his daughter Nicola who was only about 16 at the time.

The crews on here were now being integrated with the crews off the Harding, Miller and the Andrew platforms, it was a time where Management through appraisals and assessments could pick the crews best suited to do the work, in other words they could get rid of the guys they didn't want, what they intended to do was have 4 crews of men that would go round these platforms as and when needed, to do the work that was required, that was ok if you were one of the ones picked, not so good if you weren't, it was also becoming a bit of a guessing game as to who we were all employed by, in the beginning we all worked for Dan Smedvig, then it was Smedvig Offshore Europe, later it was Smedvig Technical Resources, then Smedvig Limited, some were even employed by a Smedvig subsidiary called Pro-drill. But it all began to make sense with these name changes when we started getting paid from overseas, all new starts had to sign their contracts Offshore on the rig or platform, giving the impression that there was no Management based in Aberdeen, but it was quite obvious that Management was being advised by their Accountants to run the company business from abroad so as to escape paying the Employers National Insurance Stamp as other Drilling Companies had already done,

Nobody really knew what was in the pipeline for the workforce or if they did they didn't let on until it was announced that Smedvig????? was being taken over by another Drilling Contractor called Deutag and the transition period for that happening would be sooner rather than later, this seemed to cheer the lads up, as it was common knowledge that Deutag was a top paying outfit and the sooner we changed boiler suits the sooner we would get a pay rise, but things didn't work out as the men had thought, instead of us getting a rise to equal the Deutag workforce, they were given a pay cut to equal ours, a sort of if you don't like it, lump it kind of attitude, and just to put icing on the cake we had heard a rumor that the Crane and Lifting Equipment Contract was changing hands to a firm more qualified to run the contract than us, it was a case of nobody knew what was happening to the crane op's but when they did, we would be the first to know, now where have I heard that before, I thought to myself.? We knew for a fact that Deutag didn't carry Crane Operators on their books so the future was looking bleak for us at the moment. The first casualties came in the form of the welders, Ernie Milne seen the writing on the wall and left to work on the beach, his place was taken by Ronnie Johnson until he was given a permit controllers job in the control room that only left Neil Cowie and he was later sent to work on the Harding leaving no rig welders working for Deutag on the Bruce.

Ian (Dids) Robertson from Aberdeen became my new Rousty Pusher and along with a guy from the Harding called Stevie Dowds and another new guy Tam Leahy from Dundee that was my new crew. These guys were employed by Smedvig???? but I couldn't for the life of me understand why we were still getting agency guys out to make up the crews when so many of the regular guys were either moved elsewhere or paid off. we were working a man short on the deck when Management sent us out a guy who was as green as the grass, this was the first time he had seen a rig never mind worked on one, but like everyone else you have to start somewhere, his name was Steve, and a pleasanter guy you couldn't meet, but his perception of things were quite different from everybody else's, Steve was working in the sack-store and Dids called him up to the pipe-deck to work with Tam while he and Stevie went to eat, we were busy bundling up excess joints of 5inch tubing casing and moving them from one side of the pipe/deck to the other ready for back/load to the beach, but every time we moved a bundle Steve would unhook his sling and let go of the hook so it travelled in the direction of Tam. Now these hooks are heavy fucking things and the last thing you want is to be hit by one, especially one that's travelling at speed, Steve had been told before about this but it was going in one ear and out the fucking other, he would be ok for a couple of bundles then the same thing would happen, when he let go of the hook one time just missing Tams head I was fucking raging and went down to tell him off again, this time he stood there head bowed taking in everything I was saying to him, or so I thought, but as I turned to head back up the crane, he said, Johnnie what's your favorite Stars War character, I couldn't fucking believe it, I thought surely this cunts taking the piss, I was trying to get this guy to understand that he could seriously injure or possibly kill Tam with the hook, and all he wanted to know was who I liked in Fucking Star Wars. I finally stopped the job and waited on the other guys coming back from dinner, Needless to say after his 3 trip trial period was up, it was a foregone conclusion that Steve wasn't going to make the grade, even menial tasks like working in the sack/store was a chore, he had to be supervised at all times and with the manpower we had, that wasn't always possible, it was the first time that I had to put in a negative report on anybody, but in all honesty I couldn't have lived with myself if he had hurt someone or himself for that matter while under my jurisdiction. So after filling in my report and the senior Tool-pusher agreeing with my assessment Steve was brought into the office where we had a heart to heart talk, I tried to make it as painful as possible trying to advise Steve that maybe an offshore career was not really his vocation In life, I thought that was the last I would see of him so you can imagine my surprise when at the next check/in Steve turned up at the Heliport, someone in the office had fucked up and Steve was given another 3 trip trial, that was the first time I ever witnessed that happening, but there was nothing that I could do about it, I did voice my concerns to the Tool/pushers that they were using this rig as a training ground and possibly because they also forwarded their concerns to Management that was the last time I had a brand new recruit. Inevitably Steve was moved on but I did hear through the grapevine that he was working off-shore with another drilling company, obviously one that didn't have the same standards that Smedvig demanded, all I can say is thank Fuck he's not my responsibility anymore. I could at least get decent nights sleep now.

As the year progressed and we finished the current drilling schedule there was more talk about where the crews were going, some were going to the Magnus, some to the Miller and others to the Harding, but still there was no word about the drilling crane operators, this just pissed everybody off, me included. Davy Cartwright took the bull by the horns and left, finding employment with Offshore Crane Engineering on the Magnus Platform, but Jim Brown the other crane mechanic stuck it out and was offered a job by Sparrows the new crane contactor for the platform, there was talk from the platform management that the other operators would just change boiler suits when the contract changed hands but there was never anything definite, in the end we all sent our C.V.'s to Sparrows and to be fair we did receive recognition of this, but didn't hear any more. It was a phone call from an old workmate of mine Colin Prentice who was working at O.C.E. at the time that prompted J.M. and me to send them our C.V.'s, and with Colin and Davy Cartwright's recommendation we were asked up for an interview in December, I was the last of the Drill-ing crane operators to come off here on December 15th with all my worldly goods as the saying goes, in 2 bags, I was told that I was going to the Harding as rousty pusher, there were no jobs with Deutag for crane operators so it was a case of take it or leave it, that for me was a right kick in the teeth, I don't know why I was so disappointed, I should have known better, because believe me, when it comes to loyalty it's all one sided, it's a case of what can you do for us, not, what can we do for you, Since starting with Dan Smedvig in December1997 I never once missed a check/in or was off ill in nearly 13 years and this was the thanks I got, I had been operating cranes for 10 years now and knew that that was what I wanted to keep on doing, and if it wasn't going to be with

Deutag then that was their loss, I knew what I was happiest at and working the deck again, wasn't it,

It was on my birthday Tuesday 21st Dec that I went up to Aberdeen armed with all the certification certificates that I had accumulated over the years for the interview at O.C.E, I must admit looking at these certificates impressed the fuck out of me, even the big leather bound folder that I borrowed to keep them in looked the biz, but it wasn't me I had to impress. I knew I could talk myself into a job but I was also hoping for a bit of luck and as interviews go I thought I presented myself very well. David Logan (Contracts Manager) and Rosemary Adams (Human Resources) conducted the interview and after it was over I was told that they would contact me one way or the other by early January, I felt quietly confident I had the job, but on the train journey home there was still the nagging thought of having to go to the Harding in the next couple of days, I wasn't looking forward to it that's for sure, but at least it was another months pay and who knows, maybe the New Millennium will bring something prosperous with it. (Hopefully a new job).

Bruce Drilling

11

THE HARDING

Thursday 30th of December 1999, two days before the New Millennium I set out from the digs at 6-30am heading as requested for the Skean Dhu Hotel in Dyce, the whole crew had been summoned there by top management for what I thought was maybe an introduction to management themselves as most of us had never met half of them before, or maybe it was to wish us a belated merry Xmas and good luck in the coming New Year. How wrong I was, because it was neither, the meeting started off with management stating that they hadn't brought us here to wish us a merry xmas, we were here to discuss an incident that happened out on the platform, basically they had brought us here 45 minutes before we checked in to give us an ear-bashing because some derrick-man on the rig had dropped 22 stands of drill-pipe across the derrick and rig floor and management wanted answers from us as to how it happened. and what were we going to do to stop it happening again As I said before I really didn't want to be going out to this rig and I certainly didn't need to be told off before I went, especially from this lot who were going home to put their feet up and enjoy the rest of the festive holiday while we were going Offshore for 2 weeks, so when I stopped one of these hierarchy know it all's, a guy called (Ian Shearer) in full flight with his ramblings, by saying, I think this is ridiculous,! you bring a crew of guys in here 45 minutes before they fly out to work for a fortnight, give them a grilling on something that happened when they were on leave and expect them to go out there and focus safely on whatever their doing, if that's what you call motivating men, then your all in the wrong job. You should have seen the fucking look on their faces, the whispers and nods in my direction told me they were wondering who I was, and they wanted to put a name to my face, they coughed and spluttered and tried to play down their initial hostile attitude but for me the damage was done, I told them who I was and I could see one of them writing it down.

My statement seemed to jolt one or two of the crew into action because they also voiced their opinion that it was nothing to do with us with what happened out there on the rig, but if lessons could be learned from it then we would quite happily discuss it, this seemed to calm everybody down and some good points were raised from both sides in the end. But I can honestly say management were there that day to kick ass and if you let them do that for nothing, then on your own head be it.

Walking round to Bond Helicopters in Dyce with my big mate Alan (Jenky) Jenkinson we were fuming at management's attitude, at that precise moment I could have very easily just went home there and then, but Jenky talked me out of it, after we checked in and watched the pre-flight video we were soon on our way to the Harding platform, an hour and a half's journey away. All the way there I couldn't get settled, the thought of what they fuckers tried to do to us had me seething, I tried to put it out of my head but every time I managed, it came rushing back in again, all the pent up anger of how we were treated after the 8 years service on the Bruce that we had faithfully given them, and this is how they repay us, I really wasn't focussed for going out here and I knew it, I also knew that I would be lucky to last 2 days never mind 2 weeks. I knew most of the crew I was going out with Ian (Dids) Robertson, Tam Leahy and Steve Dowds were on my crew on the Bruce and most of the roughnecks I knew as well, so it wasn't as if I was joining a new crew, it was the feeling of betrayal that kept on gnawing at me, and as we circled the rig before landing I looked out the window and saw my home for the next 2 weeks for the first time, that also pissed me off.

After landing on the platform I had 5 minutes talking to J.M.Sutherland whom I was taking over from, we quickly compared notes on how our interviews at O.C.E. went and I promised to keep in touch with him to see if there was any news from them, his parting words to me were, you won't like it here!, and he was right. I didn't.

Checking in at Heli-Admin I handed over my ID card to the guy behind the desk who looked at me and said, give it to Sooty and say hello, I said what? He said again, give your card to Sooty and say hello, that's when I noticed on his right hand was a Sooty glove puppet, I just laughed, gave my card to Sooty and said hello, this guy was called Harry Catherall from Newcastle, he was the leading steward on here and Heli-Admin was just one of his duties, he certainly had a way about him did Harry. The way he made people welcome to the platform was unique bordering on eccentric, over the next 2 weeks Harry was a focal point on the rig there was nothing he wouldn't do to make your stay more pleasant or entertaining. Full marks to him for making my stay bearable for there were times I didn't think I would last.

After the usual welcome from the O.I.M. we were shown to our rooms, the drill crew were all on the same level and the rooms were comfortable enough with T.V., toilet, shower, and double bunk beds, the only drawback was there was no lifts on here and the stairs you had to walk up and down went on forever, some fucking non-smoking wag, had put posters at every level informing you that if you climbed these stairs every day of your trip for a year then you had climbed the equivalent of some fucking mountain in Scotland, now that really cheered me up every time I got to level one and then found out that I had left something in my room 2 levels from the top, from the rooms you had 6 double flights of stairs to walk down to reach the smoking tea/shack and locker room, so it didn't take me long to cross/check that I had everything I needed, before leaving my room. On here I met my mate Jamie Wright. He was as pissed off as the rest of us with the way we had been treated on the Bruce, but even more so now that he thought that J.M. and myself might be leaving, Jamie as well as my other mate Alan Mathew from Portlethen outside Aberdeen had also put a C.V. into O.C.E. but never heard anything more after their interviews with them, at least J.M. and myself were told we would know one way or the other by early January 2000 so at least we were on the shortlist, for the moment.

As I was the only one on the crew new to this platform I was given a personal tour of it by the BP safety man, for about an hour we wandered through air lock door after air lock door, the fucking place was full of them, it was like walking about in a submarine, with always to close the door after you, and if I thought the stairs in the accommodation were a chore, outside was even worse I knew then that I hated this place and this was only my first day.

The drill crews on here were working the more civilized shifts of 6 to 6 dayshift and nightshift and as our crew were working the first week on nights we were supposed to start at 6 PM but as the rig was preparing for the big computer crash that the New Millennium threatened to bring with it we were put on a sort of standby mode until the New Year. Personnel on Board (POB) were down to a minimum so why the powers that be had the full drill crews on is beyond comprehension. I mean, that if what the boffins said was true, that all computers would not recognize the year 2000 and if that happened then there would be chaos the world over with the satellite systems, the telecommunication systems, the air traffic control systems, in fact everything that has a plug on the end of it would crash, and here we are stuck in the middle of the North Sea waiting for it to happen, remember what I said before about the workforce being the cheapest commodity out here, well this action speaks volumes, don't you think? In the end there was a lot of hype about nothing, as midnight struck on New Years Eve we were sitting in the tea/shack I won't say holding our breath but there was some concern as to what was going to happen, would the tea-urn suddenly switch off or would the fag lighter fail to work or would something happen in the galley so that the chef couldn't take the frying pan away from the heat before the sausages were cooked all the way through, that's the sort of nonsense that we were worried about and we were right, it all turned out to be a damp squib. All those firms that spent millions on new computerized systems to combat the coming apocalypse must have felt a little peeved shall we say!

The New Years Day meal was like something served up from a 5 star hotel, so I was told by Jamie, and I could quite believe him, the selection and quality of food on here was quite exceptional to what I was used to on other installations, the filled rolls at morning tea/breaks were bursting with either bacon, bacon and egg, sausage, or square slice, or there were pies, bridies, chicken legs or breasts, pizzas, all on different days mind you, but whatever was on that particular day there was plenty of it.

We were still shut down on New Years Day so most of the nightshift guys myself included went to the Galley at 8 PM to join in the festivities, Harry Catherall was the Master of Ceremonies for the night and organized tirelessly the domino, darts and cribbage tournaments, he also ran the prize raffle and co-ordinated the betting for the horse racing videos, on top of that he sang and joked his way through the whole evening, you could not ask for a more dedicated guy, he put so much of his own time and effort into everyone's enjoyment and all the thanks he got for it was for someone to kidnap his beloved glove puppet Sooty from heli/admin and hold him too ransom. The kidnapper's wanted tin's of coca cola and Mars bars in payment for sooty's safe return, For the next few days ransom notes (letters cut from old daily news-papers) were secretly left for Harry to find and ponder over, there was even a photograph of Sooty with a noose round his neck, Harry went from being the life and soul of the rig to a broken man overnight. You just had to look at him to feel the anguish he was experiencing, I knew it was my mate Mick Gower the Mechanic who was now employed by BP that had spirited Sooty away, but I was sworn to secrecy, even I didn't know if Sooty would return to Harry in one piece or not, so I couldn't ease Harry's pain, The negotiations were at a critical stage and the next few days would provide the outcome.

Things were back to normal out on the rig floor and the pipe-deck, the crews were back working normal hours again, I was told to throttle back for another couple of days by the Tool-pusher until I was more familiar with my surroundings then I was to throw myself into the job, I had no intention of throwing myself anywhere, but I did think about throwing the Tool-pusher over the side, but knowing my luck I would have been spotted, so instead I asked Did's to look after the crew as he would be taking over from me when I left, and I would concentrate on doing the crew's competency records, so they would be up to date, and for the next week that's exactly what I did.

Now and again I wandered through some of the modules not particularly looking for anyone or anything, it was just an exer-cise to see if I could find my way back to the tea/shack without help from someone, on one of these recce's I came across a glass fronted cabinet attached to a wall inside this cabinet were items on show that were the focal point of the dropped object scheme that was promoted to the hilt on here, there were things like hammers, nuts, bolts, bulldog clamps, scaffolding clips, all sorts of things that had or could have fallen from a height and injured someone, the thing that crossed my mind was, where did they keep the cabinet with the 22 stands of drill-pipe.

Periodically during that first week I phoned J.M. to find out if he had heard anything from O.C.E. but he said no, I was going to wait until I was on dayshift when I was going to give them a phone myself and on Friday morning the 5th that's what I did, the news I was given was like someone lifting a full bag of coal off my shoulders I was told if I was still interested in employment with them then could I be available on January 25th to go out to the Magnus platform on a 3 month trial basis and if successful after that, I would be taken on full time. Well you can imagine my answer, as soon as I put the phone down I phoned J.M. to tell him my news and found out from him that he too was going out to the Magnus a week earlier than me on the 18th so at least two of us had jobs, that only left Jamie and Alan, I phoned Jamie at home to let him know about J.M. and me, not to piss him off, but to put him in the picture about the Magnus crewing up, he said he would phone O.C.E. himself and find out what was happening. I was quite happy now that I knew I wouldn't be coming back to this rig and I called the deck crew together to let them know, there was no way in the world that I was going to jeopardize this move to another company by going out to possibly get injured in unfamiliar surrounding's so I spent the rest of the trip doing paper work and attending meetings. I also didn't want to leave Deutag under a cloud, (a sort of never burn your bridges kind of attitude) so I did my work, typed out my resignation giving them 2 weeks notice dated from the 13th of January 2000 and settled down waiting on crew change day to arrive. (So I could get to fuck off of here.)

Oh bye the way Harry got Sooty back in one piece after handing over an undisclosed amount of Cokes and Mars Bars to the heartless Kidnappers, and all the personnel that were on the rig for either Xmas or New Year received a commemorative watch from B.P. and those that were on for both, received two.

12

The Magnus

The day I came off the Harding some of the crew and myself went for a New Year's drink to celebrate the New Millennium and also to celebrate the fact I wouldn't be going back there, we spent a few hours touring the local bars in Aberdeen before Tam Leahy and myself headed to the train station, I was feeling pretty inebriated by the time Tam got off the train at Dundee leaving me with another 30 minutes journey before I got off at Markinch, where I caught a taxi home, the rest of the leave was pretty much spent doing nothing in particular, I was chilling out as they say, just enjoying the fact that I was back again in the comfort of my own home, over the years I had replaced nearly everything in the house with new stuff so in that respect I was lucky, but as for having bought my house, having a large bank balance and getting ready to set up a wee business of my own, That was still a dream.

The thought of the new platform and new employer was foremost in my mind and I was pretty excited about it, but this excitement turned to dismay when J.M. phoned me to give me an update on the 22nd of Jan of what it was like out there and the description of the rig and the state of the cranes didn't sound to good to me, he had been out there since the 18th and I was due out on the 25th so he had been on there for 4 days now and had plenty of time to suss things out, his exact words were, the cranes are well past their sell buy date and are so fucking slow their danger-ous, they look as if they haven't been cleaned since they were first installed out here, and the rig itself is a rust bucket. Apart from that its ok I suppose. What he meant by that I don't know, but my mind was racing for the next 3 days wondering what the fuck I had let myself in for.

A phone call from Rosemary Adams had me making my way to Aberdeen early on Monday morning, I was to attend a Computer Based Induction Course at a place called Crescent Engineering for the Magnus, then in the afternoon attend an informal introduction to some BP guys at BP's offices in Dyce with David Logan, the computer course only took about an hour, it was only a quick insight into what and where the Magnus Platform was and after it was finished there was a few questions to answer, I was out of the place by 12-30pm and as I didn't have to meet David till 3-00pm I messed about Aberdeen till then, I didn't bother going for a drink, I didn't think that would have gone down to well going to BP's offices smelling of drink. At 2-45pm I arrived at O.C.E.'s office where I met David and we both walked the hundred odd yards up the road to BP's offices, David was a guy in his early 30's he was a non drinking, non smoking, non swearing a kind of regular family and church going sort of guy, not the kind of bloke that I would normally be associated with, but at this moment in time needs must, I tried to curb my language in front of him at least until the interview with the BP guys was over, In there we were shown into a room which held 6 guys I'd never seen before but David obviously knew all of them because he started introducing them by name to me, once we were seated one of the guys I was introduced to, a guy name Joe Kaiser asked me to tell them something about myself, I didn't know what to say, I could see they had my C.V. in front of each of them so I didn't know what else they wanted to know, anyway I started off by saying that I had been married twice, that I had 4 children, and that I was actually in a bit of financial difficulty at that present moment in time, Well you should have seen the look on David's face, it was a fucking picture, he looked as if he was going to throw up, I was beginning to wonder if I had just blown this job before I even got started when Joe started laughing along with the rest of them and said, its you Offshore Experience were interested in John, we'll find out about your personal details later, I thought well done Kaiser, my mind racing back to my dog, The rest of the interview went well as far as I was concerned and outside after it David commented on my wee bit of brilliance in the way I got everyone at ease before the interview had started, little did he know it wasn't planned that way.

After picking up my 2 bags with working gear in them I was standing outside with David waiting on the taxi coming to take me to my digs, when he asked me what I had planned for my last night Onshore, "I'm going to get fucking steaming drunk", I said, but don't you worry David, I'll be there tomorrow for the

9am check/in, that sickly look appeared on his face again and although I'm sure he knew I was only winding him up, he still reminded me that the check/in was at 8am.

Anytime the Magnus helicopter landed on the Bruce to re/fuel our hearts used to go out to the guys on the flight, we all knew that the Magnus Platform lying about 120 miles north east of the Shetlands was the furthest Platform north in the whole north sea and if the wind was against you it could take up to over 3 hours before they reached there, that was a sore journey, especially on the Arse, these choppers were certainly not built for comfort, at that time in the early days the Magnus flight was nearly always a direct flight from Aberdeen only stopping off in Sumburgh Airport in the Shetland Islands for fuel or if the weather was really bad it would have to stop to re/fuel a couple of times. So getting the fixed wing plane from Aberdeen to Scatsta (also in the Shetlands) then an hours journey to the rig on the chopper seemed like I had won a prize, at Aberdeen Airport I met the guy (Tam Ramage) who was going to be my relief on the rig, he was coming out with me for a couple of days to assess me on the cranes, O.C.E. employed him from time to time as a Trainer Assessor but for the time being once he had assessed and passed me he was going to be my back to back. Tam and me arrived on the Magnus about midday and by the time we had dinner and I was given the usual platform safety induction it was about 2-00pm, we were working 6 to 6 on here so my first shift was nearly over all I had to do now was meet the rest of the OCE personnel and the Tool-pushers and crew I would be working with, The first 2 crane mechanics I met were Brian Hamilton and John Mackerron followed later on in the trip by their back to backs Roddy Macdonald and Cliff Rollinson, the crane operators were JM, Tam, George Davidson and me. The cranes were winded down that first day so I wasn't assessed in them until later. But looking up at the 3 of them from the pipe-deck it was obvious that JM hadn't glossed things over with his description of them, (they were fucking monsters) they were obviously the first of their kind, they were of the same type that were on the Bruce OS200 pedestal but were so over engineered they looked massive compared to the newer models. The first time I got to operate them was like being at the fair, they were rocking and rolling all over the place, they certainly took some getting used too. I couldn't believe how slow they were on single line fall and they were even slower when

218

changed onto double line and four line fall, there was a foot pedal switch which could be activated to give you more speed on the lines but once this was in force you lost the use of the boom, you couldn't boom up or down until you de-activated this switch, as you can imagine, trying to offload and backload a supply boat in marginal conditions, was a fucking nightmare, JM was also right about them needing a right good clean, there were more leaks in here than in a Welsh fruit and veg shop, the engine room decks were covered in oil and grease and that wasn't because they had sprung a leak the day before, but trying to get into these places to start cleaning was another matter there was no room to move whatsoever, every time you moved in here you either banged your head or knocked an elbow on something it was no wonder anybody bothered trying to clean them up.

Some other things that caught my eye were the three 50 foot tall turbine exhaust stacks on the north side of the platform they were just begging to be hit by a load coming up from or going down to the boat if you didn't watch what you were doing. Then there was the crane rest that supported the south and north cranes when they were down for whatever reason, this huge metal beam straddled the middle of the pipe-deck, if you wanted to move something from one side of the pipe-deck to the other you had to lift it about 40 feet in the air to clear this obstacle which was just a fucking nightmare especially when moving tubulars, whoever designed this monstrosity certainly didn't give a fuck about the crane operators, and then there was the gantry crane, this also straddled the pipe-deck and travelled on rails from one side of the deck to the other, this was used for moving tubulars onto the catwalk if the pedestal cranes were winded down, the only thing was, if it wasn't parked up under the crane rest when not in use, it would block the view of the deck from either the south or the north crane. Remembering back to what James Kyrle Pope said, I would certainly have to remain focussed when doing lifts on here.

The 2 day Tool-Pushers on here were Andy Kenyon and Brian (Robbo) Robinson the 2 night Pushers were Jimmy Thomson and Munster so in that respect I wouldn't have any trouble fitting in here as I knew and worked with 3 of them before, but my first meeting with the deck-foreman of the crew I would be working with and who was also the crane operator on here until OCE took over the crane contract was a bit, shall we say frosty, he made it very clear when he said, (don't expect me to let you down from the crane when your needing a break), that he wasn't happy about being demoted to deck-foreman, I think I may have rubbed salt into his wound when I said, (I won't mate, your not allowed).I wasn't giving a fuck if he was unhappy or not but I wasn't going to let him take it out on me, If he was that pissed off he should have done the same as me and looked for another job. A couple of trips later that's exactly what he did and left.

The first couple of trips on here were a bit of a culture shock after coming off a rig that I'd been on for 8 years some of the practices on here took a bit of getting used too. for years we had it rammed up us about the need to manual handle things only when absolutely necessary, then when I come on here I see that you couldn't put a container on the pipe-deck beams until you put some down 4x4 timbers to straddle the beams and support it, things like baskets and half/heights were no problem as they had the width to straddle the beams safely, but the width between the beams were just not narrow enough to support the container width safely and they weren't wide enough in places to let you put a container in between them, these 4 x 4's were about 8 feet long and heavy as fuck, so if you can Imagine putting down enough of these timbers normally 3 to a container to accommodate 10 or 20 containers then that's a lot of manual handling in my book and not to fucking clever on the spinal cord either. There were 6 bays about 6 feet wide running parallel to each other the whole length of the pipe-deck and the height of the beams separating them were about 18 inches, believe me when I tell you that after climbing over these beams from one bay to the next dragging enough 4x4 timbers with you so as to make a platform that the containers would sit safely on. You knew you had done a days work. On the plus side it was good to see that they also practiced waste segregation on here, there were different types of skips for materials the same as the Bruce but they also had special containers for waste paint, asbestos items, cardboard boxes, and bins for oily contaminated rags, inside the accommodation there were different coloured bins for empty drinks cans, aerosol tins, and used batteries, this place was a front runner in terms of trying to save the environment, the minus side was once these skips were back on the beach most of them would be sent to a landfill site, undoing all the work involved out here

After a couple of trips J.M. and myself were getting settled on here, it took a bit of getting used to working dayshift the first week and nights the last, but as we had dedicated drill crews to work with we had to work the same rota as them, although we were the drilling crane operators we had no say in the every day running of the roustabout crew that was left to the rousty pusher, the one I had at first was replaced by a guy called Dion (Dino) Matthew's, Dino was a funny cunt in the sense that nothing seemed to upset him and he always had a witty answer for every awkward question that was fired at him, there was also another more sinister side to him, Dino liked nothing better than to get dressed up for the yearly BP dinner dance, I'm not talking top hat and tails here I'm talking blonde wig, short skirt and wellington boots, the first time I saw a photograph of him at one of these dances I must admit he or should I say she looked stunning and every one else in the photo looked to be enjoying themselves too, possibly thinking that after the joke was over he would change into more proper attire, but my sources told me that Dino had no intention of doing anything of the kind, for the whole night he wandered about dressed like this to the applause of his work-mates and the looks of disbelief from the BP punters.

It was on my second leave home from here while laying in bed one night the phone rang and on answering it I was asked a question by a woman on the other end, do you know who this is, she asked? No I said, are you sure, she asked again? I'm sure, look who are you and what do you want, I asked? It's me Liz, how are you? After getting over the initial shock of hearing her voice again after all those years, we spoke for about an hour, just talking about how she was and me telling her how I was and shite like that, in the end we arranged to meet up to discuss things, past, present and possibly future, Liz and me met and talked things over admitting that their was blame to be had on both sides. We never really went into any real detail about what went on in the 7 years we had split, what happened was water under the bridge now and I wasn't going to start dragging things up from the past, she told me she was staying in Leven only 15 minutes drive away from Glenrothes, Nicky and David were also staying there although Nicky was now married with 2 children Catherine and Robert, David was still living with her in a flat and was attending University, everything was going well for Nicky and David but Liz was looking a bit on the overweight side she put this down to the tablets she was taking, she was also on Invalidity at the moment and was waiting to go into hospital for more tests. She also told me that Kaiser had developed a common weakness in German Shepherds a few years back, his back legs started to fail him at times and it was obvious he was in a lot of pain so to save him any more suffering she had him put down. I was genuinely sorry to hear that and vowed that I'd never have another dog; Kaiser was a one off and couldn't be replaced. We started to see each other regularly while I was on leave, it was like starting courting all over again, only this time we were both a little bit wiser.

My relief Tam wasn't too happy on here for some reason, and trip after trip he always said this is my last one, I kept on at him that if he was going to leave then at least give the office plenty of notice because I wasn't one for doing extra time, I like my 2 on 2 off rota and I won't do extra time unless it's absolutely necessary, anyway, usually on my last nightshift I would phone him to make sure he was ok for coming out and to give him an update of what was happening on the rig, but on this particular night in April he didn't answer, I waited a couple of hours and tried again, still no answer, after several attempts I gave up, next morning waiting to check/in I heard the P.A. system calling me to the phone, before I answered it I fucking knew deep down that it was either about Tam or it was Tam himself saying he wasn't coming out and I was right, the story was, as Tam was driving into Aberdeen in plenty of time to make his check/in, a low flying Kamikaze Seagull went head first through the windscreen of his car, the seagull suffered massive injuries resulting in it's demise(the last thing to go through it's head was it's Arse) and Tam was so badly shaken by the whole ordeal that he had to go home, hopefully he should make the check/in on the Wednesday, I wasn't giving a fuck I wanted go home and in the end that's what I did. As far as Tam was concerned he must have been stricken with remorse and ended up going to the seagull's funeral because he didn't make Wednesday's check/in either.

He did eventually return to the Magnus for a couple of more trips but had a few wee incidents concerning the crane and he eventually left making a position available for my new back to back Phil Meach from Dundee, I knew Phil from the North West Hutton days.

Munster and me had started up our old arrangement of travelling together, but this time round we hired a car, Wee Betsy had been put down, all those years driving up and down to Aberdeen finally took it's toll on her and she finally gave up the ghost, we shared the cost of the hired car with another two guys Tam Leahy who joined my crew from the Harding and Graham Wood from Glasgow he was one of the chefs on here, this arrangement lasted over a year until Tam was finished offshore after being taken ill and Munster moved to the Andrew Platform while Graham changed his crew change date. After that I started taking the train spending Monday night in Aberdeen or Liz would drive me up to Aberdeen and pick me up on the way home.

The crews on here were changing all the time, working on the Magnus was not everybody's ideal choice of platform in all honesty when I first came on here I felt as if I had made a bad move. The place was falling to bits, it took hours to get here, and as we were the furthest platform North it was always fucking freezing, you could never depend on getting off on your regular crew change because of the weather or the planes and choppers breaking down, (just a technical hitch) I wish I had a week off for every time I heard that warbler, you could get all four seasons in one day out here, not really much incentive to want to be here as they say, especially if there was work to be had further south on some of the newer platforms, people used to be asked what they had done wrong to be sent up here as punishment,

When the crew I was working with eventually settled down, on the deck were Dino, Tam and Gary Johnston from Elgin. later on a fourth member would be introduced on the deck for manpower safety reasons, The rig crew were Tony Smart (Driller) Finbar (Fin) Paterson as AD, Jeff Freeman (Derrick-man) Steve (Sumo) Simmons, Duncan Blake, Paul Armstrong, Brian Gardiner, and Robbie Anderson who replaced Jeff as Derrick-man when he was promoted to AD when Fin went to work in Russia in 2002, these were a fine bunch to work with but as the years went on the crew changed from time to time as they always seemed to do,

This platform was no different from any other that had a Drilling team on board, we were always struggling for space to put things, if a bay became empty for some reason then it was quickly filled up with something or other, there was never enough room on the pipe-deck and never any space on the lay down area of the top deck where they kept chemical tanks, containers, baskets, skips, and anything else they could fit in, it seemed to be as soon as one of the boats that came once every three days was off/loaded and back/loaded we were still struggling for room to put things, we were bringing onto the platform more than we were putting off, to try and give us more space all the tanks were double stacked even the skips were doubled up, we were double stacking everything that had the facility to do so, and even some that didn't by putting 4x4 timbers between them, but it was getting beyond a joke on here, you could hardly move and it was verging on being dangerous.

July was looming up on us and the decks were becoming quite empty, all the drill pipe, collars, jars, etc,etc were being prepared for back-load to the beach for their yearly inspection, soon the decks would be empty and the majority of the drill crews would be off for the annual shutdown, this would normally last about six weeks so it fell in nicely for their three week change over, it meant that they either had 5 or 7 weeks off then came back to work on the opposite crew change to the one they were working, one or two of them would be kept on here to help the maintenance department so obviously they would have to do their 3 weeker but for the rest of them it was holiday time, with pay.

During this period when drilling were off we thought that as we were the drilling crane operators we would get some time off as well, but no such luck, we were told that we would be needed on the platform to do lifts as required, I wasn't too bothered about this but it would have been nice to have some extra time off, in the end we did a week and week change over to put us on the correct crew change for when our respective crews came back again.

The shutdown itself was for the platform to do work that couldn't normally be done when drilling was working and of course the scheduled work planned for this time of year. But this year was an extended shutdown as far as the drill crews were concerned it was planned to renew some sections of the drag chain and the power cables that were supported by it (this chain was like a big conveyer belt that carried the power cables to the rig and when the rig was skidded this chain moved along with it) this would probably take from August until the end of the year all things going well, but first they had to scaffold out the whole area and that meant miles of scaffolding poles, boards and fittings, this was a summer job being done in the winter.

It was around summer time that someone from the office staff on the platform was trying to introduce a Healthy Eating Campaign, this was sanctioned by the Management so it went ahead, looking around I didn't notice anyone that looked obese or in any great need to go on a diet apart from the one that was introducing this campaign, they could certainly have done with missing a meal or two, but to introduce the rest of us into it, was a bit much as far as I was concerned, it wasn't as if we had much choice in the matter, as soon as the campaign started there was only hot soup and hot filled potatoes on the menu at dinner times, the only other thing you could have was salad or a salad filled Baguette, to say I was unhappy at this is an understatement, and the rest of the keep fat club weren't too happy either, I'm a steak and kidney pie man with plenty of butter through my mash potatoes if I can get them, so coming in for my dinner and having the take it or leave it choice of rabbit food didn't go down to well, don't get me wrong, if people want to diet that's up to them, if they want to go on an exercise craze that's also up to them, just don't fucking drag me into it,

Liz stayed at her flat when I was away, but stayed with me most times when I was at home, I remember one day my big mate Pitcairn came down for me and Liz opened the door too him, I could sense he was uneasy and didn't know what to say until I broke the ice and laughingly told him that I was just explaining to Liz that everything in the house could be hers, as soon as I went offshore, the only one that didn't see the funny side of that one was Liz, we were getting on better than ever and we started going out together during the day, me having a drink and Liz going the messages then coming back to spend a few hours in the pub with me before we went home, it was like old times us being together in the pub, the only difference being she wasn't setting up the vodkas like wee soldiers like she used to, I was strictly a single glass man now, there might have been a double in the glass but it was a single glass just the same.

The drill crew thought that they had won a prize when they heard the news about the extended shutdown, it was looking more like January before they would be back up to full strength, but it didn't work out that way, they were either sent elsewhere or were put on courses some were left on here to help with the maintenance and help out with the drag chain, By the time July came round it was time for me and the other 3 crane OP's to change our rota, as I said before I hated doing 3 weeks so I did a week on then a week off then back on for 2 that put me on the opposite shift to what I had been working, only this time when I had already been on for a week and was only going home for one the fucking fog rolled in, it lasted from Tuesday till the Thursday night when they sent a chopper from Norway to take us back to Bergen then fix wing us to Aberdeen on the Friday morning, travelling with me was George Davidson and another 15 blokes heading to a hotel somewhere in Norway once we landed in Bergen, it was over an hours journey to this hotel from the Airport and we were fucking knackered after being up all day praying for the fog to lift, but in true offshore worker style we all got a new lease of life when we arrived at the hotel at 10 30 pm that night, once everyone had checked/in to their rooms (George and me were sharing) we headed straight for the bar to find that it cost 4 Krona for a beer that was about £5 a pint and it tasted like dish water, we were about to complain when the BP rep appeared and told us to order what we liked within reason, and he would meet the bill, well, all of a sudden the beer didn't taste that bad and the more we drank the better it tasted, I remember George telling me that, I sat up all night drinking what was left of a case of beer, and serenading the seagulls with my best Sidney the Swine voice until I fell asleep just as the phone rang to tell us the bus was waiting to take us back to the airport, I vaguely remember the flight home to Aberdeen, and when George dropped me off in his car at Dundee I was just sobering up, Liz picked me up from there and the rest of the week-end flew in, I wasn't going to be home long enough to cut the fucking grass before it was time to go offshore again on the Tuesday.

Liz had been for various tests over the months but it was when she was referred to a Rheumatology Consultant for the constant pains in her joints and back she was told she had Renal Cancer, this was a blow to both of us but she was determined to fight it as only a woman knows how, for the rest of the year she attended various hospitals for treatment and seemed to respond to the medication.

With the crews still off or working elsewhere in early November the ones left on here

on my crew included Fin, Tam and Dino, Fin a Bermondsey boy from London was in charge of sorting out the permits for the guy's working on the drag chain and power cables, Tam and Dino were helping out what with banking the crane and slinging up loads, the Drag Chain was taking shape although it still had a long way to go before completion. They had also started to renovate the galley making it a more open plan design and they were hoping to have this finished for Xmas, but from the looks of it at times we thought it might be ready for the following year. The contractors doing the work were cordoning off a section of the galley at a time and for weeks it looked as if it was never going to be finished. But in the end it was, but not completely until January 2001.

November was the start of the Cycle Challenge that was going to be a yearly event out here, it was to last for about 6 weeks and it involved not only here but other installations in the north sea, to see which rig or platform could clock up the most miles in the allocated time, this was our first attempt at it and as we were nearly up to full POB on here it looked like we could possibly have a chance of winning it if everybody took a turn and kept the wheel turning 24 hours a day, but it wasn't as easy as it looked, I had a go at it and it wasn't like riding an ordinary push bike like I remembered, it was fucking hard going trying to maintain what was the norm of 20 miles an hour for the allocated 15 minutes at a time you were allowed. Tam and Dino were regular goers on it and I applauded them every time they went on, but Fin and me were spectators quite happily watching, we had no intention of going on it until one night we were goaded into it, we decided that the two of us wouldn't last 15 minutes each, but we might manage it if we split it between us, so we put our names down for the following night, I wasn't to keen on this but when the time came I went on and started peddling like a fucking nutcase until I thought I would faint, Fin kept me informed of the minutes to go urging me to keep going, I could feel the sweat running down the cheeks of my arse and my face felt scarlet, the minutes seemed like days I kept asking him how long now and he would reply in his cockney accent just another few minutes Johnny boy, when I finally fell of the bike my legs had turned to Jelly, I didn't have the strength to stand up never mind light the fag he handed me, I just lay on the sofa and watched Fin endure his torture for a gruelling 8 minutes, by the time he came off I still hadn't got my breath back. Later on as we hobbled back out to work we vowed we would never put ourselves through that again for anyone or anything, although we did receive a lovely tee shirt each at the end of the challenge for our efforts. The Magnus won the challenge at the first time of trying but I'm not so sure they would have if it hadn't been for Fin and me.

Some of the biggest changes in late 2000 early 2001 that took place out on the deck for us were the replacing of the lay down area on the top deck. This deck was really rusted to fuck, there were holes in the deck that you could see through, you had to watch where you were walking in case your foot went through one of the holes, the deck crew were always laying down 2x2 timbers to spread the weight of the loads, it wasn't a complete renewal of the deck, that would have caused to much upheaval, what they did was they cordoned off areas at a time and welded new plates of sheet metal onto the existing ones, but it took a couple of minor injuries on the pipe-deck before top management finally took notice of the manual handling practices that the boys had to do with the 4x4's before landing containers, at great expense, so we were told, they had manufactured a portable deck to fit over the existing one doing away with the need to handle these 4x4's. When it finally came out a year later it was in 4 sections and when bolted together it made one large section that covered about a quarter of the pipe-deck, this was a godsend for the guys it was such a simple idea that it was a wonder they didn't think of this years ago, there would be no more dragging these heavy fucking lumps of wood about every time you wanted to land something, the only time we would need the 4x4's now was when we were laying out tubular's to give us a 4 inch clearance between one row and another so we could get the slings underneath them,

By the time January 2001 came round the drag chain was all but finished and the crews were up to full strength again, it was speculated that the Gain Share payment for the contractors would be around £1500 this was the same bonus system that was worked on the Bruce and some of the other BP installations it certainly gave everyone a boost knowing that this payment would be either be in our wages at the end of the month or the following at the latest, in fact it was the end of march before we were paid out, but it was a great feeling just the same, Robbo had the men on a painting mission, just to get them back into the swing of things again before the drilling program started, the rule of thumb was if it didn't move paint it, the place looked like new for a couple of weeks then it was back to normal again, from then up to July was spent either doing work-overs on the wells (taking the old completion string out and replacing it) or doing wire-line work to inject new life into under-performing wells, whatever was happening we were kept busy.

There was a few changes in the first half of the year in the Tool-Pushing department, Andy Kenyon moved on to take up a company man's position elsewhere, he was eventually replaced by Bob Anderson as Senior Pusher after a couple of temporary guys had stood in, Munster moved to the Andrew platform and Eddie Slater who I knew when he was a Driller on the Bruce took over as Night Pusher, Robbo injured himself and was replaced for a few trips by Munster then eventually by my big mate Steve Mackay he had certainly done well for himself, the other night pusher was Jimmy Thomson and from what I could see the crews on here were lucky to have so many decent pushers on the same platform. Robbo once he was better eventually moved to the Scott platform as Senior Pusher.

The topic on the rig was the new project that was starting in the late second quarter of 2001, it was the Enhanced Oil Recovery (E.O.R) this project once completed was going to give a new lease of life to the Magnus Platform and possibly extend it's current life span by up to 15 years or more, the cost of this project was in the region of $550 million. The enormity of this project was reflected when we found out that new pipe lines from Sullom Voe to the Magnus had to be installed and once the work on the platform was completed, gas from the West of Shetland was transported via Sullom Voe down these pipes and into the Magnus reservoir to enhance oil recovery This was a massive project in work terms and would affect the drill crews in the sense that they would be stood down for as long as it took to allow bed space for the Bears when they came out,

The drilling program for 2001 was to be in 2 phases one part was to take us up to late May then the crews were going to the Forties Echo until late September and the next one was planned from October onwards, the time in between was left open for work to be started on preparing the steel foundation work that was going to support the new E.O.R. Module.and bring on the rest of the equipment that was part of the E.O.R.project itself, the whole project was supposed to take 18 months and in that time there was going to be a lot of heavy and awkward lifts on here.

On July 18th the worlds largest pipe-laying ship the Solitaire came alongside the platform and started laying the pipes (that was going to carry the gas) on the sea bed from here to Sullom

Voe, when it arrived it's size wasn't exaggerated, on the horizon it looked large but when it got close to the platform it was massive, I stood looking in amazement at the size of this floating assembly line watching it drop section upon welded section of pipe from it stern as it slowly moved away towards the Shetlands.

June through to October saw the platform with hardly any free deck space, everywhere you looked was filled with 20 foot open top containers, half/heights, baskets, containers, tanks, anything that could carry equipment was utilized and sent out here it was like a war zone, as soon as the containers were empty they were sent down to the dedicated supply boat and another one brought on to take its place, this supply boat was here for months bringing out cargo and sending it up as we needed it, there was so much equipment coming out that we had to store some on the Thistle platform which was only about an hours sailing time from here, the POB on here during this time was up to the maximum of 196 this still wasn't sufficient for the personnel that was needed on here so another 30 Bears were shuttled back and forth from the Thistle on a daily basis, believe me this was one busy place 24 hours a day.

Although the Magnus had 3 cranes only 2 sides of the platform North and West were used to offload and back/load supply vessels, the reason for this was there were production risers on the sea bed situated on the south side of the platform and because of the danger of something falling into the sea and damaging them, it was normal procedure never to bring boats in to this side, however after a lot of discussions and Task Risk Assessments (TRA's) it was deemed more feasible to bring certain awkward and accessible lifts onto the platform from this side rather than have to move the lift 2 or possibly 3 times with the other cranes before the lift was installed in place. What could take an hour to do a lift using the other cranes to get it off the boat and in reach of the south crane; the south crane could pick it off the boat and slot it straight into place in minutes.

Some dates of events that have happened while I was working offshore had been imprinted in my memory, the Piper Alpha, the Lockerbie Disaster and the Cormorant Alpha tragedy, another was added to them when I got out of bed on the afternoon of Tuesday 11-9-2001 to get ready for nightshift, I had just switched on the television and was watching what I thought was a trailer for an action movie, in fact what I was watching was something very real, it was a live news broadcast of the events that happened that morning in America, Terrorists had hijacked 4 planes, 2 were flown into the Twin Towers of New York's World Trade Center, and one smashed into the Pentagon, both resulting in the deaths of more than 3000 innocent people, the fourth had crashed.. I couldn't take in at first what was going on until it sunk in; I stood there watching this broadcast thinking to myself what is the fucking world coming too? Then in answer to my own question, that if we don't get our act together, it's going to come to an end.

When the drill crews came back in late September one of the regular guy's Tam Leahy was missing off our crew, seemingly while waiting on the shuttle chopper to take the crew from the main field of the Forties to the Echo platform Tam blacked out and collapsed, he was taken to the medics where he was kept under observation until it was deemed they should return him to the beach for a more detailed look as to what caused this, speaking to the crew when they came on here I was told that they had been weathered down on the beach for 3 days and they had spent their spare time doing what nearly everybody else does when this happens, (they go on the drink) Tam was no exception to this procedure and according to Fin they certainly had their fair share by the time the weather abated and they went offshore, Tam was sent for a medical to try and determine what caused this blackout and because there was nothing physically wrong with him it was deemed it could be mental, in the end the root cause was put down to possible epilepsy and since that was a no, no as far as working offshore went Tam's career offshore came to an end, in true offshore fashion the drill crews and certain others rallied round and a collection of £700 was raised just before Xmas time and I hand delivered it personally to Tam, Fin and myself visited Tam in Dundee later in 2002 to find out how he was doing, and according to Tam none of the offshore medical doctors he had attended at any time would say he was definitely epileptic, even his own doctor scoffed at the idea, but then again none of them would sign their name to anything to say he wasn't, to this day Tam has never had another blackout, he said when it happened he was feeling ill with the drink and just keeled over, I can believe that, but I'm not the one who has the say as to whether he works offshore again or not.

Dino went on the sick shortly after coming back from the Forties and was never seen again working offshore, the last I heard he was working as a fireman down in England somewhere although whether that was true or not remains to be seen, I don't think dressing up as a woman every time the fireman's ball came round would go down to well with them. Still every man to his own as they say.

The EOR project was coming along nicely, it was still a skeleton of what it would look like when it was finished but it was taking shape as the months went by with pieces being added to it all the time,

I was just about to go for dinner one nightshift in late November when the tannoy system came to life calling out my name and asking me to call the control room as there was an outside call for me, my first reaction was to ask myself, who the fuck is that, I didn't get outside calls because it can generally only mean bad news, I always said to Liz never call me out there unless it's absolutely necessary and even then as a last resort. If the house is burning down don't phone me phone the fucking Fire Brigade there's nothing I can do about it when I'm out there, you can always tell when someone gets a call from the beach whether it's good or bad news by the look on their faces when they come back from the phone, as soon as someone's name is called and he's not a regular at getting them, people will say to each other (I hope it's not bad news), anyway the call was from JM informing me that Sparrows had offered him a job and he wasn't coming back, he wanted me to be the first to know before informing the office, I was happy for him but also felt a sense of loss, JM and me had worked together since the North West Hutton days and had a formed a friendship that was more than just work mates, I still keep in contact with JM and at least once a month we will talk on the phone just to see how the other Sutherland is doing.

November through to January was the coldest spell I'd witnessed offshore since I started working out here, sometime it was minus 5 degrees centigrade but that felt colder in the 40 to 50 knot winds we were all wrapped up like fucking Eskimo's, when the temperature did rise a bit and it started snowing there were 3 and 4 foot snow drifts on the deck, some days when we came out to work we had to clear the snow off the equipment before we started, the lumps of ice that were falling periodically from the derrick and the flare tower would have knocked you out if one of them had hit you, it used to piss us off when someone from the control room would put out a tannoy warning everybody about this hazard and informing them to take care and not to venture outside the accommodation unless it was really necessary, he didn't actually say(drilling personnel excluded) but that's what he meant, also if it was really windy he would tell you to remember to wear your chin strap in high winds, I've never heard of anybody getting hurt by not wearing their chin strap, but getting clobbered by a lump of fucking ice, or getting blown off your feet when your standing on top of some tubular's, that I've heard of.

Liz was taken into hospital where she had a her left kidney removed this seemed to knock her for six for a while but she perked up again later on, for months she visited the hospital for more treatment and seemed to respond well.

I did my RGIT refresher and Medical again at the beginning of the year that was me set up for another 4 years on the refresher and two on the medical, soon I would have to do the Medical every year when I reached fifty, surely I would be out of here by that time.

I had no hesitation in putting Jamie Wright's name in the frame when my boss at the time Dave Robertson, phoned me and asked if I knew someone suitable to replace J.M., Jamie was duly interviewed and started in February 2002, JM must have started a craze because before the year was out most of the Crane Mechanics had also joined Sparrows or went elsewhere, they were slowly replaced by Campbell MacAskill, Stuart Campbell, Daniel Graves and Jim Johnson, John Laing and Willie Pigdon would come out regularly to stand in as relief operators, while Doug Stephen and Dan Toye were the in-house Training co-ordinators.

I wasn't one for going to Xmas dances even if it was held in March, but when I found out that this year they were holding it in Newcastle I thought I could kill two birds with one stone as the proverb goes, it would be a nice change for Liz to stay a couple of nights in a 4 star hotel and I could go and visit my mate John Stubbs in Sunderland, I set the wheels in motion by phoning Robbo and Jenky to let them know I would be coming for a visit and to make sure Big Stubbs was there, but not to tell him I was coming, on the Friday morning Liz and I boarded the train at Kirkcaldy where we met Fin, Craig (Homer) Davis, one of the stewards, Russell Love, the welding inspector and their respective partners, Homer kept everyone in our carriage amused with his under sized Kilt and SEE YOU JIMMY bonnet and ginger wig on his head, offering cans of beer to anyone that wanted one not knowing that Homer had shaken the tin like fuck until they opened it only to lose half the tin on the ceiling, thankfully everyone took it in good spirit. My mate Sam Graham who was the cementer on the rig picked Liz, me and Homer up in Newcastle and drove us to the Gosforth Park Hotel, near Newcastle's racecourse, once we checked in and got settled we spent the night drinking and partying, with Sam his wife Maureen, Liz and me heading into Newcastle city centre to sample the night life, as arranged the next morning Mick Casey who was working on the rig as a deck hand and Steve (Sumo) Simmons came and picked up Fin, me and the Magnus BP company rep Charlie Sutherland Robb, then the 5 of us leaving the women to go shopping at the Metro Centre in Newcastle headed for Sunderland with Charlie giving us his best rendition of Gerry and the Pacemakers most of the way, the club we were supposed to be at just after opening time was the Plains Farm Club that's the one John and Robbo left the night of their accident, Mick knew how to get there so there was no problem finding it, we arrived about 11-15 and went straight into the bar, we were all sat at a table that couldn't be seen as you came through the door, so after about 15 minutes when Jenky and Robbo came through it with Robbo holding the door open for John he didn't see us sitting there, I heard Robbo asking John where he wanted to sit as there were people sitting in his regular seat John turned to look at us and when he recognized me he nearly fell off his crutches, there was an emotional few minutes with hugs and hand shakes and if I had a pint for every time he said (I don't fucking believe it) I wouldn't have made the dance at night, everybody knew each other and that made it more enjoyable, Robbo's wife sent down cheese, biscuits, cooked sausages and cooked chicken legs for us, it was like an indoor barbecue, but it all ended to soon, we had to get back and get sorted for the dance at night, we all agreed that we could have spent the whole day there but by 4pm we had to make our way back, it was sad seeing John like he was but hopefully through time he will be able to do some of the things he treasured doing but can't at the moment for obvious reasons. The rest of the weekend was very enjoyable it was nice to spend time with people you work with away from the work place, if you know what I mean.

Jamie was settling in fine, he was slowly getting the hang of the cranes just as the rest of us did when we first came here, there was no point in trying to rush things the cranes didn't respond to that sort of harsh treatment, everything just flowed along nicely, we were always being told that if we weren't happy with something or other then we could stop the job and discuss it, Time Out For Safety (TOFS) was what they called it and it was and is a good tool to be used when someone is unhappy about any part of the operation or task their carrying out, I personally use it when I deem that something's not right or if I'm not happy about an operation that's going on, and more importantly it's there for anyone to use.

There were another few additions to the crew to make up for the loss of Tam and Dino, mainly agency guy's, Gary was rousty pusher for a while until Brian (ploo) Clark from Keith arrived from the Forties to take over, then came Scott (Scotty) Gordon from Lossiemouth closely followed by Mike Marson from Whitby in North Yorkshire, that's the crew that would be here for a few more years to come.

Ever since my father died I made a point of phoning and visiting my mum whenever I could, for a long time now she was not in the best of fettle and was attending the Western General hospital in Glasgow for Radium treatment twice a week to try and reduce a tumour on her brain, it was a foregone conclusion that things weren't getting any better after weeks of this treatment, she kept complaining of headaches and of being tired all the time, she didn't like the colour or shape of the wigs the hospital gave her to try on even though she picked them, Deep down I knew she wasn't long for this earth so I arranged with Liz to travel down to Greenock and bring her up to stay with us for a while just to take her mind off things, the day before I went home from here Liz had picked her up and took her through to Glenrothes and the next day drove her up to Aberdeen to meet me off the plane, I had told the boys on the crew that she was there and was proud by the way they made a fuss of her when they met, as you can imagine they towered over her with most of them being about 6 foot tall and my mum kicking the arse out of 5 feet 2inches, you wouldn't have thought she was unwell the way she knocked back the wee brandies as she called them that the lads were setting up for her and to be honest she couldn't finish them all and used Liz's empty coke bottle to put some into for later. At home I had her and Liz out everyday showing her the sights and finishing the day off by playing her at her favourite game of pool in my mate Tam Adamson's pub The Station Hotel in Leslie, she thrived on the attention

Tam and the rest of us gave her but by late afternoon she began to get tired and was usually bedded by tea time, she spent the whole 2 weeks with us that time home, and my sisters Jane and Angela remarked on her new lease of life when Liz finally drove her back home, although the whole family expected it, it was still a shock when on the 5th of May 2002 she peacefully passed away in her sleep at home. Tam and Jim Pitcairn travelled down to Greenock for the funeral to pay their respects and once again I thank them for their concern.

The rig was doing another work-over that would take them up to the planned shutdown in June, there was going to be an extension put on it this year so they could bring on more people for the EOR, the crews wouldn't have to do their 3 week changeover they were going home for 16 weeks with full pay but as usual the crane op's would do their own thing working 1on 1off as normal, as I said before this time was normally used to do planned maintenance and the rig crew would give the maintenance guys a hand, some of them had been on here for years like the electricians Les Bell, Peter Atherton, Colin Watson, Bill Coulthard and Derek Printer. The Mechanics were also mostly long term guys Eric Gilroy, Ronnie Hutton, Alan Smith, Trevor Allum and new comer Maitland Baff who replaced Cliff Bell, anyway one day during the first week of the shutdown I was standing looking over the handrail down at something in the water, I didn't know what it was at first but it had what seemed to me to be flippers or short wings, at first I thought it was a young bird struggling to fly then I watched it go under the water and come back up again, now you may think that I should have learned my lesson on the North West Hutton about telling people about what I saw in the water, and I did, this time I went into the maintenance office where I found Les Bell, on asking Les what he knew about sea-life?, he asked me why? I told him to come outside with me and I'll show you, looking at the water this thing was still there but Les didn't know what it was, do you think it might be a small turtle I asked him? Could be he said? Later on my mate Campbell MacAskill asked me if I had seen any turtles lately, I knew he was taking the piss so I told him that Les had also seen it, but when we questioned Les later on he denied ever seeing anything, I called him all the lying Bastards under the sun but he wouldn't admit to seeing it, I wasn't giving a fuck whether they believed me or not, I knew what I saw. Later on in the galley I was having my dinner when I noticed Les and Campbell standing at the counter with what looked like brand new Cycle Challenge tee shirts on but on closer inspection it wasn't a picture of a bike that was on them it was a picture of a fucking turtle with the slogan of, is it a bird, is it a plane, no it's a turtle, they had gone to the medic and got 2 tee shirts and super imposed a photo of a turtle onto them, I tried not to let them wind me up but it was hard not to bite, it didn't make it any easier when Val Stevenson one of the catering crew put a small plastic turtle in my bed for me to find. I promised myself again that never under any circumstances would I tell anyone what I see in the water ever again.

In the years I've worked offshore the wild life I've seen out here beggars belief, believe me when I tell you I've seen all different kinds of migrating birds, homing pigeons that have lost their way, owls and cormorants, I've seen hawks hunting their prey in pairs, I've seen whales, sharks, schools of porpoises and seals with fish in their mouths teasing the seagull's, but if I see any of these again will I tell anyone, will I Fuck.

The EOR was looking like it would be finished by September and for most of the Bears working on it, it would mean a change of venue if there was somewhere else for them to go that is, a few of them would be kept on for the inevitable teething problems but as for the rest they would be scattered around the North Sea on other rigs, there was talk of an end of project bonus to be paid out once the plant was up and running, but whether that materialized or not remains to be seen, I did know that after this Year's Gain Share payout if there was one, there wouldn't be another, not for the contractors anyway. BP stated that it was now up to the individual companies to pay out any accrued bonuses if the targets and qualifying dates for the year had been met, that didn't go down too well with the guys, after all, we thought we were supposed to be working as a team, but obviously the contractors were the reserves.

BP were obviously planning for the future when they started the EOR project this platform was 19 years old and they were looking at another 19 so after the upgrade of the galley in 2000 the rest of the accommodation looked pretty dismal in comparison so for the next couple of years we saw the renovation of the Cinema, the Recreation room in level 4, the smoking lounge, the smoking TV lounge, the Gymnasium, the Sauna, and later on all the tea-shacks on the platform. All this cost a fortune but they were badly needing done up. Another huge project that was on the go working Parallel with the E.O.R project was the Temporary Refuge (TR) on level one of the accommodation, this place once it is finished in the 2nd quarter of 2004 is to accommodate the full POB on the platform in case of a full blown emergency, the walls, doors and ceiling are all blast proof, it has its own command and medical centre, it also has its own personal power and ventilation supply, basically it is fully independent and self sufficient and once the doors are closed we have a minimum 2 hours of intense heat protection. After that??????

It was when there was a couple of fatalities on other installations involving the cranes that we held what was called a (safety stand down) on here, what this involved was, getting everyone together that had anything to do with the movement of cargo and equipment with the crane, discuss what had happened and determine if it could happen on here, (one man was crushed to death by a 50 foot basket, another was killed when a chemical tank that was double stacked became foul hooked by the crane and toppled on top of him) the outcome was, although our deck management procedures were first class, it was decided that because of the latest events we would no longer double stack anything, if it was deemed that we had no option but to double stack, then a T.R.A. would be held, a lifting plan had to be submitted, and a permit had to be issued beforehand, what this meant was we would never stack anything on here again and if we did it would only be as a last resort, this was good and bad news for us, the good news was we wouldn't have the hassle of trying to fit one item onto the top another and balancing like fucking acrobats while trying to stack tanks, the bad news was we were always struggling for space on here and that was even though we were double stacking things, it was going to be a fucking nightmare if they still brought out the same amount of cargo with less space to put it in. this point was raised at the regular meetings between management and deck-crew and would be addressed as top priority, all the heads of departments were supposed to get together to plan ahead what cargo and equipment was really needed so as to avoid congesting the decks, but in true offshore fashion the decks were still as full as ever.

Another point that was raised at these meetings was the manpower working the decks, at one stage there were only 3 guys on deck including the Deck/foreman but this rig was no different from any other in the sense that one of the rousties would either be away mixing chemicals or on the rig floor relieving, therefore leaving 2 guys on the deck to manhandle the cargo, this was ok until the management changed the rules of handling loads suspended from the crane. What they deemed sufficient in the terms of a cargo handling team were 3 men, one of them being the crane operator, one the banks-man and the other the handler, but to throw a spoke in the wheel as they say, the banks-man (wearing a yellow fluorescent jacket) must never touch the load, the handler (wearing an orange Fluorescent jacket) must not touch the load until it was at waist height, and nobody without an orange jacket and the proper qualifications could give him a hand. This took some getting used too, especially when its human nature to step in and help, when you see someone struggling with something like landing a container squarely, there were several times when guys were reprimanded for doing just that and in the end they just said fuck it and kept on walking, BP always said that there was no job so important that time can't be taken to do it safely, and in the end that's what the guys were doing, if it took 2 men to land a load then they would wait until there were 2 men, there was no point in getting your arse kicked for trying to get on with the job if it meant breaking the rules, eventually another guy was introduced to the crew which helped enormously, especially if we were doing lifts from one level of the platform to another.

The rest of 2002 was spent doing work-overs on existing wells and the lads wondering what new procedures would be in force in the New Year. It seemed that every couple of trips there were new rules to adhere to and it was becoming a bit of a chore try-ing to remember them all, since BP brought in their 8 golden rules it was common practice to make sure you never broke any, because hell mend you if you did, but these coupled with your own companies working practices made you wonder if it was sometimes better to stay in the accommodation (if you could get away with it) than venture outside looking over your shoulder to see who was watching you, initially some of the lads were get-ting paranoid about doing something wrong because the feeling on the rig was, the powers that be wouldn't be happy until they ran somebody off (N.R.B.) for breaking or infringing the rules, periodically I would spot the fair weather people (that's what the office staff are known as because they hardly ever come out in the rain) from the crane, hunting in pairs looking for some poor unsuspecting bastard to pounce on, I would put the lads on the deck wise to them being out and about, to make sure they were doing everything above board, but like any new regime people get used to changes and although it may take time they will eventually conform to the different ways of working than what they've been used to in the past.

The start of 2003 saw the EOR up and running, to me it didn't look as if it was worth $550 million but that's the Oil industry for you, I wondered how long it would take before BP and it's partner's re-couped that, then again when you think that to drill a well from start to completion costs in the region of £9million and on here at the moment there are 20 wells, that's a lot of money to lay out, but I'm sure they'll get all that back plus interest in the future.

Liz was once again taken into hospital, after months of tests and scans it was decided she should have her gallbladder removed to try and stop the cancer that was eating away at her, all these visits and treatments seemed to take their toll on her but she responded once again and seems to be doing well

Just to make sure the guys were not getting too complacent trying to conform to the new working practices on the deck another new procedure was brought into force in the form of more paper work, this is how it worked, before crew changeover times the crew starting shift will attend a pre-shift tool box talk to discuss the planned events of their 12hours, they will go through the relevant Drilling Operation's Guidelines (DOGS) to make sure that they know the procedures for the ongoing operation they will be doing, after that the rig crew will have another meeting on the rig floor to discuss how they will perform their tasks and bring up any points their concerned about, then they will all sign any relevant documentation, the deck-crew will hold their own meeting and fill out the relevant Task Risk Identification Cards (TRIC) for the operation they will be carrying out, this card has 12 tick boxes that must be filled in to identify any risks or hazards that could be encountered while carrying out this specific operation, and if so what measures are taken to combat these, if they start a different operation then another TRIC must be filled out, to let you follow what I mean, if for example were working a boat a TRIC card will be filled in to acknowledge this and signed by everyone involved, if we stop this job and start another like emptying chemical containers, then another card must be filled in to acknowledge this, and so on, it's a wonder we get any fucking work done at all what with filling in cards all day, waiting on permits and Work Control Certificates (WCC's) I know that these procedures are in place to keep a record of the work fronts about the platform but I feel that maybe there's to much emphasis on the paper trail, but that's what the company wants and they pay the wages.

The drilling program for the year was pretty much the same as we had been doing in previous years, it was planned to do some sidetrack wells (cementing in one well then kick off and drill another using the same slot) do some coil tubing work to inject new life into under performing wells, and later on in the year try again and successfully drill a multilateral well (have two wells using one slot), this was tried in early 2000 but without success, multilateral basically meant with only one slot available per well they would use a tool shaped like an upside down Y called a whip/stock, this tool once in place and the wells drilled would have two completion strings at the bottom merging together at the top.

Since starting offshore in the late 80's I've noticed some major changes in the industry, gone are the days when people were terrified to speak up for themselves, the dinosaur pushers have either retired or been moved on by the companies not prepared to put up with their Victorian attitudes, Safety is now paramount on most of the installations where as before the job had to be done regardless, I used to laugh when the OIM would tell us the Motto of (No job is so important that time can't be taken to do it safely) where was he when the driller or pusher was screaming at the guys, WHAT'S THE FUCKING HOLD UP. You hardly hear any of that now; well not on any of the platforms I've been on lately (I can't say the same for semi- submersibles,. it's head down Arse up on these rigs) The non-existent recreation facilities and 4 man cabins are a thing of the past; those were the days of the first up best-dressed rule. Days when guys would stay up most of the night playing cards, it was not uncommon for someone to lose a trips pay at these sessions, Days of not knowing who you were sharing a room with and the only way to find out who was using your shampoo was to put some hair remover in the bottle then wait to see who was impersonating Kojak, These are some of the plus factors about the industry but there's also the minus, Manpower levels have been cut drastically over the years but not the work-load, nearly everyone on an installation will have at least two duties to perform possibly more, take a scaffolder for

241

instance apart from his own job he will possibly be part of the heli-deck team, a painter when not painting will either give the scaffolders a hand or go fire-watching for the welder, the crane mechanic will be the lifeboat engineer and part of the heli-deck team, but the one that will do the most duties in any one shift is the roustabout, he can be a forklift driver, a chemical mixer, a cleaner, a roughneck, a painter, a slinger banks/man, heli-deck member, generally a jack of all trades, the drilling companies won a prize when this breed of guy came to work offshore, but true to form their the least thought of and the lowest paid.

Gone are the days of visiting the medic for a minor ailment (unless its within surgery hours) or seeing them out and about re-stocking the first aid boxes or the eye wash stations as they used to do because now their not just first aiders, their titles have been changed to Occupational Health Advisors (OHA's) don't get me wrong they still administer first aid and give you medicine when your feeling poorly (why is it the medics think Lem-sip drinks and Solpadeine tablets cure all ailments) but they can't give you an injection to ease the pain without first contacting a qualified doctor on the beach, their role has been changed to more of an advisory capacity, Seminars are held periodically to advise us on things like Heart Disease, Stress Management, Holiday Health and Manual Handling, then there's Drink and Drug abuse post-ers on the walls, don't they realize that coming out here for two weeks is like checking into the Betty Ford clinic for most of us and we don't need reminding of the damage were doing to our-selves, then there's the Dental Health Theme, that one doesn't affect me as my teeth are usually sleeping in a tub of water half an hour before I am, there's also Foot Health, how to be kind to your feet after keeping them sweating like Fuck inside a pair of Wellingtons for 12 hours, all the things that most people really don't give a fuck about, but the theme that gets up everybody's nose (pardon the pun) especially the smokers, is the No Smoking Campaign, I'm all for giving people that want to stop encourage-ment to do so, by all means give them access to Nicotine Patches, Nicotine Chewing Gum and loads of Cold Turkey, if they want to give up good luck to them we wish them all the very best of health, but for fucks sake leave us Lepers in peace, let us social outcasts enjoy our cigarettes, be as happy for us we are for you, after all, its not as if were breaking any rules and infringing on your air space, when we're having a fag it's in the designated smoking area, anybody that doesn't want to come in there needn't come in, surely if it bothers them so much they can always go two levels up or down to find a tea point without forcing themselves to endure the passive smoking tortures that seem to annoy most non-smokers, two points that come to mind, The first one is, if the head of B.P. Sir John Browne came on here and lit up a cigar in the conference room who would ask him to put it out or get up and leave, the second one is, at the various functions I have attended you don't see the anti hash brigade sitting in a non smoking area enjoying the pleasures of fresh air, their usually all at the bar enjoying the free drink and blowing smoke up other peoples arses.

The drilling program up to July was near enough on schedule then there was an incident with one of the cranes, the mechanic who had just joined the company damaged some boom lattices when putting the crane in the rest, the damage was pretty bad and by the time everything was up and running again the crews had nearly 10 weeks off, when they came back in September the plan was to start drilling the Multilateral well and this was going to take us up to the end of the year. There were also rumours of a big planned shutdown in 2004 only it wasn't going to last a couple of months this one was going to last a year, the reason for this was they were planning to extend the slots on the platform by another 8 giving a total of 28, even though this was just a rumour it had an affect on the crews, being realistic they knew that BP wouldn't keep them sitting idle on the beach with full wages, not for a full year anyway, and to be unemployed for a year hoping to get brought back when the drilling program started again was not an option, people were starting to look elsewhere for work

It was during the extended shutdown that a new procedure was implemented for the nightshift crane operator, we were given computer training on the platform permit system so we could take out a Work Control Permit (WCC) to allow us to perform certain duties like re-fuel or grease the cranes on nightshift, it also allowed us to counter sign other peoples permits if their work scope was going to be affected by any crane work near by, in other words it was an arse covering exercise, if I counter signed their permit admitting I knew they were working nearby then did a lift over the top of them, then it was my fault entirely, punishable by a severe boot up the arse, the WCC was no hardship to take out but the only reservations I had was having to go to the central control room (CCR) every night to implement it, in the past on other platforms depending on who was in charge you could stand there for long enough before anybody would make eye contact with you, I would look into the computer screen to see if I could see my reflection because I was obviously invisible to everybody else, it was like being at fucking school again waiting on an audience with the headmaster, or waiting like a leper to get a different coloured dinner ticket than everybody else for a free school meal because my father wasn't working, I used to get really pissed off at this and these cunts knew it so they did it all the more, it wasn't as if you could pull them over the table and slap some civility into them, all that would have done was get you the next chopper and tagged with the dreaded N.R.B. But if the truth be known I've never witnessed any of that on here, the CCR supervisors have always given me the same courtesy as I've given them, the likes of Laurie Kelly, Bali Singh, Simon Carey, Rob Mackay and Glen Connelly as soon as they finish their nightshift crew brief they will attend to me and the other guys waiting, a couple of times when the brief ran over time Jim Gallagher went out of his way to get me sorted, but maybe Jim who could see I was getting agitated took pity on me and helped out a fellow Greenock man, The majority of the BP production guys were just like us out here to do a job and get home again, don't get me wrong, there's still one or two that think the platform can do without the contractors and that this place would be better off without them, but their just being small minded as far as I'm concerned and with attitudes like that, I know who the platform would be better off without .

The Magnus Platform celebrated its 20th birthday this year in August and to commemorate this the catering crew put on a special meal, they really excel themselves at times like these with T Bone Steaks, Sirloin, Beef Wellington, Salmon, Lobster, and Crab on the menu and the presentation would be first class but as my mate Fin would say in true Drilling fashion as the Head Chef stands proudly over his trays of delicacies (their only multicoloured troughs to me mate) on top of that everyone onboard here received a commemorative bottle of Speyside Malt Whisky sent to their home to acknowledge it,

The Multilateral well was finished in December as far as the drilling side and the running of the completion string was concerned all that remained now was for the wire-line crews to run their guns and blow holes in the tubing to see if we had a gusher or not, the outcome was, it wasn't a gusher but it was a success, the office staff out here and on the beach were delighted, this was the first of its kind and now they were looking to do more, Possibly one before the shutdown in 2004.

I had celebrated my 50th birthday with Liz and my mates in the pub two days before the correct date of the 21st this fell on the Sunday and I didn't want to travel to Aberdeen feeling like a bag of shite on the 23rd, the change-over I did in July meant that I would spend Xmas and New Year offshore, that didn't bother me because my back to back Phil had a young family and as mine were well up it could be Xmas and New Year anytime I was home, apart from that, if I was still here next year I would get them both off, my mate Homer came on the rig on the 24th with the news that I had won 10 bottles of spirits in the pre-Xmas draw that they held every year in the Spiders Web pub in Dyce I only bought £20's worth of tickets so thought myself lucky to win anything at all never mind two prizes, Xmas was the same out here as in previous years, Xmas tree, Decorations, cans of non alcohol Kaliber and plenty of cracker pulling, as usual I didn't bother with Xmas dinner although I believe the catering crew did the guys proud with the spread they put on, the drill crew were given a couple of hours off after their dinner but were back at work before their relief's came out at 6-30pm, the same happened at New Year, the rest of the platform apart from some of the BP production guys had most of the day off, this was par for the course for the drill crew and it didn't put them up or down, they knew that if the Pushers could give them the day off then they would have but well operations restricted that, I was in the crane on New Years night when I heard my name being called over the PA system asking me to call the CCR as there was an outside call for me, as I said before I didn't get outside calls so my head was buzzing as I climbed down the ladder on the way down to the phone, wondering who it could be, when I eventually got through to the CCR and gave the guy the phone number I was on I hung up waiting on him ringing me back to connect the call, it seemed to take for ever then it rang, giving the distinctive double ring that identifies a call from the beach, normally it would give one long intermediate ring if it was from somewhere on the platform, on answering I recognized the distinct voice of Dave Robertson from O.C.E's office, after wishing each other a happy New Year Dave said he had some bad news for me, my first thought was, my back to back

Phil wasn't coming out, I went on the defensive and said, I don't give a fuck Dave I'm not staying on, it's not that he said, Liz has tried to get through to the platform without success and eventually phoned me to try and contact you, your sister Janet has died, as soon as he said the name I felt a rush of adrenaline hoping against the odds that it was someone else he should be phoning not me, but deep down I knew he had the name wrong, it was Jane, she hadn't been well for a long time and whether by mistake or a search for relief for the constant pain she was going through daily, the tablets she was taking mixed with the New Year celebration drinks proved to much for her frail body and she died in her sleep just like her mum and dad. For two days I mulled over what had happened, there were no scheduled flights until the 3rd of January although Derek Furlong the Chief Steward and Helicopter Administrator tried his best to see if there was anything flying in our vicinity, so I had to sit it out till then, watching films but not paying any attention to the plot, going from one level of the accommodation to another just for a change of scenery, I noticed guys side stepping me because they didn't know what to say, watching the clock every hour on the hour as the time dragged by, I wasn't allowed outside the accommodation for fear that as my mind wasn't focussed on the job for safety reasons it was better to stay indoors, I got off on the Saturday and Liz picked me up and took me round to the Spiders Web where I picked up my choice of spirits, (10 bottles of vodka), then we drove home, we buried Jane the week before I was due back offshore, (remember what I said about outside calls).

When we came back to the platform on the 20th January we were greeted by the news that as the Multilateral was a huge success there was going to be a bonus payment of £1000 for the drilling team and £500 for the crane operators, this well added to the other producers gave the platform a production figure of over 60,000 barrels of oil a day that's not bad for a 20 year old platform, but it's still well short of the 180,000 barrels a day it was producing at it's peak in the early 90's, when you work it out that there's 42 U.S. gallons of oil to a barrel that's a lot of black gold.

In the Offshore Oil Industry you get people from all walks of life, Doom and Gloom merchants, Hypochondriac's, Comedians and Walter Mitty's, these people and many others are tolerated because for one reason or another their an essential part of everyday life on an oil rig, if it wasn't for them we wouldn't have anybody to laugh at or bitch about, but there's one low life that nobody puts up with and that's a Thief, I'm not talking about someone who's fucked off with the only monthly TV guide on the platform, I'm talking about the compulsive sticky fingered bastard who would take the sugar out of your coffee if he could, the guy who would rifle your locker when he knew you were on shift and take everything that couldn't be traced back, luckily enough there's not a lot of them but the reason for that is if their caught red handed and before the management get to hear about it he is dealt a swift justice and advised to seek alternative employment elsewhere, if management do get to hear about it and the culprit is found as so often happens, then he is swiftly dispatched back to the beach with either the police waiting on him to press charges, or his Employers being informed of him receiving the dreaded NRB which with the OIM's recommendation would most certainly mean the sack. This is exactly what happened when a guy who was in a position of trust abused it, at one of the regular horse racing nights that was held to raise money for a work colleague who was off sick it was found that certain discrepancies had crept in, what happens at these nights are tokens for various amounts are bought for cash and bets are placed on the horse of your choice with the tokens, if it wins then you hand back your tokens and your paid out in the cash value, a couple of guys are selected to run the race night and to monitor the tokens that are bought and cashed in, as there are only a certain number of these variously priced tokens allocated at the beginning of the night once the race night is finished and the winnings are paid out then the tokens once collected should be the same number as at the start and the winning cash bets paid out should match up, the rest is profit, but at the end of the race night it was found there were more tokens than originally allocated and hardly any money left, so suspicion fell on innocent people until it was found that this particular guy had been pleading poverty the day before saying he didn't have a spare £5 to buy a lottery bonus ball and although he had tokens at the race night the guys selling the tokens couldn't remember him buying any but remembered him cashing in a few, in the end he was questioned and tried to say he had kept the tokens from the last race night but later he admitted to stealing tokens from the place they were kept and he had access too, it was ironic in a way because he actually won a couple of hundred pounds at the race night and if he had taken the loan of money he was offered earlier by a work mate of his then he might just have gotten away with it, but fate has a certain way of working it's magic and he was relieved of his ill gotten gains and returned to the beach branded a thief, I wouldn't like to be in his position as I have said before these rig's are like Wee Villages and no matter what story he tells his friends and family about why he gave up his job just as a New Year was starting the truth, as so often does, will come out.

The morale on the platform among the Drilling guys is at an all time low, come August 2004 the majority of the guys will either be paid off or have left for alternate employment, the reason behind this is the go ahead of the Magnus Extension Project (M.E.P.) this project is expected to last for about a year and will add another 8 slots to the 20 already in use, once this is complete it will possibly mean another 5 years drilling for the contractor, not necessarily the one on here at the moment, this is all very well and can only be good for the life expectancy of the platform, but in the meantime it holds fears for the men about what the future may bring, nobody can afford to be idle for a year hoping that they may be taken back on again in the next drilling phase, promises don't pay bills, but this is the drilling game and everyone involved in it is well aware of what can happen at the drop of a hat, over the years I've had so much smoke blown up my arse what with broken promises that now I take every trip as my last one.

Looking back over the years working offshore I've achieved about half of what I started out to do. I've bought my house, although that came from my fathers insurance claim and by the time 2005 comes we'll find out if the policy I took out in 1994 really will give me a better return for my money than the High street Bank or Building Society, (up to now it's not performing too well) the Wee Business is not looking too promising either, but apart from that everything else is ok, Liz is bearing up and her cancer is in remission, I go every year now for a medical (M.O.T.) I call it and it's not looking like I'll be giving up the Offshore life in the near future, unless the Lottery turns up trumps, still I can't complain, I've experienced the Highs and Lows of the Roller Coaster ride and although it was a longer ride than I expected I wouldn't give up a day of the High times for anything, I've made a lot of lifelong friends working out here and if it wasn't for some of the Low times I would recommend working offshore to anyone with the stamina to go the distance, as long as they remember, It's only the best job in the world when your on the Helicopter going home and if their like me and countless others they will soon find out that whatever goals they set themselves at the start, it will seem for a long, long time that they are working in, "The Fields Of Dreams".

Magnus Crew (l to r)
Robbie Anderson, Steve Simmons, Steve Mackay, Mick Groom,
Sammy Graham, Brian Clarke, Scotty Gordon, Gary Johnoson,
Les Bell, John Sutherland

Supply Boat as viewed from crane on Magnus

Congested deck on Magnus platform

3 exhaust towers on Magnus Platform

The Solitaire, a pipe laying ship

Magnus platform

Magnus platform

ISBN 141202696-2

9 781412 026963